SAVE ME
THE LION'S

EXPOSING HUMAN-WILDLIFE CONFLICT IN AFRICA

C O M P L I M E N T A R Y   C O P Y

R160.00

Recommended South African retail price

July 2012

South African publishing date

Tel: +27 (0)11 484 3538 ■ Fax: +27 (0)11 484 6180
Isle of Houghton, Corner Boundary Road & Carse O'Gowrie, Houghton, 2198
PO Box 2002, Houghton, 2041 South Africa
mail@randomstruik.co.za ■ www.randomstruik.co.za

BY THE SAME AUTHOR

NATURAL HISTORY
Man is the Prey (London, New York 1968)
Focus on Fauna (Johannesburg 1970)
The Bushman (Johannesburg 1971)
Our Fragile Land (Johannesburg 1974)
The Environmental Crisis (Johannesburg 1974)
Bottero's Wildlife Art Collection (Johannesburg 1978)
Mountain Odyssey (with David Coulson) (Cape Town 1983)
Roof of Africa (with David Coulson) (New York 1984)
Survival Guide to the Outdoors (Johannesburg 1987)
Sabi Sabi (Johannesburg 1990)
Back to Earth (Cape Town 1991)
Coming Back to Earth (Cape Town 2001)

HISTORY
Like it Was (Johannesburg 1987)
An Extraordinary 20th Century (Johannesburg 1999)

ANTHOLOGIES
The Bedside Star – edited (Johannesburg 1988)
Back to Bed – edited (Johannesburg 1989)
Bedtime Again – edited (Johannesburg 1990)
Laugh, the Beloved Country (with Harvey Tyson) (Cape Town 2003)

HUMOUR
The Yellow Six (Birmingham and Johannesburg 1994 & 2006)
S*x for the Extremely Shy (Johannesburg 1995)
The Search for the Great South African Limerick (Johannesburg 1996)
Great South African Limericks (Johannesburg 1997)
Enclosed, Please Find (Johannesburg 1999)
Clarke on Your Stoep (Johannesburg 2005)
The Funny Side of Golf (Johannesburg 2005)

TRAVEL
Blazing Saddles – the Truth Behind the Tours de Farce (Cape Town 2007)
Blazing Bicycle Saddles (Amazon/Kindle 2011)

SAVE ME FROM
THE LION'S MOUTH

EXPOSING HUMAN-WILDLIFE CONFLICT IN AFRICA

JAMES CLARKE

Published by Struik Nature
(an imprint of Random House Struik (Pty) Ltd)
Wembley Square, First Floor, Solan Road,
Gardens, Cape Town, 8001 South Africa
PO Box 1144, Cape Town, 8000 South Africa

Reg. No. 1966/003153/07

Visit **www.randomstruik.co.za** and subscribe to our
newsletter for monthly updates and news

First published in 2012 by Struik Nature

1 3 5 7 9 10 8 6 4 2

Copyright © in text 2012: James Clarke
www.jamesclarke.co.za
Copyright © in published edition 2012: Random House Struik (Pty) Ltd

Cover design: Flame Cape Town

Reproduction by Hirt & Carter Cape (Pty) Ltd
Printed and bound by Interpak Books, Pietermaritzburg

All rights reserved. No part of this publication may be reproduced,
stored in a retrieval system, or transmitted, in any form or by any
means, electronic, mechanical, photocopying, recording, or otherwise,
without the prior permission of the copyright owners and publishers.

ISBN 978 1 92054 475 1

To the fallen

ACKNOWLEDGEMENTS

I owe a lot to Alan Calenborne for helping with this book. Alan is an old friend with a zoological background and a great deal of experience in the African wilds, as a recreational hunter and as an active conservationist and one-time trustee of the Endangered Wildlife Trust. As a collaborator he has been valuable in helping research the habits of animals that prey upon humans and putting me on to many useful sources. One of those sources was of tremendous value – Dr Jeremy Anderson, the first director of Pilanesberg National Park and co-director and founder of International Conservation Services (ICS). Another important source was Johan Marais, one of Africa's top herpetologists, who read through the snake and crocodile chapters.

Dr Rolf D. Baldus, president of the Tropical Game Commission of CIC and a world authority on Tanzania's wildlife, was generous with his time, as was Dr Paula A. White, director of the Zambia Lion Project of the Center for Tropical Research at the University of California, Los Angeles. I received some useful advice from Jeff Gaisford, recently retired public relations man with Ezemvelo KwaZulu-Natal Wildlife, and Russel Friedman of Wilderness Safaris.

Nevertheless the views expressed in this book are purely my own and do not necessarily reflect the views of those who helped me.

I have also my wife, Lenka, to thank for reading the manuscript in its various stages and offering valuable criticisms – not to mention the way she tolerates the hours she spends alone while I beaver away among my books. My daughter, Julie Clarke-Havemann, who is well versed in the field of rural development in Africa, was, as always, on hand to advise. My other daughter, Jenny Nourse, a biologist and educator, was, as always, a great help.

I owe a great deal to Lesley Hay-Whitton, eagle-eyed and meticulous, for editing this book and to Pippa Parker, publishing manager at Struik Nature, for her patience and advice.

There are scores of others who helped with suggestions and data – they know who they were and they know how much I appreciated their help.

JAMES CLARKE

WHAT THIS BOOK IS ABOUT

This book investigates the increasing conflict between people and wildlife in Africa and what needs to be done about it.

It describes the human suffering and perceptions of those who live outside the reserve fences among man-eaters and marauders, yet are excluded from the economic benefits accruing from the wildlife around them.

It provides evidence of a growing resentment among rural communities, especially near game reserves, and warns how it is threatening the existence of Africa's game reserves.

The book suggests that many in the northern hemisphere who support African wildlife conservation are blind to the seriousness of the situation. Some African states – notably Kenya and Tanzania – adopt wildlife policies to please donor countries from whom they receive millions of dollars. Thus government policies – many of them patently disastrous and certainly detrimental to rural Africans and to wildlife – are dictated from middle-class homes across Europe and North America.

Fortunately there is a growing international lobby that is seeking solutions.

I would be disappointed if this book were taken as an indictment of wildlife conservation. I have been a conservationist, wildlife observer and science writer for more than half a century, and am one of the three founders of South Africa's largest and most effective wildlife conservation movements, the Endangered Wildlife Trust.

POLITICAL MAP OF AFRICA

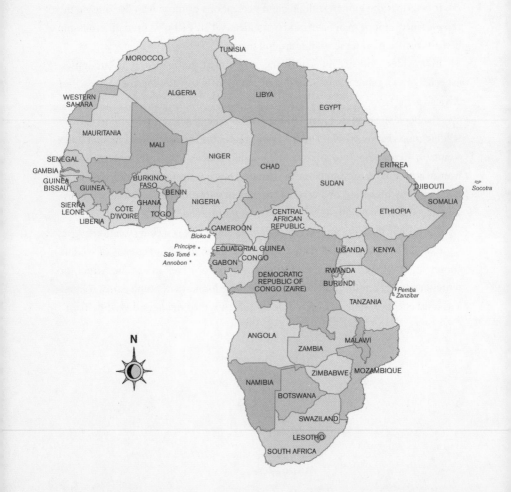

CONTENTS

1 THE CONFLICT

Save me from the lion's mouth

– Book of Common Prayer

Those who study human evolution in Africa ponder how the diminutive apemen and early humans – fangless and clawless and, one imagines, lacking in fleetness of foot – survived and eventually flourished in the African savanna. After all, the grassland was picked over by huge sabre-toothed cats; its waterways were ruled by crocodiles and hippopotamuses and the veld was the ancient domain of heavyweights such as the elephant, rhinoceros and buffalo. Our naked ancestors appear to have been singularly ill-equipped for survival in Africa of all places. Yet that is where humanity began.

Since the 1960s I have taken an interest in Africa's wildlife and in its fossil-rich regions with their unique opportunities for the study of human evolution. This resulted in my first book, *Man is the Prey*[1], which was an investigation into the methods and motives of man's natural enemies. More than forty years on I am still collecting data but years ago the angle of my interest diversified: I began to look at the impact of wild animals on the day-to-day lives of millions of people and the sad fact that, right across sub-Saharan Africa, many people 'fear and detest' elephants and lions[2]. They look upon wildlife as either edible or dangerous. Indeed, throughout much of the region, the all-encompassing word for wildlife is *nyama* – meat.

A gulf in understanding has been allowed to develop between those who live in the wilds and those who, laudably, want to assure the survival of Africa's amazing variety of wildlife.

It must be borne in mind that 80 per cent of Africa's wild animals live outside game reserves. Wildlife and humans are competing for the same habitat, with serious losses on both sides. The people don't deserve it. Neither do the animals.

The antagonism between humans and wild animals is particularly pronounced on the eastern side of the continent, which is by far the world's most hazardous rural environment for humans. Yet this eastern side is precisely where humans evolved. Somehow our much smaller pre-human ancestors, with brains a third of the size of ours, not only survived but thrived in an environment 'bristling with menace'[3].

Wildlife television programmes and their depiction of the African wilds and the creatures that inhabit them tend to give the false impression that elephants are friendly creatures (while they are indeed noble beasts, they are at best indifferent to our presence), and that you can cuddle lions and make pets of hyaenas. The hippo is often seen as a rotund comical character, when in fact it is the most unhumorous animal God ever created. Few programmes, brilliant though many of them are, focus on the reality of rural Africa or help us empathise with those who live every day with wild animals as neighbours, and who not only lose livestock and crops to wild animals, but who also lose loved ones and neighbours to them. Annually, throughout Africa, many thousands of deaths are caused by lions, leopards, hyaenas, crocodiles, elephants, hippopotamuses, rhinoceroses and buffalo, and tens of thousands are killed a year by snakes, according to the WHO.[4]

I am not suggesting that Africa is one giant Jurassic Park or that all of wild Africa is traumatised by wild animals, but there is a continuity of deaths in many regions that has been unceasing since the very beginning of humankind. Today, for various reasons, the situation poses a challenge to all who call themselves conservationists, since it might ultimately threaten the continuance of Africa's great game reserves.

Wild Africa is an exciting and marvellous wonderland containing the last vestiges of the real Eden, but the wonderment and beauty of it all is lost on millions who live in this wonderland and who, in the end, will one way or another decide its fate.

'Save me from the lion's mouth' chanted the psalmists and church congregations over the centuries; even today the cry is part of Christianity's *Book of Common Prayer*, as shown by these excerpts:

> O Lord, how long will you look on?
> Rescue me from the roaring beasts ...
>
> O God, break their teeth in their mouths;
> pull the fangs of the young lions, O Lord.
>
> O Lord my God, I take refuge in you;
> save and deliver me from all who pursue me ...
>
> Lest like a lion they tear me in pieces
> and snatch me away with none to deliver me.
>
> They lie in wait, like a lion in a covert;
> they lie in wait to seize upon the lowly ...
>
> Save me from the lion's mouth.

This is pretty earnest stuff.

Since the first hominids emerged, the big cats – whether in the form of sabre-toothed cats, tigers, lions or leopards – stalked us and ate us as part of their diet. For at least eight million years *Homo sapiens* and our australopithecine forebears, and those before even them, have been the natural prey of carnivores. Today in Africa *millions* still live under these conditions. In sub-Saharan Africa people are daily and stressfully aware of their own vulnerability, whether from predators that eat their stock and their neighbours, or from marauders that trash their crops – marauders such as elephants, hippos, bushpigs, baboons, grass cutters (cane rats), dense sun-blocking swarms of locusts and quelea finches that can wipe out an entire season's crop and leave a community starving.

In many parts of Africa a 'front line' has developed between humans and wild animals. It began many generations ago when the colonial powers appropriated wildlife to the central authority – a policy that most African countries have seen fit to retain. To the colonial powers, wildlife was a resource to be commercially exploited – like minerals. Today's governments view it as a revenue-earning commodity via tourism and hunting. And, in common with the colonialists, the current authorities allow those who live among wild animals almost no part in their control, so that rural communities traditionally regard wildlife as government-owned. Throughout much of Africa they pursue bushmeat at the risk of going to jail – this after millennia of having the right to do so. They view national parks and game reserves as places set aside exclusively for the entertainment of rich outsiders. The authorities, with few exceptions, are doing too little to alter that impression. As a result there is today something like a guerrilla war being waged by many communities along this front line. On a daily basis bands of poachers, armed with AK47s, cross it and invade the reserves for meat, ivory and rhino horn. Annually hundreds of poachers on the one hand and game guards on the other lose their lives in what has become an intensifying bush war. And annually vast numbers of wild animals are killed.

There have been, since 2003, some significant if sporadic moves within Africa by scientists, officials, game lodges, safari companies, politicians, community representatives and field workers to formulate a policy to alleviate human-wildlife conflict, of which the public, particularly outside Africa, is unaware. The challenge to conservationists is no longer simply a case of 'saving our wildlife heritage'. By raising funds to put up fences and aiding zoological research, they have done wonders. But little is being done to win the hearts and minds of those outside the reserves so that they feel safer; so that they receive compensation for the loss of livestock, crops and lives to wild animals; so that they perceive wildlife in a positive light and at least receive tangible benefits from its presence.

Too few involved in conservation recognise the real threats in wild Africa – especially those conservationists living in Europe and North America, who so generously fund Africa's efforts and who, because of their funding, have been able to wield enormous influence. Many countries in Africa mould their wildlife policies to please donor countries. Kenya's wildlife is in an appalling mess; numbers have fallen disastrously since hunting was banned a third of a century ago, at the behest of animal lovers in Europe. Lions are now considered vermin by rural dwellers in that country and have never been so low in numbers. The loss in revenue from hunting is around $20 to $40 million a year, but the Kenya Wildlife Service (KWS is mandated to manage the country's wildlife and national parks) appears unconcerned because Western donations can amount to as much as $400 million a year. Thus, as one Kenyan observer put it, wildlife policies in Africa are being dictated from TV-watching middle-class homes in Europe[5]. As a result of a misreading of the situation, their efforts have done nothing at all to alleviate the central problem – the conflict between the communities and the wild animals around them.

There is also the question of tourists to consider. The number of tourist casualties is rising as more and more people seek 'adventure tourism' and want to walk in the wilds and see the 'big five' – elephant, rhino, buffalo, lion and leopard – and want to be taken closer and closer. And, as the reserves strive to cater for this relatively new but rapidly growing demand, it is becoming increasingly obvious that they are unable to recruit and train enough game rangers and game guards capable of handling fraught situations. Thus, week in and week out, there are tragedies involving tourists and those who cater for them.

2 THE FRONT LINE

Most of the time there is no recognition
of the fact that communities
are always on the front line of the
battle between man and beast.

– Charles Jonga, Campfire Association Zimbabwe[1]

It had been one of those hot and humid days in southern Tanzania and, as the lowering sun set the western clouds ablaze, the temperature showed no sign of dropping. The villagers noted that the lion they'd spotted in mid afternoon was still there, 500 metres (550 yards) away, head resting on its front paws. They weren't particularly worried because the big cats – sometimes as many as a dozen – often passed by. Sometimes quite near. If they showed an inclination to go towards the cattle kraal, the men would rush at them shouting and banging anything that came to hand, and the dogs would go frantic. The lions would then move away.

And this lion showed no interest in the kraal.

Nevertheless Aiha Iddi called her four small children inside. It would soon be dark anyway and, once the sun goes down, few villagers venture out of doors.

Aiha's husband, Mizengo, a woodworker, did not share his wife's concern. There had been a man-eater 20 kilometres (12 miles) away near Kwtende in the west, where a young goatherd had been taken. But that was two weeks earlier. The lion was said to have moved even further west towards Nampungu where it killed a woman. This was some distance from where the Iddis lived south of the A19 road that runs from the interior to Lindi on the coast.

TANZANIA & SURROUNDING TERRITORIES

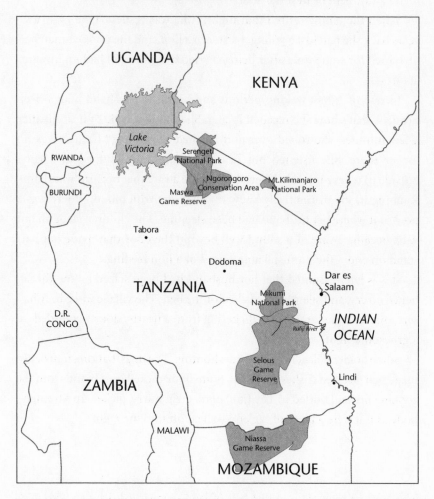

Although Aiha would have preferred to close the heavy sliding door, Mizengo felt it safe to leave it open to allow the evening breeze to cool the hut. The family slept on a wide, slightly raised platform strewn with three blankets on a thick pad of cardboard packaging. When there were man-eaters about, Mizengo would keep the door closed and, if he needed to urinate, he would do so rather noisily in a bucket inside the hut. So would everybody else. Aiha slept between her children and her husband who, a metre away, slept nearest the door.

When the family retired that night, Aiha was restless. One night two years back she had lost a younger sister to a lion, and the poor woman had screamed for some time after being carried off. Aiha still had nightmares about it.

In one of Aiha's waking periods she heard her husband take a deep breath – that's how she recalled it later. She thought little of it until, after a few minutes, she rolled over and reached across but Mizengo was no longer there. She listened but heard nothing and assumed he'd gone outside to relieve himself. Then she became aware that her arm was damp. Rubbing it, she instinctively knew it was sticky with blood – there was a pool of it where her husband had been sleeping. The children slept on but Aiha became aware of a sound well beyond the door that made her hair stand on end – the unmistakable sound of a lion feeding.

It was later assumed that her husband had been seized by the throat, hence no cry, and silently lifted clear of the bed. The village woke to Aiha's screams. A single torch beam flickering from a nearby doorway settled on a gruesome sight.

Some bolder villagers rushed out shouting. The dogs, barking frenziedly, made half-hearted rushes at the cat. Somebody picked up a brand from the cooking fire and hurled it. The lion, in no great hurry, picked up Mizengo's body as if it were a piece of rag and walked off into the night.

The incident took place in that belt of land sandwiched between Tanzania's Selous Game Reserve to the north and the Ruvuma River, which marks the Mozambique border, to the south. On the south side of the Ruvuma is the Niassa Game Reserve. The two game reserves – each bigger than Switzerland – are the two largest in the world. Between the two is a 160-kilometre-wide (100-mile) corridor, along which elephants and lions and other wild animals travel, sometimes passing through some of the 27 villages. The region has the world's highest incidence of man-eating – more than 500 victims have been killed by lions alone in the last few years. It is also notorious for crocodile attacks, mostly on women and children, because they are the ones who draw water from the river and streams.

Hyaenas and leopards also take people from time to time. Many say the elephant is the greater nuisance because a herd can, overnight, wreck a village's entire crop of maize or cassava, leaving scores of people on a starvation diet. They sometimes raid the grain storage bins after harvest time, when it is too late to plant again. They also kill. They mostly kill men because it is mainly men who venture far and who move about after dark. Many are killed trying to scare elephants off when they threaten the community's crops.

Yet, as is the case in most of Africa, these villagers have had no say in how wildlife in their region is managed. Wild animals, they will tell you, belong to the government.

North of the Limpopo, most of Africa's large mammal species share their habitat with humans. Only a fifth of Africa's wildlife is inside protected areas. And, while the presence of potentially man-eating lions or crocodiles adds a tingle of excitement to the foreign visitor's experience in Africa, it is the bane of many who live there.

The majority of Africans are totally unaware of the economic benefits of wildlife, yet the national and regional income from wildlife is supposed to trickle down to the people. In much of Africa, it trickles up.

Vast areas of Tanzania, including the Selous Game Reserve, are still prime examples of wild Africa. Tanzania has some of the best virgin landscapes that remain of this magnificent continent. Mainly because the country is so poor, its beautiful reserves are still more or less as they always were – for instance, the Serengeti and Ngorongoro Crater – and the uniquely rich biodiversity is intact. But there has been a price and the price is borne to a large degree by the surrounding villages.

There are varying statistics regarding how many people are killed by lions in Tanzania. According to Professor Craig Packer, who heads the Lion Research Center at the University of Minnesota's College of Biological Sciences, 563 Tanzanians were reported killed by lions north of the Ruvuma River between 1990 and 2004[2]. An often-quoted number is 200 deaths by lions a year (reliable statistics are hard to come by in Africa's developing states; in many cases deaths are not reported because villagers attribute them to supernatural forces). A few specialised man-eaters have been identified, including the notorious Osama (named after Osama bin Laden) that ate at least 34 people and terrorised thousands along the Rufiji between 2002 and 2004.

Packer found that more people are killed and eaten by predators wherever the population of smaller animals – the preferred diet of all the cats – had been reduced by bushmeat hunters and poachers. Paradoxically, there is another spike in man-eating when bushpigs are abundant. The reason for this is that bushpigs raid croplands and so villagers will sleep out in the fields in flimsy shelters to protect their crops – 'and that is where [lion] attacks take place and where lions learn to eat people'[3].

Hyaenas and leopards also take a steady toll – steady enough to keep many villages in a state of anxiety.

Most deaths are in the south of Tanzania, which has Africa's largest population of lions, and most victims are taken at night when they are sitting in temporary shelters, either protecting their food storage bins from elephants or, especially at harvest time (March and April), protecting their crops from bushpigs. South of the Ruvuma River lies Mozambique whose northern province, Cabo Delgado, is where carnivores – mainly lions – in and around Niassa Game Reserve in 2008 and 2009 are known to have killed 116 people. In this same province crocodiles take scores of people a year. It was pointed out that this was only 'a partial survey' in a small section of a large region, and that in many cases attacks were not recorded because the locals believed the victims had been taken by ancestral spirits. Further south, in August 2009, the situation was worsening in Mozambique's central provinces Manica and Sofala, to the point that it was becoming a political issue[4]. The governor of Manica, Mauricio Vieira, announced that a militia had been put together 'to protect people and their property'. It comprised 66 trained community wardens and 'six brigades' aided by five hunters. National president Armando Guebuza saw fit to attend the extraordinary session of the Manica provincial government and said it 'made no sense that Mozambicans were still being killed by wild animals'.

Packer says that in two years (July 2006 to September 2008), of 265 Mozambicans who were killed by wild animals, 31 were killed by elephants, 24 by lions, 12 by hippos and one each by buffalo, snakes and baboons and most of the rest by crocodiles. Sixty-one were killed by 'species unknown'[5]. Many cases are not reported because people have little or no incentive to report them and because the deaths are attributed to witchcraft. And in even more cases people – possibly victims of predation – simply disappear and, if their disappearance is recorded at all, they are merely listed as 'missing'.

An indication of how bad the situation is in northern Mozambique came in a 2010 FAO (Food and Agricultural Organization of the United Nations) report citing various research papers. In Cabo Delgado Province, between 1997 and 2004, 48 people were killed by lions and 70 more in 2000 and 2001. Forty-six people were killed in Muidimbe district on the Makonde plateau in 2002 and 2003 and in the Niassa Reserve 'at least 73 lion attacks, with at least 34 people killed and 37 injured since 1974 and at least 11 people killed and 17 injured since 2001'[6].

Dr Jeremy Anderson, who has spent many years studying the situation, believes crocodiles alone kill 300 Mozambicans a year – more than double the official estimate[7].

The rural African's main interest in wildlife is meat – a point that was stressed in the 2009 FAO report[8]. The report focused on the 'human-wildlife conflict' (HWC, an acronym that is increasingly being heard at 21st-century conservation conferences). An important step towards finding how rural dwellers perceive wildlife, it was published in the hope of finding ways to alleviate the suffering being experienced in Africa where people compete for living space with potentially dangerous animals. The idea is to achieve some sort of conciliation between humans and wild animals. Wildlife, after all, is the mainstay of Africa's highly lucrative tourist trade and is a major source of protein. In the remote parts of Africa it is the *only* potential source of income for rural communities.

Poverty is a factor in man-eating. The FAO report gives the example of fishermen so desperate for food that they knowingly risk crocodile attacks every day by wading into rivers or lakes. Shortly after the FAO report was published, a grim example was announced in Harare, Zimbabwe. In a period of two weeks eight people were killed by crocodiles while illegally catching fish in Lake Chivero, not far from Zimbabwe's capital. The poachers feed their families with the fish and sell the surplus door to door. Their deaths failed to deter other destitute poachers from wading waist deep into the lake with their fishing spears[9]. Another report said that, in 51 cases of crocodile attacks in neighbouring Mozambique, 39 of the victims had been fishing and presumably knew they were taking risks – although they might have underestimated the probability. They did so in the absence of alternative foods or livelihoods[10].

Poverty sometimes makes it impossible for villagers to protect their crops with elephant-proof barriers or lion-proof fences, or even for those working in the veld to afford shoes or boots or long trousers to protect their legs against snakebite. It is estimated that snakes in barefoot Africa kill at least 20 000 people a year[11].

One of the most respected voices in East Africa is that of Dr Rolf D. Baldus[12] who has more experience than most when it comes to HWC in Tanzania, where he was in wildlife management for many years. It is a region of Africa he loves dearly. He believes that, unless communities in the major wildlife areas of Africa are allowed a significant say in the management of the wildlife around their villages, they will see no point in conserving it and Africa's famed biodiversity will become greatly reduced. He is a strong advocate of sport hunting as a means for communities to derive sustainable income from the wildlife around them, arguing that it not only brings in millions of dollars a year, and a lot of it directly to the communities, but it does more to conserve wildlife than any punitive measures can achieve. Once lions, for example, have a value – and hunters pay tens of thousands of dollars to shoot just one trophy lion – the locals no longer poison and trap them. Kenya, under pressure from animal rights groups and other well-meaning overseas pressure groups, banned hunting more than 30 years ago, since when it has experienced an alarming decline in lion numbers. Since lions in Kenya no longer have a material value, cattle owners now regard them as vermin. Although they are not allowed to shoot them, not even to protect their cattle, many are killed – a surprising number by spears – and left to rot.

In 2007 Kenyan land-use economics researcher Mike Norton-Griffiths chastised the government-controlled Kenya Wildlife Service (KWS), virtually the sole owner of all of Kenya's wildlife, and Europe's wildlife societies for the lack of realistic and effective governance regarding wildlife[13]. Kenyans who live among wild animals have little chance of being heard on HWC issues and no opportunity to earn revenue from the animals they are expected to conserve. He says landowners have no rights regarding wildlife and receive no compensation for destruction and damage to life and property. The West's wildlife 'protectionists' are 'deeply at fault for they are too focused, obsessed even, on topical single issues that rarely concern the economics of producing wildlife'[14]. Norton-Griffiths suggests that animal lovers in Europe are ignorant of the market forces that determine land use and production decisions in rural Africa 'and they are often too reticent in challenging the government over policy issues'. We can add that the KWS is equally reticent in challenging its funders in Europe, who then attach strings to their funding – strings that reflect the desires of TV watchers in middle-class European homes, rather than the needs of people living in the real Africa.

Rolf D. Baldus has campaigned for years for communities in wild Africa to be in charge of their own natural resources and to be empowered to host overseas hunters, but under strict ethical conditions.

It has been found that most attacks on people by lions, leopards and hyaenas, and on their crops and livestock by elephants, hippos, buffalo and bushpigs are concentrated around the game reserves. The people's reaction is to retaliate, especially if they had been removed from ancestral lands to make way for the reserve, which is often the case. Many feel justified in killing or indiscriminately poisoning wild animals, as well as in poaching inside protected areas. If the government fails to protect rural dwellers, then they will protect themselves in any way they can. A particularly interesting example was a few years ago when the people of Makoko village on the western border of the Kruger National Park were found 'roasting meat of four lions' that had come from the park. The lions had come under the fence and killed eight cattle. The villagers had then removed 500 metres (550 yards) of the park's high multi-strand fence and used it to protect their village and crops[15].

Packer says the term 'wildlife-damage' is nowadays so much in use that there's a tendency for rural dwellers to blame predation and marauding on wildlife in general and 'to take it out on even beneficial species'. He shares Baldus' view that adverse perceptions of wildlife are particularly pronounced near game reserves, where wild animals inflict daily costs on local communities – costs that are being increasingly resented[16].

This view echoes a 2002 report on elephant–human conflict in Mozambique's Niassa Game Reserve, which discussed how elephant–human conflict had become a significant problem, not only within the reserve but outside the reserve in nine of the 15 districts of Mozambique's far north. It had become, according to the report, a priority issue for the provincial administration and incidents were rising. A provincial meeting of administrators and chiefs on local government 'was largely hijacked by discussions on elephant crop damage. In Nipepe district it was estimated that 18 tonnes of maize had been lost this year in the fields around the district centre and this had contributed to the recent riots in which the community attacked the administration.'[17] In the following decade various FAO reports indicated the problem was still unresolved[18]. Such reports make it clear that the future of conservation will depend on the relationship established by the wildlife authorities and those bearing the brunt along the front line. There is a lot of ground to be made up because most rural dwellers, understandably, regard elephants and lions only in terms of the damage they do to their crops and stock, and they bitterly resent being powerless to retaliate.

There is a consensus among those scientists and non-government organisations involved in redressing the situation that, whatever the answers are, they must not come as top-down edicts but as strategies jointly created with the communities themselves. Wildlife-management agencies, donor groups, conservation scientists, land-use planners and developers and law-enforcement agencies are all in their various ways responsible for the situation. Nor are the communities themselves blameless.

In South Africa, which is far more developed than the rest of sub-Saharan Africa, man-killing and man-eating is on a small scale but is increasing, and even the leopard appears to be changing its spots. The leopard has been a rapacious man-eater in India and sometimes in Africa, but prior to 1990 I had not heard of a single case of man-eating leopards (as opposed to man-killing) in the whole of South Africa. And then a series of incidents began just over 20 years ago[19]. It was around this time that lions in the Kruger Park began living off Mozambican border-jumpers who were fleeing the internecine war to the east. Leopards might also have turned to man-eating at that point, having discovered how weakened refugees travelling by night were easy prey.

But is there something else afoot?

There have been suggestions that we are witnessing a global heightening of aggression among large animals towards humans. Richly deserved perhaps, when you consider what humans have done to Africa's wildlife over the last three centuries. In 2008 London's *Daily Telegraph*, reporting a killer elephant terrorising a village in Assam, northeast India, made this observation:

> Elephants haven't always behaved like this. But in recent years, in India and all over Africa, too, some menacing change has come over them. And not just elephants – it's almost any species. This disquieting pattern has only recently been detected, in part because it is so disparate and weird. But it's now widely accepted that the relationship between humans and animals is changing.

One of the world's leading ethologists [specialists in animal behaviour] believes that a critical point has been crossed and animals are beginning to snap back. After centuries of being eaten, evicted, subjected to vivisection, killed for fun, worn as hats and made to ride bicycles in circuses, something is causing them to turn on us.

It's happening everywhere. Authorities in America and Canada are alarmed at the increase in attacks on humans by mountain lions, cougars, foxes and wolves. Romania and Colombia have seen a rise in bear maulings. In Mexico, in just the past few months, there's been a spate of deadly shark attacks with the *LA Times* reporting that, 'the worldwide rate in recent years is double the average of the previous 50'. America and Sierra Leone have witnessed assaults and killings by chimps who, according to *New Scientist*, 'almost never attack people'. In Uganda, they have started killing children by biting off their limbs then disembowelling them.[20]

The writer's implication that there is some sort of international telepathy among predators seeking revenge on their tormentors is pure fantasy. Yet there is no doubt that incidents of human-animal conflict are increasing throughout Africa and across India and North America. On Lake Victoria in East Africa, where crocodiles were so docile during most of the 20th century that local people had no fear of them and even swam among them, crocodiles now kill people regularly. At Bwonda on Lake Victoria, hippos are increasingly attacking homes and killing people. Elephants, where they still exist in large numbers, are showing increased aggression. There's evidence that today's elephant populations are suffering from chronic stress brought about by prolonged habitat reduction, ceaseless poaching, culling and mass translocations. People who have had experience with these intelligent creatures know that elephants, like whales and dolphins, are sociable animals with strong family bonds and have an ultra long-range communication system. As a result dealing with the elephant overpopulation in parts of Southern Africa is proving to be extremely complex[21].

Human-wildlife conflict is receiving unprecedented publicity, partly because the communications revolution is bringing stories from places that, in the past, were barely covered by the news media and because reporting has become far more penetrating, comprehensive and analytical – and, one supposes, people are becoming more interested in what's eating them.

As C.A.W. Guggisberg put it:

It is easily understandable that human imagination is always stirred by stories of man-eaters, be they big cats, wolves, crocodiles or sharks. One experiences a by no means disagreeable shudder – provided there is no chance of being chosen as the next meal – as well as a feeling of outraged amazement that lowly animals can have the effrontery to gobble up the 'lord of creation'. From this feeling probably stems the strange effort to show the man-eating habits, especially of the big cats, as something absolutely out of the ordinary – something almost monstrous. Thus a very eminent scientist compares the man-eating lion with a homicidal maniac. I admit that I am unable to follow his reasoning ... a man-eater does not harm individuals of his own species. He kills other animals, only those victims are for once not zebras or wildebeest, they belong to that strange species known as Homo sapiens. Why should this be so monstrous?[22]

The 2009 FAO paper mentions how some people blame colonialism for 'ruining traditionally harmonious relations between wildlife and local people'. But was there ever a harmonious relationship? There might have been, in the sense that we ate wild animals and wild animals ate us, but that is poetic rather than harmonious.

I am being facetious: the fact is there are, as we shall see, many instances of harmonious relationships. And there are even instances where rural dwellers have philosophically accepted that it is their fate that predators would eat them and pachyderms would trample their crops. Many people to this day rationalise it by blaming deaths from man-eaters on the supernatural. Many will not kill man-eaters for this reason.

It is hardly surprising, as human numbers grow and as people and wild animals compete for space and food, that the conflict has become more bitter and bloody. In 2008 in Tanzania's Rombo district, which includes a great deal of Mount Kilimanjaro, 20 people were killed by elephants. Yet that year was shrugged off as just an 'average year'[23]. During the year this region suffered crop damage to the tune of $500 000, which for a mainly peasant population is a considerable amount.

It is difficult for conservationists living in Baltimore or Wolverhampton to visualise what it is like for villagers during the night to hear a herd of elephants destroying their crop of cassava or maize, just before it is ready to harvest – which is when elephants are most attracted to a field. For farmers and their families it means months of hunger, even starvation – having to ration each day's food carefully. This explains why so many villagers try so desperately to defend their fields. We cannot blame the elephants – there's not an ounce of malevolence in an elephant under normal circumstances – but to the subsistence farmer the elephant can spell death.

Most African countries do not pay compensation for damages caused by wildlife. They argue that a compensation scheme can do little to reduce the conflict and might even encourage communities to relax precautions. The International Union for Conservation of Nature (IUCN) African Elephant Specialist Group and the Human-Elephant Conflict Task Force recommended against compensation for elephant damage, arguing that it can at best address only the symptoms and not the causes. Some governments, which have tried and abandoned compensation schemes, prefer to assist villagers by improving their defences.

The 2009 FAO report said:

> The failure of most compensation schemes is attributed to bureaucratic inadequacies, corruption, cheating, fraudulent claims, time and costs involved, moral hazard and the practical barriers that less literate farmers must overcome to generate a claim. Additionally, they are difficult to manage, requiring reliable and mobile personnel and logistics to verify and objectively quantify damage over wide areas.

A study of elephant damages in the region of Boromo (Burkina Faso) in 2001/2002 revealed that 98 per cent of the damage caused by elephants was not reported to the administration because the farmers knew there would be no compensation.

In Namibia, the Ministry of Environment and Tourism subsidises funeral costs (approximately US$710 per victim in 2007) for people killed by elephants, crocodiles and hippos 'under conditions where the affected persons could not reasonably have been expected to defend himself or to avoid the incident, and where the family has to incur costs for a funeral'. In Ghana, while no compensation is paid for crop damage by wildlife, the Wildlife Division and the Ministry of Food & Agriculture assist victims to adopt both mitigation and crop-improvement techniques. In 1991 in Burkina Faso, the victims of elephant crop-raiding were preferentially contracted as workers to maintain the infrastructures in the Deux Balé Forest Reserve. This operation involved 127 farmers who received about US$40 each – the equivalent of three 50-kilogram (110-pound) bags of millet. 'This compensation scheme was very much appreciated and sensitized the villagers to conservation.'[24]

Either we co-exist with wildlife or we continue to assist calculatedly in the extinction of the world's lions, tigers, leopards, jaguars, elephants, rhinos, bears, gorillas and wolves. A positive step forward came in Durban in September 2003 at the IUCN's fifth World Parks Congress. A 30-person workshop, comprising conservation scientists, field workers, sociologists and other disciplines from across the world, was convened by the IUCN to examine the topic 'Creating coexistence between humans and wildlife – global perspectives on local efforts to address human-wildlife conflict'. The workshop's deliberations were presented to the nearly 3 000 delegates at the congress – a congress that, in retrospect, has proved to be a landmark event in HWC. It addressed not just Africa's HWC problems but also those in other parts of the world, for instance problems with bears in North America, jaguars and crop-raiding animals in South America, India's tigers and elephant, crop-raiding gorillas in Uganda and dingoes in Australia. Right across the globe, as populations grow and protected areas become hemmed in, there are conflicts between humans and wild animals. What was significant at the congress was that, generally speaking, few saw the rifle as a solution and all saw the importance of conserving what is left of the world's wildlife and wild places. Scientists, sociologists and field workers sought to find some sort of strategy towards reconciling the aims of conservationists and the needs of those outside the reserves. The idea was to review progress and suggest a course for the next 10 years and beyond – 10 years being the gap between each World Parks Congress[25].

The workshop defined the problem of HWC, saying that, as populations grew, incidents involving conflict were increasing in frequency and severity worldwide and were likely to escalate. HWC involves more than problems with man-killers. It involves crop damage; the death or injury to domestic stock; the loss of crops and the consequent anxiety and frustration. HWC involves conflict not just between humans and wild animals but between humans and humans. Measures to counteract it can be divisive among communities and can involve retaliatory measures by desperate villagers, not only against problem animals but also against sluggish authorities who are often perceived as being unsympathetic. Generally, rural communities, especially in Central and East Africa and the Indian sub-continent, are powerless against, for instance, elephants and the big cats, either because they do not have the weaponry or because the law forbids them to take physical action. In such cases resentment builds up and the communities feel, understandably, that the authorities favour wildlife over human well-being, which in certain regions is probably true. In this situation are the seeds of bitter strife sown. It could in the long run be the death of Africa's unique biodiversity.

If those who took part in the Durban congress came away with a common perception of the problems and solutions of HWC, it must have been that the situation is far more complicated than anybody imagined. There are few simple answers – just a lot of possible measures involving national, regional and local politics; cultural idiosyncrasies; economics; sociology; education, ethology;

psychology; land-use planning; policing; climate change; the possible extinction of endangered and threatened species and a plethora of other biological challenges. And, whether in Asia, South America or Africa, the weighting of these factors differs, not just from region to region, but from locality to locality, even village to village and sometimes among those within a village.

There are also prejudices. Stray cattle might cause more destruction in a field than elephants. But the resentment against the marauding elephant is bitter indeed for the simple reason that the community has no control over the elephant, whereas straying cattle would have been their own fault.

The park conferences are important in more ways than one. A common characteristic among scientists who enjoy working in the field and people such as game rangers is that they often work in isolation and, indeed, are frequently loners by choice, who abhor having to visit cities and put on suits and becoming involved in formalities. Much of their knowledge is never disseminated because they get so few opportunities to engage with other disciplines. The Durban congress and subsequent sponsored seminars brought many of them out of the bush to mix with others, and it provided opportunities to add to the global ideas exchange. The deliberations indicated that what works, for instance, in counteracting crop-raiding baboons in South Africa's Western Cape might well have application in India or Brazil with quite different species. It was perhaps inevitable that the congress' most important conclusion was that constant dialogue and the global sharing of information was essential. With the revolution in electronic communication, this was now possible. Three years later, and arising directly from that suggestion, the Human-Wildlife Conflict Collaboration (HWCC) was established in Washington, D.C. In November 2006 more than 50 conservation professionals from 40 different institutions across the world met there and resolved to form an ideas exchange. One hundred organisations now participate in this global network and the HWCC has a two-person secretariat and has established a web-based resource. It also offers courses, among them a three-day training programme in 'conflict resolution leadership' techniques, and it processes a three-day critical skills training programme for all conservationists dealing with HWC[26].

The acute situation in some regions of Africa has to an extent been engineered. In trying to conserve Africa's unique variety of wildlife, governments have been compressing wildlife into isolated 'island' reserves – and there's then a tendency to pave and plough in between – right up to the fences. Little room is left for buffer zones where land owners can erect lodges or conduct hunting safaris and there are few uncontested corridors for animals to move from one protected area to another. There are now attempts in Southern and East Africa to create protected corridors joining national parks and smaller reserves into contiguous zones, so encompassing a maximum variety of habitats and thereby preserving a maximum variety of plant and animal species. As far as conservation, biodiversity, job creation and land-use planning go, this is fine – but it might also exacerbate HWC. 'Wildlife corridors' are sometimes possible.

This is certainly so in Tanzania where, in 2012, there existed more than 30 opportunities to link protected areas, none of which was likely to exist in a few years' time. There is plenty of scope too for lucrative buffer zones on community-held land, particularly outside the Selous Game Reserve, but the Tanzanian government, riddled with nepotism and corruption, will not release its grip on the multi-million-dollar income from the hunting industry[27] and it brooks no opposition from outside the reserve. The wildlife and tourism ministry wants to have its hands on all hunting and photographic tourism and, in particular, it does not want to share proceeds from hunting on village land with the villagers. It would also like to control private tourism operators. Hunting regulations require all companies involved in tourism in any wildlife area – including non-protected areas – to obtain permission and licences from the ministry. Yet the ministry seems incapable of handling this. One community that wanted to build a tourist lodge waited 10 years for permission.

The government's attitude has caused massive retaliatory poaching and, according to the World Wildlife Fund (WWF), the Selous and Mozambique's Niassa Game Reserve are today's major source of illegal ivory being shipped out of Africa.

The Kruger Park, which is the size of Belgium or Massachusetts, long ago took down the barbed wire and electrified barrier between it and the thousands of square kilometres of private game reserves on its western flank. More recently it did the same on its eastern side, thus incorporating within the South African protected zone a vast portion of protected Mozambican bushveld, to form the Great Limpopo Transfrontier Park. There has been talk of developing a belt of reserves extending westwards up into the high Escarpment, which divides South Africa's temperate Highveld from the hot Lowveld. There has long been talk of linking the scattered reserves of Zululand[28] (already linked from Maphelane to the Mozambique border) northwards into Mozambique. Then, via a chain of reserves, to the Great Limpopo Transfrontier Park and even further northwards (with Zimbabwe's cooperation) to the Zambezi River. It is feasible then to link this complex – which would be the largest protected wildlife area on Earth – westwards along the wild valleys of the Limpopo and Zambezi to the large desert reserves in Namibia and Angola, offering unrivalled opportunities for safari lodges, wildlife viewing, birding, hiking, motoring, hunting and fishing (both fresh water and marine).

It is within the realms of possibility to link Southern Africa's parks to Kenya and Tanzania – a concept first articulated by the South African statesman Jan Smuts in the 1930s. When Dr Richard Leakey revisited South Africa in the post-apartheid era and I introduced him to a meeting of the Institute for the Study of Man in Africa, I mentioned this and suggested that existing villages could be incorporated because to tourists they were a fascinating part of natural Africa. I was surprised by Leakey's violent reaction. He said, 'We don't want to be stared at like animals by tourists!' This was hardly a valid objection – it is rather like villagers in England's protected Cotswold Hills or on America's Appalachian Trail resenting being part of those heritage areas.

There's also talk in the Peace Parks Foundation[29] – though nothing more than that so far – of joining the huge Selous Game Reserve in Tanzania to Mozambique's Niassa Game Reserve incorporating the 160-kilometre-deep stretch of community land in between[30], creating a trans-border reserve of around 110 000 square kilometres (42 480 square miles). But, as long as those living outside develop up to their boundary fences, so the propensity for conflict remains and grows. Many reserves are already bordered by intensive agriculture and in places by dense human settlements. The Kruger Park's southeastern flank is an example. The division is absolute: two different antagonistic worlds separated by barbed wire – the front line.

Mothers living outside Pilanesberg National Park[31] not far from Johannesburg warn their children that if they misbehave they'll be put over the fence. I doubt that this threat (which is obviously not meant seriously) is confined to those living around Pilanesberg but, in populated areas with an isolated 'island reserve' in their midst, it is leading to a generation of children growing up to view wildlife more with terror than wonder. The 2009 FAO report refers to rural dwellers 'hating' wildlife – especially elephants[32]. But we must be cautious about interpreting that as Africans 'hating and detesting' elephants or lions. There are significant and hopeful inconsistencies. In Uganda in 1999 a survey seeking rural views on the best way to deal with 'problem' lions found, surprisingly, only 37 per cent (out of 156 respondents) felt lions should be exterminated. An almost equal number (35 per cent) said a game-proof fence should be erected around protected areas. The rest felt people should be taught how to avoid lions. In Tanzania's Rufiji district villagers who had, in a few short years during the 1990s, suffered 92 lion attacks, nevertheless had a 'high tolerance for lions because the lions helped control the bush pig population'[33].

In Namibia, Garth Owen-Smith, who has an intimate knowledge of the situation in the arid but intensely beautiful northern region where elephants share precious waterholes with cattle and humans, says resentment flares when they damage windmill water pumps and tanks and many elephants are killed in retribution. In contrast he writes of an old man, nicknamed Old Kaokoveld, who complained bitterly of the damage done by elephants in his area. Although there was a spring nearby, elephants chose to drink from the reservoir next to his house. Owen-Smith suggested the only solution was to have them shot, to which the old man replied, 'No one must shoot my elephants!' Owen-Smith, a courageous conservator, commented, 'At the time I started to think that getting the local communities' support for stopping [elephant] poaching was a hopeless task but Old Kaokoveld's response made me believe it was possible. The key was – whose wild animals were they?'[34]

That unresolved question alone deserves the undivided attention of the IUCN's future World Parks Conference.

Since the Durban accord there have been a few tentative signs from the usually sluggish and often devious government bureaucracies that their political consciences are being pricked regarding protecting villages and sharing with them the economic benefits coming from the natural resources around them. The Tanzanian government held a national workshop in 2009 'to prepare a national action plan for lion and leopard' and made noises about letting communities in on wildlife management. But progress in the field is hard to find. The wildlife ministry still stifles private enterprise. A share of the millions of dollars from hunting inside and outside of the Selous Game Reserve – including on village land – does not go to those along the front line.

The former Zambian government frequently vowed to step up efforts to see that rural dwellers helped in the control of problem animals and often appeared to be trying to devolve power regarding wildlife to local communities. It achieved almost nothing and in September 2011 was defeated at the polls. The new president, Michael Sata (a former policeman and trade unionist), immediately disbanded the board of the Zambian Wildlife Authority (ZAWA) and also released 670 prisoners, who had mainly been convicted of poaching. He claimed that 'the previous administration valued animals more than hungry humans'[35]. ZAWA provides national parks with armed scouts and rangers.

Sata warned during the opening of parliament that he would invoke bold measures: 'In order for us to preserve our wildlife for tourism we must also put measures in place to control the problem of human-animal conflict in game management areas which has led to increased levels of hunger and poverty among our people.' He announced, 'I have today dissolved the ZAWA board and I have to look at it, to reconstitute it.'

Sata's move shocked many and was widely seen as a green light for poaching. In the following hiatus two game guards were shot dead and a scout post was put to the torch, though the motives were unclear. The new Minister of Tourism, Environment and Natural Resources, Catherine Namugala, found it necessary to state that the new government would 'deal strongly with individuals caught for poaching'. But Sata's announcement was largely seen as an understanding that the law would be lenient towards those who hunt bushmeat to feed hungry families. Indeed some of the freed prisoners were mothers.

The *Cape Times*' Tony Weaver, who knows Zambia well, claimed ZAWA's board was dysfunctional and corrupt anyway and that the previous government fell because of corruption and gross incompetency:

> Of those released only a few are commercial poachers. Most are villagers living on customary land; land supporting the wildlife owned by government from which they receive no benefit, being abused by the agents of the state for eating some duiker meat, and living unprotected from the depredations of wild animals. Zawa has been implicit in the bushmeat and (illicit) ivory trade in Zambia for 30 years or so and [protective of] the 'Big Man' networks... Sit back and watch a lit candle in the African dark.[36]

Other African governments have announced intentions to decentralise wildlife controls, but such statements of intent have been heard for the past 20 years. Judging by the lack of follow-up, the pronouncements appear to be aimed at appeasing overseas conservation lobbies and international donor agencies. Very little has been achieved after years of talking.

In 2011 there was an incident in South Africa that was a warning to all involved with HWC. A frustrated community in Zululand breached the front line. Rural dwellers tore down the fence of one of Africa's prime game reserves

– Ndumo on the Mozambican border, which is a beautiful wetland where five per cent of the world's bird species can be seen. They moved in with their cattle, chopped down trees and defiantly tilled the land for crops. The intervention of 50 policemen failed to budge them. The standoff was solved diplomatically but it was a shot across the bows.

We then have to consider the tourist element. Visitors, well protected in their vehicles, cross the front line daily in their thousands. In recent years 'ecotourism' and 'adventure tourism' have increased enormously because tourists want to get closer to the animals. They want to experience wilderness but, understandably, more and more want to do so on foot. They are willing to take chances; they are looking for thrills. Some merely want to regale their friends back home about their adventures; some are seriously passionate and very knowledgeable about wildlife and plants and are interested in the minutiae of the educated class' growing enthusiasm for ecology. The trend towards hiking in the bush is excellent news for reserves – if visitors walk rather than use vehicles it means more tourists and less impact.

Since visitors want to see 'the big five', more and more small reserves are finding it commercially advantageous to reintroduce these animals. As a consequence the big five are today far more widely spread, especially in the southern third of the continent and most certainly in South Africa, than they were a century ago.

The danger to tourists is increased by the lack of suitable game rangers and game guides. Scientist and former game park warden Jeremy Anderson, with his 40 years' experience as an international wildlife management consultant, mostly in Africa, says that many people have been elevated into the position of game rangers before they are adequately trained[37].

The Kruger Park has run 'wilderness trails' for tourists for the last 30 years and Zululand's reserves, which pioneered the concept, have organised trails on a daily basis for 40 years. Several visitors have been injured but not one has been killed inside these particular reserves, though there have been tourist deaths in the private reserves. The trails, relaxed affairs taking up to five days walking in areas untouched by development of any kind, are led, single file, by an armed ranger and followed by an armed assistant.

After a series of attacks on trails in 2004 the Johannesburg *Star* newspaper reported that 'animal attacks are increasing as tourists dare to get closer to the animals. Already this year eight attacks by wild animals have been reported [on Kruger Park trails] while only five were reported in 2003 and three in 2002.' Although none of these attacks was fatal, in 2009 the Kruger Park suspended some of its trails. This was shortly after a ranger, escorting eight hikers, was severely mauled after spotting a lioness with cubs just outside the Metsi-Metsi Trails Camp, not far from the popular picnic spot Tshokwane. Despite two warning shots, the lioness attacked but after clawing and biting the ranger she ran off. The tourists, after recovering from the shock and with a new ranger, continued their hike.

While there have been no tourist fatalities on wilderness trails inside national parks, it seems just a matter of time before there are. There have been plenty of close shaves, including when a Kruger Park white rhino – a normally docile animal – charged into a line of eight walkers, injuring two.

In many parts of Africa hiking in the bush accompanied by game rangers or guides has become a daily occurrence; tourists are sleeping in tents and even in the open in lion and elephant country. The new growth and expansion of wilderness trails has outstripped the availability of experienced rangers and guides. Gone are the traditional rangers who, in their long years of apprenticeship, patrolled wild regions on foot, sometimes alone for weeks on end. Gone, mostly, are the cool-headed dead shots who were allowed to lead wilderness trails only after they had experienced many encounters with big game. An essential part of their training involved tracking down and shooting an elephant as part of a culling operation. But trainee rangers today are merely required to have shot, accurately, a pop-up life-sized effigy. The question is how would they react in a dire situation? A friend travelling around Madikwe National Park[38] in an open tourist vehicle noticed the ranger did not have a gun. The ranger explained he was waiting for a police permit allowing him to possess one.

Perhaps the most hair-raising of all groups who go into the bush are the television crews who put pressure on rangers to take them closer to animals. Jeff Gaisford, recently retired public relations man with Ezemvelo KwaZulu-Natal Wildlife, has had much experience accompanying TV crews. He explained how 'old hand' rangers would put them firmly in their place if they made demands that entailed undue risk, but 'the youngsters' often give in. 'Heaven knows, I have had the same pressure on me when guiding some film crews – "make the animal move", "get us closer so we can get a better shot". And when the animal in question disappears in a cloud of dust or a great splash of water they complain, "Gee, a pity you were not more careful".

'The fact that there have been so few tourist injuries and deaths is an enormous tribute to the good behaviour of the animals.'[39]

3 THE NATURE OF THE BEAST

It's not so much a case of problem animals – it's often
a case of animals under fire. To say wild animals pose
a problem for humans overlooks the fact that we
pose a bigger problem for them.

– Julie Clarke-Havemann, environmental analyst

Wild animals under normal circumstances do not pose a threat to humans. Quite the opposite. Whatever the species, they invariably move away as soon as they see a human. Lions, elephants, buffalo – even crocodiles when encountered on dry land – move away at our approach. Some, including lions, even flee. This doesn't say much for humans. Significantly, they do not shy away from other species – buck will graze quite close to resting lions. The fact that animals in the wild will flee at our approach is not, however, an immutable rule and it could be fatal to assume so. The problem is that, these days, 'normal circumstances' do not prevail over much of Africa. We have to sow crops and so we attract herbivores; we have to have livestock and so we attract carnivores and, as Africa's human population grows, we have to establish villages and towns and invade the habitats of other large species – some bigger and toothier than we are – and so a conflict situation arises. The more clumsily these conflicts are managed, the worse the consequences for both animals and humans.

Many overseas tourists have a perception of wildlife heavily influenced by television programmes such as *Mad Mike and Mark* who, in the African wilds, perform flamboyant and pointless antics, getting perilously close to dangerous animals, seemingly to show off like circus lion tamers who put their heads in lions' mouths. Other programmes depict wild animals in an anthropomorphic way, often insinuating there can be a sort of Doctor Dolittle bond between humans and wildlife. Their naivety can be chilling.

A few years ago some Southeast Asian students driving in a South African lion park saw a group of lions; two of the students got out of their vehicle and casually walked over to them to pose for photographs. One was instantly killed. In 2000 I was driving a Hungarian visitor in the Kruger Park and stopped because there were elephants in the road. My guest leapt out of the car and ran towards the elephants gesticulating for me to take his picture. Fortunately the elephants fled.

This naivety about bonding with wild creatures was epitomised in 2003 in Alaska when Timothy Treadwell (46) and his girlfriend, Amie Huguenard (37), were killed and partially eaten by a grizzly bear or bears near Kaflia Bay in Katmai National Park, about 480 kilometres (300 miles) southwest of Anchorage. Treadwell, a popular self-styled 'eco warrior', would on Discovery Channel, get up close and unarmed to bears and call out, 'I love you.' The couple decided to camp in bear country to prove the point that bears would not harm you if you did not harm them. Soon after the tragedy a man was witnessed in the same national park luring bears with food offerings and then whacking them with a stick. He explained, 'I'm teaching them that humans are bad.'

Equally hard to live with is the other extreme epitomised by that segment of the hunting safari industry catering for redneck American hunters, whose holy grail is to hunt in Africa. It was revealing to see their reaction when a cyclist was killed by a mountain lion (cougar) in Orange County, California, in January 2004 and a young woman hiker was dreadfully mauled by the same cat. Many people felt the lion should not have been shot. This sentiment incensed the hunting fraternity's Smith & Wesson Forum on the Internet, which carried many vitriolic comments describing such people as 'weirdos', 'commies', 'perverts', 'liberals' and, presumably the worst of all, 'anti-gun lobbyists'! One hunter said he'd never enter a national park without a side arm. This would certainly bar him from entering any African national park that I know of.

Yet even highly knowledgeable people can overlook the unpredictability of animals. Daphne Sheldrick of Animal Orphanage fame in East Africa reared an elephant and set it free. Years later she came across the elephant with a new calf. She walked up to it, calling its name, and then touched it. It hurled her aside, breaking her hip.

In fact, there are more positive stories of humans making friends with potential man-killers than there are negative ones, for instance Joy Adamson and her friendly lions in East Africa and her estranged husband, George, and his friendly lions in northeast Africa. Ironically both Joy and George met their deaths at the hands of humans – both were murdered in Africa. Patently, we can make friends with lions when they are brought up on the bottle, even romp with them; we can tame African elephants enough to ride on their backs. But in the wilds no bond exists between us and them. Wild animals in general live in fear of humans and even the sable antelope, tsessebe and giraffe have been known to attack, lethally, out of defence.

Nature is neutral. As John Burroughs (1837–1921) wrote, 'Nature does not care whether the hunter slays the beast or the beast the hunter. She will make good compost of them both and her ends are prospered whichever succeeds.'

While every continent has its share of dangerous wild animals, some places are more dangerous than others; the most dangerous place on Earth is that vast ocean of golden savanna on the eastern side of Central Africa. It is significant that for well over three centuries this area was traversed by caravans of Arab slaves being escorted in chains to the coast, for shipment and sale in Eurasia and the Americas. Every year thousands were left dead and dying along the route, to be eaten by wild animals. During the 19th century the East African slave trade grew enormously, due to the demands for slaves by plantation owners in the French, British and Portuguese colonies. The slave traders penetrated into Malawi, and their southern routes leading back to the coast converged on Lindi on the Indian Ocean in southern Tanzania and on Sofala (Beira) in northern Mozambique.

Between 1501 and 1820 slave traders took 8.7 million Africans in chains to the western hemisphere. In the 68 years before the final abolition of slavery (Brazil was the last country to set its slaves free, in 1888) 2.3 million more were transported. A total of 11 million men and women came from Africa – 70 per cent owned by either British or Portuguese traders. An unknown proportion came from the central-eastern side of Africa. They were shackled together in small groups sometimes attached by iron collars. If any showed signs of exhaustion, they were abandoned to their fate and even hacked from the chain and left by the wayside. Nobody will ever know how many died along these routes, but it seems likely that, over the centuries of the slave trade, carnivores in those regions developed a taste for human flesh, which they retain to this day. The situation has been aggravated by bodies lying around after internecine wars and the custom among some communities, even today, of leaving their dead and, in the recent past, even their dying in the bush, to be consumed by carnivores. That region, that knot of countries embracing northern Mozambique, southern Tanzania, Malawi and eastern Zambia, has more problems than anywhere else in the world regarding conflict between wild animals and humans. There seems to be a genetic predisposition among the big carnivores in the region to seek human meat.

Man-eating hyaenas, uncommon outside this region, became a particular nuisance in southern Malawi around the mid 20th century and the Royal Air Force based in what was then Nyasaland was asked to bomb their caves in the Mount Mlanje region. They remain man-eaters to this day. Lions and leopards still frequently take humans in this region.

Coincidentally perhaps, baboons and chimpanzees in this same area have been known to kill and eat children.

Other casualties in the region result chiefly from attacks by elephants, hippopotamuses and crocodiles. Snakes take a steady toll as they do throughout the barefoot world. Another of this region's bizarre records is that here was the biggest toll taken by a mammal in one go – a rhino is said to have charged a file of 21 slaves chained together by their necks impaling a person near the centre of the line and breaking the necks of the others[1]. But I wonder if this is not an urban legend.

Of all potentially dangerous animals, snakes are by far the biggest killers. The next in the order depends on the region but will always include hippos, crocodiles, lions, hyaenas or elephants. The Nile crocodile is probably the most persistent man-eater throughout Africa (as opposed to man-killer). W. Robert Foran, one of Africa's more famous big-game hunters in the first half of the 20th century, felt that crocodiles kill and eat more people than any other large animal[2]. Jeremy Anderson tends to agree, saying that this is certainly so in Mozambique. It is probably so in South Africa.[3]

Of the world's five big cats (tiger, lion, leopard, mountain lion and jaguar), the tiger in Asia was probably the bigger danger in the recent past and was eating as many as 2 000 people a year throughout the first half of the 20th century. Pro rata the tiger in India, even though it is becoming rare, takes a disproportionate number of humans compared with the more numerous lion in Africa because, I believe, tigers are presented with more opportunities and Indians have fewer firearms; in addition, Indians seem to have a more fatalistic attitude towards man-eaters. The Gir Forest lions in western India – the only lions left in Asia – seem far more inclined to eat humans than lions in Africa.

African hunters refer to 'the big five', which refers to the five most dangerous and sought-after big-game animals – the elephant, buffalo, rhinoceros, lion and leopard. The rhinoceros refers specifically to the rather maligned 1.5-tonne black rhino (*Diceros bicornis*) and not to the much heavier, 2.5-tonne white rhino (*Ceratotherium simum*), which is generally less aggressive[4]. The hippo, a formidable animal and a notorious man-killer, is not included among the big five because it is not considered a 'game' animal – 'game' denoting creatures desired by recreational hunters.

THE NATURE OF THE BEAST | 35

There is an interesting divergence of opinion regarding which of the big five is the most dangerous to hunt. The late George Rushby, a hunter of renown, found lions were 'dull stuff in comparison to elephants'[5]. Major H.C. Maydon, one of the most experienced hunters in Southern Africa in the early 20th century, stated, 'The elephant is by far the most dangerous beast to tackle.'[6]

Advances in rifle and ammunition technology have changed perceptions regarding which is the more dangerous to hunt. Most 19th-century hunters would certainly have declared elephants as the most dangerous quarry but the modern rifle has considerably lessened the chances of the hunter being killed. During the 20th century hunters such as Bronsart Von Schellendorff, Denis D. Lyell, E.A. Temple-Perkins, and John F. Burger were citing lions as the most dangerous. Foran, who hunted all 'big seven'[7] around the mid 20th century, considered the tiger and the African elephant equally dangerous and placed them above the lion. C.J.P. Ionides, who did a great amount of shooting in Africa, put the leopard on top, as do a few other hunters. They argue that, if you mess up your first shot with an attacking leopard, you rarely get a chance for a second because it is small and very fast and it comes low against the ground. The records contradict these hunters.

Jeremy Anderson, who during control work in recent years has had to shoot both lions and elephants in large numbers, suggests the fairest way to assess which is the most dangerous African wild animal is to consider the numbers of hunters killed by that species and the frequency with which that species is hunted[8]. His formula reveals the lion to be the more dangerous. Anderson cites colleagues who have shot up to 2 000 elephants in culling operations without injury yet, although very few lions have to be hunted in wildlife management operations, death and injury from lions crop up fairly frequently.

The hunting fraternity's views regarding the relative dangers of hunting grizzlies or tigers, lions or elephants will depend, not only on the period, but also the type of terrain in which the hunters operate. Somebody hunting elephants in Africa's savanna country would feel a great deal more confident than somebody hunting elephants in a forest. Surprisingly, no professional hunter rates the African buffalo as the most dangerous yet, as the chapter on buffalo will reveal, it can be a formidable and cunning adversary that has killed many hunters.

Reports of hunters killed by their quarry and the Anderson formula would suggest that the most dangerous animals to hunt are (in descending order): lion, elephant, buffalo, rhino (both species together) and leopard.

There is also a tendency among a few latter-day big-game hunters to make hunting sound more dangerous than it really is in order to justify what they do. As has already been stated, the big five are normally passive animals if left alone and are quick to retreat. And none under normal circumstances would stand a chance against a well-placed bullet fired from a modern firearm.

Aside from the hazards facing hunters, Louis Leakey, the Kenyan palaeo-anthropologist, suggested towards the end of his days that the big cats generally avoid humans because of our repulsive smell. He argued at a press conference in New York in 1967 that 'nature endowed us with something of either a nasty taste or smell where the carnivores are concerned'. It is far more likely that our smell *became* repulsive to the big cats only after we had established ourselves as a dangerous species and generally as not terribly nice creatures. Since man first flung a stick or a stone at an animal, he has been preoccupied with weapons. To survive, he had to be a smart hunter with a smart weapon. By the time the Stone Age was in full swing, not even the biggest creatures on Earth were safe from this bold little hunter. The first Americans – 15 000 to 12 000 years ago – drifted in from the Asian steppes using the temporarily exposed Alaskan Land Bridge. Armed only with stone-headed spears, they killed four-tonne mastodons and mammoths. These now-extinct North American pachyderms may have felt no reason to retreat from these puny Asians with their funny little sticks – the first humans they had seen – and so they paid the price for failing to adapt to new circumstances. As humans migrated down the Americas, so they extinguished the megafauna; this spelled the end of the large scavengers that had depended on their remains as a food source – the dire wolf, the giant hyaena and others. The sole survivor into the 21st century is the condor vulture.

In most parts of the wilds, the faintest whiff of humans now triggers a fear response in the mightiest of creatures. But I don't think Louis Leakey was right about our 'nasty taste'. There are indications that, once a lion has killed its first human (usually accidentally, such as when a herdsman gets in the way of a predator that was stalking his cattle or sheep), it finds the taste agreeable. Having once tasted a human, a lion might well attack again and become addicted. Some man-eating lions have chalked up an extraordinary toll and have weaned their cubs on human flesh for several generations.

At Swartkrans – a hominid fossil site 40 kilometres (24 miles) northwest of Johannesburg – there is evidence that the first human species, *Homo habilis*, knew the controlled use of fire as early as 1.4 million years ago[9]. It surely would not have taken man very long to discover that generally animals are nervous of fire and for him to have used it to keep the big cats at bay. There's little doubt that *Homo* used fire to drive animals over cliffs or into pit traps and cul-de-sacs.

But the use of an ordinary camp fire to keep away wild animals is overrated. In the wilderness of America and the bush of Africa, camp fires are usually not only ineffective in keeping the really dangerous animals away, but sometimes even attract them. In Africa the hippopotamus and the black rhinoceros have both been known to charge camp fires. In the United States grizzly bears have deliberately charged camp fires and mauled campers sitting around them. There are many instances of man-eating lions and tigers snatching up victims sleeping around a fire, and there are cases in Central Africa where hyaenas have, with one hasty bite, torn off the food-smeared faces or hands of people sleeping beside fires.

The infamous pair of man-eating lions of Tsavo, which killed so many people in 1898 and 1899, disregarded fire. Almost nothing would stop them once they had selected their victim, not even firebrands hurled at them. In fact, they were so disdainful of fire that they ate some of their victims in the light of it.

Big-game hunter John Taylor, who had a great deal of experience in Central Africa, found fires useless but swore that his 300-candlepower storm lantern was effective – 'even the most determined man-eater would never venture into the dazzling blaze of light'[10].

Oddly, the sound of a human voice has been enough to frighten off dangerous animals. In a magnificently pedantic work, the Reverend J.G. Wood refers to 'a certain Mr. Cumming' caught by a wounded lion saying to it, 'Take it easy!' The lion dropped him and fled[11]. Richard Perry says, 'Man's noise was particularly upsetting [to the tiger] and noise is the one deterrent that will keep the most confirmed man-eaters at bay.'[12] When at night lions walked into the vegetable garden of Colonel James Stevenson-Hamilton, warden of the Kruger Park from 1902 to 1946, he would go outside and, in his high piping voice shout 'Shoo!' (and, no doubt, other words) to get rid of them[13].

Africans resort to shouting to keep lions, hippos, elephants and wild pigs off their crops at night, and there are instances when shouts have turned charging rhinoceroses. Clapping too can help. In 2008 Alan Calenborne was in the Okavango where the inhabitants spend a great deal of their time on the water in *mekoro* (dugout canoes), fishing and cutting papyrus for their huts. He recalls:

> One can be quite vulnerable in these dugouts because all you have is a pole for propulsion and that's pretty slow especially when in the vicinity of an aggressive hippo or croc. We were confronted by a bull elephant in a channel which we had to get through. He refused to move but was not aggressive. We were told to start clapping our hands quickly, upon which the elephant immediately moved off. I'd never experienced this before, but was told that this was a common and safe practice used in the delta.[14]

South African farmer R. de la B. Barker, writing in *African Wild Life* magazine many years ago, told how one of his African workmen turned a buffalo nine times in succession by screaming at it. Big male baboons will repulse a hunting leopard in the same way. Ian Player, who was for many years wildlife conservator in Zululand, was with a group of editors in Umfolozi Game Reserve (now part of Hluhluwe-Imfolozi Park) when a white rhino charged. There was one tree and, while the editors stood one behind the other behind the tree, Player stood his ground and shouted, '*Voetsek!*', a South African word meaning 'Scram!' that seems to be universally recognised by most animals. The rhino veered away[15].

Most animals have predictable flight-or-fight distances – the distance at which they decide whether to flee or take aggressive action. F.J. Pootman, writing of his experiences 60 to 70 years ago, calculated these distances and came to the conclusion that lions retreat when a person gets to within 80 metres (87 yards), elephants at 150 metres (164 yards) (in open country) and crocodiles at 150 metres when discovered out of water. He said most antelope rush off at about 20 metres (22 yards). This last one, if it were accurate for those days, which I doubt, certainly no longer applies.[16]

Flight distances depend on many factors. In game reserves where animals feel safe they can have the flight distance of cattle if approached by a vehicle. Outside protected areas most antelope flee at 200 metres (220 yards) and in hunted areas at 300 to 400 metres (328 to 437 yards).

It is interesting to consider why Africa's megafauna – its elephants and rhinos and many herd species – did not go into the same cataclysmic decline experienced by, for instance, the bison of America and the saiga antelope of the Steppes, both of which were reduced to small remnant herds because of uncontrolled hunting. I believe it is because the wildlife of Africa saw man evolve from the rock-throwing australopithecine (apeman) through to *Homo* (true humans) and, as humans developed more and more efficient weapons, so the animals increased their flight distances and survived. Only when the long-range firearm appeared on the scene did the continent's wildlife experience wanton slaughter[17]. It soon resulted in the extinction of the blue buck (*Ozanna leucophaea*) of the oryx family, the zebra-like quagga (*Equus quagga*) and the Cape lion (*Leo leo melanochaitus*), all of which were shot out in South Africa in the 19th century.

A course in a Mpumalanga college for prospective game rangers or ecologists offers advice on what distances various wildlife species will remain and not feel threatened once they become aware of one's presence[18]. To move to within a certain distance will cause an animal to display displacement activity – just as a domestic cat (or even a lion) when uncertain about a situation will pretend to groom itself while deciding what action to take. An elephant will make as if it is feeding and then, as you draw closer into its flight-or-fight zone, it will decide whether to attack or flee.

The hippopotamus, throughout its range, has been indicted as Africa's most predictably dangerous mammal. As humans encroach on its habitat, the hippo is coming more and more into conflict with people. The Nile crocodile too, as more and more people encroach on its habitat, is taking a considerable toll and individual crocodiles, having found humans easy to catch, begin specialising in man-eating. In one small dam in South Africa's Limpopo Province, crocodiles killed 11 villagers in 2002[19].

In many parts of Africa, refugees from flood and famine, but mostly from conflict, have fallen prey to predators. How ironic that humans, under certain circumstances, feel safer among lions than among their own kind. Unknown numbers of African refugees have been killed by predators as a result.

Even while writing these words, I received reports of attacks within a morning's drive from where I live, on the northern edge of Greater Johannesburg. In a matter of weeks there were five attacks by elephants on staff and visitors in reserves, resulting in four deaths. There were three attacks on villagers by hippos, of which two were fatal; a tourist was killed by a lion; a youngster was dragged from his tent and killed by a hyaena; another youngster was killed and partly eaten by a leopard near the busy staff village at Skukuza, the Kruger Park's main camp. Similar incidents in undeveloped parts go unreported, not the least reason being that they are so commonplace. In particular, human deaths are increasing from encounters with animals such as elephants and buffalo left wounded by poachers.

Until just over 20 years ago I knew of no instances of man-eating involving leopards in South Africa. Yet, since the 1990s, five staff members in the Kruger Park have been killed and partially eaten by leopards. This was probably the result of leopards becoming used to human flesh, after encountering weakened and starving refugees fleeing neighbouring Mozambique's civil war towards the end of the 20th century crossing through the park at night. An unknown number of these refugees were eaten – mainly by lions.

In parts of Africa north of the Limpopo River, where law and order periodically tend to break down, poachers wielding AK47s – the Russians' shameful legacy to Africa – have greatly reduced the numbers of herbivores, and as a consequence predators sometimes renew their interest in their one-time natural prey – humans. Several FAO researchers referred to the way chronic political instability in Africa impedes conservation and how there have been 30 wars and 200 coups d'état since the 1970s. 'As a consequence 500 million light weapons are readily accessible' – one gun for every two people in Africa or several for each male adult. The availability of guns enables villagers such as those living around Chad's Zakouma National Park to supply neighbouring towns and cities with bushmeat.

No wild animal is entirely predictable. The giraffe, for instance, despite being a singularly placid and timid beast, has been responsible for a few fatal incidents. In May 2010 a giraffe killed 25-year-old Merike Engelbrecht on a game farm in the Mopane district near Musina, just south of the Limpopo River. One of her dogs had menaced a female with a calf and Engelbrecht, in trying to control the dog, was kicked and died instantly of a broken neck. In June 2002 an American visitor, James Gregory, was killed by a blow to the head from a giraffe at the Aberdare Country Club north of Nairobi. James Drysdale, manager of the club, said a ranger had been killed there by a giraffe a few years earlier. I recall an incident on the Mombasa–Nairobi road 40 years ago, when a giraffe put its giant forefeet through the windshield of an approaching car, killing the driver instantly (giraffe when defending their young kick out with their front legs).

Once we realise just how many cases there are each year where people are killed by wild animals, we get an inkling of what it must have been like before we were adequately armed against our natural enemies and without medicines to fight infections from wounds – yet we successfully competed with large predators for food.

Some authorities have argued that only *Homo sapiens*' capacity for reproduction saved our species from being extinguished by predators and insect-borne diseases. I don't believe that our successful genesis was because of our ability to reproduce – nor in fact was it because we were 'born killers' as Raymond Dart[20] and Robert Ardrey[21] have suggested. We survived on the

African savanna because our single most important talent is our ability to cooperate. In some respects we behave like herd animals, looking out for each other. Cooperation was the secret of our survival in Africa, where the first humans evolved and from where they eventually migrated across the world. We hunted in highly organised packs, with weapons fashioned by highly skilled craftsmen, and while on the hunt we had the ability to plan tactics and communicate by complex signals and vocalisations. Beyond a pack of wild dogs there's no animal quite as determined and intelligent as a group of humans hunting something down.

4 THE LION

The lion's skin is never cheap.

– John Ray, *English Proverbs*

The lion, Africa's icon, is now down to possibly as few as 25 000 individuals over the entire continent. A major reason is that there is less and less space for them. And, where cattle are around and no trophy hunting is allowed, lions may be regarded as vermin.

In Kenya, where trophy hunting has been banned for a third of a century, there are fewer lions now than in the country's history. Those that survive probably represent a tenth of the lion's population in the mid 20th century.

A consensus of expert estimates indicates South Africa's Kruger Park has up to 2 000 and Etosha in Namibia between 250 and 750. Botswana's Okavango Delta, which lies more or less in between the two, could have as many as 3 500. The Serengeti Plains, which extend over 30 000 square kilometres (11 600 square miles) from northern Tanzania down to Kenya, have about 2 700 and the Selous Game Reserve around 5 000. The remaining 10 000 or so live outside the big reserves.

The now-illegal East African Maasai ceremony of spearing a lion is well documented. A young Maasai, to prove his courage and to become a *moran* (warrior), had first to provoke a lion into charging and, as it sprang, plant his spear point uppermost firmly into the ground and guide it in such a way that the lion impaled itself. Later the ceremony became one of communally spearing the lion and the man who first pulled its tail would get the honours. The ceremony, practised openly right up until the second half of last century, was often fatal to the Maasai and occasionally several men would die from wounds and infection.

In Zimbabwe there was a cultural ceremony where a Matabele youth would attract a charging lion and then fall beneath his body-length shield and, while the lion tried to tear it away, the other youths would place their assegais against the lion and push them home together. Then they would work them up and down in the wounds. Fatalities among the participants must have been common[1].

The spearing of lions, not necessarily ceremonial, still goes on in East Africa[2]. Kenyan pastoralists, for instance, speared 27 of the 40 lions that were killed in Nairobi National Park in 2003[3].

A charging lion is a disconcerting sight. Try to imagine the heavy cat standing with black tufted tail flicking and its yellow eyes blazing. Slowly it bounds forward – bounding rather like an enormous dog – and as it draws near it contrives to flatten itself against the ground and for some odd reason appears to shrink in size. It halts and, in a second, gathers itself and leaps forwards and upwards, teeth bared and massive claws unsheathed. The fascinating thing about this action is the bared teeth. Bared teeth are a sign of nervousness and fear. Lions don't bare their teeth when attacking an antelope or even, in my experience, when tackling an animal twice their size. This could explain why many claim that the charge of a lion can be checked – even without a gun. Guggisberg mentions in *Simba* that Heinrich Lichtenstein, the 19th-century German zoologist who lived for some time in the Cape, quotes Cape farmers as saying that an unarmed man was in no danger if he

> ... stared the charging lion in the eye with perfect steadiness and composure ... the lion is then supposed to become confused, retreating slowly at first and then faster and faster ... Hasty flight by the pursued person, on the other hand, was said invariably to induce the lion to take up the chase, the unfortunate person soon being overtaken and killed ... I cannot help feeling that the experiment has not very often been made.

Guggisberg comments on Lichtenstein's remarks:

> The advice was quite well founded ... although standing absolutely motionless may not be a complete guarantee of safety, it is certainly much

better than running away. On more than one occasion a charging lion has turned aside only a short distance from a hunter who did not move, to chase after one of the hunter's companions who had lost his head and run away.[4]

One man who successfully tried the standing-still-and-staring method was George Rushby – the lion pulled up at 15 paces, turned tail and fled[5]. Lt-Col J.H. Patterson, who wrote *The Man-Eaters of Tsavo*[6], also observed that a charging lion – a normal lion – would stop and slink away if its intended victim stood still and stared.

Pliny the Younger, who, like most of Rome's intelligentsia, became unhappy about Roman 'blood sports' (men pitched against wild animals in the arena), wrote of the lion:

The lion alone of all wild beasts is gentle to those who humble themselves to him and will not touch any such upon their submission, but spares whatever creature lieth prostrate before him. Fell and furious as he is at other times, he discharges his rage upon man before he sets upon woman, and never preys upon babies unless it is from extreme hunger.[7]

It is all rather fanciful but Conrad Gesner, who wrote *Thierbuch* in Zurich 1563, is quoted by Guggisberg: 'So peaceful and mild is the lion, that he does not wound anybody who throws himself on his mercy.' Tell that to the Christian martyrs who were forced unarmed into the Roman arenas to face lions. Mind you, the lions were first starved. However, there is the story of a Kenyan mother who, in 1960, was walking along a track near her home, carrying one child and leading the other by the hand, when she saw a lioness and her cubs coming towards them. The woman became rooted to the spot. Lionesses are extremely nervous and may be aggressive when they are with cubs. The lioness advanced upon the terrified woman. The lioness stopped just short of the trio and eyed them in that dispassionate way that some lions have. She then returned to her cubs and withdrew them from the track. What made the lioness so apparently empathetic? Perhaps it proves nothing more than, if you stand still when approached by a lion, there's a good chance it will back off. The average lion certainly does not see humans as a preferred prey species.

Rural Africans have a deep respect for lions. The lion, generally speaking, has an even deeper respect for humans. Even in the mid 20th century in some parts of Africa, men would chase lions from a kill – once they feel that the lions are more or less gorged – and take away the rest of the meat. They probably still do. Pigmy-sized Bushmen will also rush at gorged lions and rob them of meat. An acquaintance, cracking a whip, approached a group of feeding lions. The lions fled.

Lions will usually slink away as soon as they catch the smell of a human. If you stumble on a resting lion in the bushveld, it will invariably scramble to its feet and move off at a fast trot. On one of the early exercises in 1963 to capture and relocate hippos along the drought-stricken Olifants River in the Kruger Park – using drug-darts fired from a shotgun – I witnessed a ranger, who was running through long grass following a darted hippo, run physically into a lion. It is difficult to say who was more startled or who made more noise as they took off in opposite directions.

In the 1970s, while I was attached to a lion-darting-and-tagging team in the Kruger Park's central region, one night I witnessed rangers dart a pride of more than 20 lions in a group feeding at a carcass wired to a tree. Rangers then had several minutes to ear-tag them before the drug wore off. Some lions were stirring from their tranquillised state and had to have a little extra anaesthetic. This was done by pulling on the sleepy cat's tail with one hand and using the other to inject into its rump. Somebody asked about the one and only black-maned lion that had been darted, which had obviously slipped away in the darkness. Armed with a spotlight and preceded by two rangers, I helped in the search. We caught up with the lion and a ranger tried to grab its tail to re-inject it. But the lion moved into a faster trot, all the while looking nervously over its shoulder. After about two minutes we decided it was obviously too wide awake and gave up the chase. Then we heard a shout behind us to say the darted lion had been found close to where the others were. We had been pursuing a perfectly awake lion. It confirmed in my mind that lions will retreat rather than attack when they do not understand a situation – as will most wild animals.

The majority of people killed by lions are killed by being ambushed rather than after a long charge – I am told that three-quarters of lion victims buried in Nairobi Cemetery died in lion ambushes.

There is some evidence that suggests man-eating lions are more likely to attack after full moon and also between sunset and moonrise – bright moonlight not being conducive to successful hunting[8].

Panthera leo, the second-largest member of the family Felidae (next to the tiger) can, in exceptional cases, weigh up to a quarter of a tonne – 250 kilograms (550 pounds) [9], and measure three metres (10 feet) from nose to tail tip. According to Guggisberg, it has the strength of 10 men and has been seen to clear a four-metre (13-foot) *skerm* (cattle kraal fence), when driven by desperation, and to cover 12 metres (40 feet) in one bound[10].

The savanna down the east side of Central Africa suffers more than any other area when it comes to man-eating and man-killing. Ecologist Professor Craig Packer of Minnesota University – a man who has studied lion behaviour in Tanzania for many years – believes that nowhere is the human-wildlife conflict more of a threat to the lives of both humans and wildlife than in Tanzania, where, he says, lions 'currently attack over 120 people a year'.

In a 2007 report on HWC published by the FAO is a section dealing with lions, which cites a 2006 research paper by Packer[11]. The FAO report says:

> Since Tanzania is home to the world's largest lion population, this [HWC] conflict not only threatens human lives but also the country's economic growth through risks of indiscriminate retaliation against the lions ... Between 1990 and 2004 lions killed at least 563 people and injured more than 308. The problem has increased dramatically over the past 15 years with the majority of cases occurring in the southern part of the country where lions enter agricultural areas and villages in search of human prey. Tanzania has the largest remaining population of lions in Africa[12]. Considering the magnitude of the problem and the emotions it elicits, it

is surprising how little is known about carnivore attacks on people …
Understanding the context of attacks is crucial for designing effective
mitigation strategies to prevent future attacks.

Simple precautions can reduce the risks. Clearing bush and grass near
villages deprives lions of cover. The animals are more likely to attack lone
people than those walking in groups. Sleeping in fields to protect crops is
particularly risky.[13]

The region has bred such delinquents as the man-eaters of Njombe.
Dr Rolf D. Baldus, who directed the GTZ Wildlife Programme in Tanzania
until 2005[14], completed a case study of lions that had killed 35 people in
eight villages in the Rufiji district. He is of the opinion that one lion was
chiefly responsible for the deaths, though it might have been accompanied
by others that were eliminated mainly by snaring early on. The man-eating
stopped only after a particular lion was killed[15]. The episode lasted from
August 2002 to April 2004 and the toll surpassed the Tsavo man-eaters,
which killed 28 in a similar period of time during 1898–99. They were
immortalised in J.H. Patterson's classic *The Man-Eaters of Tsavo*[16]. Rufiji
Valley villagers named one of the lions Osama and it was later found to be
a young lion that had almost certainly been weaned on human flesh by its
mother. The Rufiji killers took men, women and children, often after having
broken through the walls of a hut or clawed through the roof. The killings
occurred not far from Tanzania's capital, Dar es Salaam, and east of the
Selous Game Reserve.

Baldus cites George Rushby who recorded 1 500 people killed by man-
eating lions in the Njombe region between 1932 and 1946 in a relatively small
area of 2 000 square kilometres (770 square miles).

Forty-two people were killed in 1986 in the Tunduru district on the
edge of the Selous Game Reserve – the district game ranger among them.
Between July 1994 and September 1995 Baldus mentions 29 people killed
and 17 injured in Liwale district south of the Selous Game Reserve.
Two years later, between January and November 1997, 17 were killed in
Mkuranga less than 50 kilometres (30 miles) from Dar es Salaam. In the

Lindi district during 1999 and 2000 at least 24 people were killed and a similar figure injured – all near Lindi airport. Lindi is a coastal town where slaves were taken in the 17th, 18th and 19th centuries, which again suggests a genetic predisposition for man-eating that goes back to the slave trade. The area is still one of the worst-hit in Africa. The local people have a special drum called *Ngula Mtwe* ('a man is eaten'); its sombre beat comprises two short thumps followed by a long one.

Baldus says one common method of attack is to snatch people off their *wadungu* (platforms in the fields for those guarding their crops from bushpigs at night). He said the victims were virtually 'presenting themselves as live bait'.

Brian Nicholson, the first warden of the Selous Game Reserve, believed that the Njombe man-eaters were more interested in cattle – they killed around 3 000 – and that most people killed by them were not eaten. There are various calculations about the annual toll taken by lions in the region, which is probably around 200, double the figure offered by Packer.

South of the Ruvuma River separating Tanzania and Mozambique is the province of Cabo Delgado where in 1908 Austin Roberts and Vaughan Kirby hunted down four man-eaters that were said to be eating 20 people a month. In some parts villages were abandoned from time to time when man-eating became really bad, and even the local style of architecture shows certain modifications to allow for persistent man-eaters that might try to rip open a hut to get at the inhabitants.

Over a period of 18 months between 2001 and 2002 lions killed 70 people in Cabo Delgado, mostly around harvest time when villagers tended their crops and slept out in the fields in temporary grass shelters. Lions pull them out while sleeping. Packer found in a case study of 60 victims that, while 13 were killed working in the fields and a dozen were going to or coming from the fields, most victims (35) were attacked in these temporary shelters.[17]

Jeremy Anderson was at a meeting in an adjacent province, Nampula, in 2002 when a pair of local delegates arrived two hours late. They had spent the night in a tree to escape a man-eater that had eaten four or five people. 'Let's go and shoot it,' somebody suggested. 'No! No!' said one of the men. 'People must just be careful.' This odd attitude is often expressed because many feel that man-eaters are demons that are immune to bullets and will take revenge if shot at.

One of the worst areas in Central Africa has been the Luangwa Valley in Zambia and central Malawi where in recent years a single lion ate 14 people in a month. East of that region John Taylor shot five man-eaters in a single night after an outbreak of man-eating at Nsungu. He shot three as they tried to tear down the door of a hut[18]. Apart from Central Africa, there are other areas that, from time to time, become decidedly unhealthy from a man-eating point of view.

The Tsavo area is familiar enough to those who have read Patterson's *The Man-Eaters of Tsavo* or have seen the 1996 Paramount movie about the Tsavo lions – *The Ghosts and the Darkness*. At the end of the 19th century many workers were eaten during the building of the railway from the coast of East Africa through to Nairobi. The Tsavo episode was not by a long chalk the most horrific in modern times – just the most publicised. Some people believe that the series of man-eating was triggered by the number of fever victims whose bodies had been discarded in the bush to save burial. There is also the possibility that the spike in the death toll had to do with the 1890s outbreak of rinderpest that wiped out tens of thousands of ungulates, including livestock, from East Africa right down to South Africa, though the Tsavo area had a history of man-eating long before that, which persists today. A generation ago W. Robert Foran shot four man-eaters in a day near this area after they had killed 50 people in three months. Tsavo's lions are particularly large and broad of shoulder, after generations of pulling down buffalo.

The Ankole district of Uganda, just west of Lake Victoria, has a bad name. In 1924 in the Sariga area of Ankole, following a rinderpest epidemic, two prides of man-eaters roamed over hundreds of square kilometres, during which period one pride accounted for 84 victims and another for 44. Their depredations spread to Entebbe on the north shore of Victoria. This particular reign of terror ended after 17 lions had been shot. But 14 years later another began. Guggisberg attributed the outbreak to yet another rinderpest epidemic that killed off the lions' natural prey, forcing the lions to eat cattle and so come into contact with humans. They partly lost their fear of humans and probably began man-eating by accident. Within a year 80 people had been killed and more than half a dozen man-eaters were operating.

One hundred and fifty years ago David Livingstone noted that some areas were notorious for man-eating – and these same areas remain notorious today. I suspect that they were being picketed by man-eaters centuries before Livingstone explored them, the most probable reason being the Arab slave trade. Indeed Livingstone came across a dying woman who had been shot or stabbed by her Arab captor because he felt he had overpaid for her. He found another tied to a tree. For more than three centuries Arab slave traders left tens of thousands of unwanted captives to die around their sacked villages and thousands more were left to die along the well-beaten slave trails. Practically all of them were consumed by lions, leopards and hyaenas. And, as the Arabs were taking only the cream of men, women and children, the few old men or sick villagers left behind were powerless to keep the wild animals at bay. Man-eating became habitual among the big cats and, in parts, frequent episodes of man-eating continue. John Taylor observed that on the Revugwi River near its confluence with the Zambezi one could shoot out all man-eaters but sooner or later they would reappear, suggesting a genetic predisposition[19]. There are, of course, several other contributory factors, for instance the rainy season. When the monsoons come and the grass grows too high for the lion to hunt its normal prey, some turn to killing cattle and sometimes people. Another factor is the disappearance of the lion's normal prey through hunting, snaring and veld fires. In so many studies it has been suggested that two of the best ways to ameliorate the lion versus human situation is to improve the corralling of cattle at night and to avoid an overkill of antelope and small mammals, which lions prefer to humans.

A contributing reason for man-eating must be the custom some East African tribes have of not burying their dead, but leaving them in the veld to be disposed of by wild animals. The Maasai sometimes wrap bodies in hide smeared with ox blood and fat, to ensure they are quickly found and eaten

– usually by hyaenas – because there is shame attached to families whose dead are ignored. These days the Maasai sometimes bury their dead, but in general burial is reserved for chiefs, while the common people are simply left outdoors[20]. Sometimes the lion that doesn't turn its nose up at eating carrion gets there first and acquires a taste for people. Man-eating frequently flares up after human catastrophes such as wars or epidemics when dead or dying people can be abundant. Man-eating lions were extremely rare in the Kruger Park until Mozambique's internecine war after the 1960s Portuguese revolution[21] when refugees from the former Portuguese colony began crossing through the Kruger Park at night to seek sanctuary in South Africa. The 2009 FAO report says, 'Nobody knows how many stragglers were eaten but it is likely to have been scores or even a few hundred.'[22]

In 1998 a ranger found 11-year-old Emelda Nkuna wandering in the bush near Punda Maria. The *Telegraph* reported:

Officials and rangers in Kruger National Park are concerned over the frequent attacks by lions on Mozambicans trying to get into South Africa in search of work. Illegals, on foot in unfamiliar territory, have no defence against the big cats, especially at night when the animals are on the hunt.

Last year field rangers became concerned for their own safety after five illegal immigrants were killed by lions in the north of the Park close to Punda Maria camp. At one point, three illegals were killed within three weeks. The cats seemed to have developed a taste for the flesh of easy human prey so seven of the man-eaters had to be destroyed.

'One of the lions was emaciated and was most likely to attack people,' explained the Park's General Manager of Nature Conservation, Dr Willem Gertenbach. Gruesome pictures of the lion's stomach contents show the remains of human hands, fingers and tongues. Bits of clothing and a wallet were also found. Gertenbach warned that the lions should not, however, be demonised. They were acting naturally in their own habitat.

The horrors of a lion attack were etched into the face of an 11-year-old girl found in the bush near Punda Maria early last month. Emelda Nkuna was lucky – the attacks are rarely discovered as there are seldom survivors and

THE LION | 53

hyenas eat what remains of the victims. 'There is a very good possibility that many more refugees have died because sometimes we find abandoned luggage and torn clothes, but we don't find bodies, not with the hyena population in the Park,' explained Gertenbach.

Last year, two illegal Mozambicans died in a Northern [now Limpopo] Province hospital after being trampled by elephants. Countless others were killed and eaten by crocodiles while crossing rivers. But it is the frequent lion attacks in the north of the Park that concern park officials most. 'Once lions lose their natural fear of humans, they become a danger to our own field rangers,' explained Gertenbach.[23]

It is significant that a great many hunters describe man-eaters as being in good condition. South African ranger Peter Turnbull-Kemp, quoted by Robert Caputo, found 91 per cent of man-eaters (he researched 89 cases) were in 'good' to 'fair' condition. Only 4.4 per cent were aged or injured[24]. The Njombe man-eaters were healthy specimens. In Uganda, out of 275 lion attacks described, 86 per cent were the work of healthy lions[25]. The theory that most man-eaters are too old or crippled to hunt game has long been abandoned. Sick lions do turn man-eater and may remain man-eaters even if they recover, but it is not as important a factor as many believed. A number of man-eaters have hunted no other quarry but humans – they were weaned on human flesh and taught the art of stalking men. These can be the most difficult to hunt and some are never caught and die of old age.

Many man-eaters display idiosyncrasies that are not found in 'normal' lions. One of the most pronounced is their habit of moving as far as possible away from the kill before dawn. They might cover 30 kilometres (18 miles) after eating a victim, ranging over hundreds of square kilometres. It is difficult to know whether they do this because they realise it must make it almost impossible to pin them down or whether it is because, having struck at a village once, there is little chance of catching another victim so easily. Although the Njombe lions killed 1 500 humans and also preyed upon 3 000 cattle, some man-eaters are reluctant to eat anything but human flesh and may show enormous patience in seeking it. This is in contrast to the tiger in India where even the most notorious man-eaters will frequently switch to other prey. Perhaps the oddest characteristic of all is the extraordinary lengths to which lions go to get a particular victim. They will step right over a sleeping man in order to get at one beyond him. Ionides wonders whether it is a difference in each man's smell. He claims lions show a preference for black people rather than white and that in selecting a victim lions tend to ignore whites[26]. Does this strengthen the theory that the African lion is genetically predisposed after centuries, millennia in fact, towards eating Africans? This possible predisposition was born out during the Chirundu man-eating episode in Zimbabwe, which is described later.

Quite often, once a lion has set its sight upon a particular victim, it will attempt to tear down doors to get at that person. Burning torches and shouting will not deter it. Ionides describes how, in Kenya, a man-eater entered a ring of blazing fires to snatch up a sleeping man, and there are many stories of lions going to some pains to snatch a particular man. Taylor describes how in Kenya a man cycled down a hill straight in between two man-eaters but, ignoring him, they pulled down the cyclist behind him and ate him. Guggisberg gives another example: a man near Fort Mangoche, Malawi, was attacked outside his hut, which was isolated from the village. His wife rushed at the lion with a firebrand and the lion dropped the man. The woman dragged her husband inside and bolted the door, but he died a few minutes later. Meanwhile the lion was attacking the door, trying to tear it away. The woman picked up a firebrand once more and rushed out into the night. The lion re-entered the hut and carried off the dead man.

Ionides describes how stealthily a lion can select a victim. Heinedi Ngoe, his tracker, was given a break from hunting a man-killer in Tanzania. The lion was held responsible for the death of 43 people and the hunt for it had been long and arduous. Ngoe, who decided to take advantage of his break to get married, became victim number 44 and, although he was snatched as he lay beside his sleeping bride, nobody heard a thing. The alarm was raised by the bride who woke up during the night to find her husband no longer with her. As she felt for him she discovered his pillow was blood-soaked. She screamed and villagers had to restrain her from going into the bush to find Ngoe. Next morning, by reading the tracks, Ionides deduced that the lion had waited just outside the village for a considerable time with its victim before going deeper into the bush to devour him.

A classic incident, which again illustrates the tenacity and unnerving cunning of a man-eating lion, happened in June 1900 when a man-eater entered Kima Station in the Congo, west of Africa's Great Lakes system. The lion attempted to tear through the corrugated iron roof of a station building and eventually succeeded in carrying off a railway worker. Later the same cat tried to ambush a railway driver, but the man managed to squeeze into a galvanised iron tank. For several minutes the lion tried to hook him out by placing its paw through a hole like a bear at a honey pot. Superintendent Ryall of the Railway Police decided to have a try at shooting it and had his personal railway carriage shunted into the siding. Two others joined him: Hübner and Parenti. The three men occupied one compartment. Ryall took first watch sitting on a bunk in the compartment and keeping watch through the open window. The two others slept, Parenti on the floor and Hübner on a bunk above Ryall. Ryall must have nodded off to sleep. The lion, either through luck or incredible intelligence, entered the carriage undetected at one end, padded softly down the corridor and slid the door open. Hübner woke up and saw the lion below him straddling Parenti, who was lying motionless but awake. The lion reached across the compartment, swiped Ryall across the side of the head (probably killing him instantly) and then sank its fangs into his chest near the left armpit. Hübner leapt over the lion's back and tried to escape through the sliding door leading into the corridor, but frantic people, knowing what was inside, were keeping it shut. Suddenly there was a crash and Hübner looked over his shoulder to see the lion leap through the open window with Ryall in its jaws. Parenti, who had been trapped under the lion, also leapt out of the window. The man-eater was later caught in a trap and was put on show, before being shot a day or so later.

It is most unusual to find a successful man-eater careless enough to get itself caught in a trap. Usually they are extremely wary and display an uncanny anticipation. It is vital when hunting a man-eater to hunt it down quickly – if the first few attempts to kill it are abortive, then the lion will most likely have learned some valuable lessons in evasion. Successive failures do worse than that; they tend to encourage locals to believe even more fervently than before that the man-eaters are under the orders of the witchdoctors and are immune to efforts to kill them. Doubtless these beliefs go back centuries and perhaps millennia. They are a very real handicap to the authorities and lead local people to refuse to cooperate, in case the bewitched lions come for them. They will even go so far as to erase the spoor so that hunters cannot follow it. They reason that by doing so the man-eater, out of gratitude, will grant them immunity.

No book gives as vivid a description of the terror created by man-eating lions as *The Man-Eaters of Tsavo*. Patterson's book immortalised its author as the man who rid the Tsavo railway of a pair of particularly notorious man-eaters, which, at the peak of their career, were cause for comment in the British House of Commons. Patterson describes a typical raid, which also serves to show the absolute fearlessness of some man-eaters:

> ... the two brutes made a most ferocious attack on the largest camp in the section, which for safety's sake was situated within a stone's throw of Tsavo Station and close to a Permanent Way Inspector's iron hut. Suddenly, in the dead of night, the two man-eaters burst in among the terrified workmen, and even from my boma, some distance away, I could plainly hear the panic-stricken shrieking of the workers. Then followed cries of 'They've taken him; they've taken him' as the brutes carried off their unfortunate victim and began their horrible feast close beside the camp. The Inspector, Mr Dalgairns, fired over fifty shots in the direction in which he heard the lions, but they were not to be frightened and calmly lay there until their meal was finished.

In the morning Patterson and some others set off to track the lions. Dalgairns believed he had wounded one and pointed to a dragging trail, which could have been a lion's foot.

> After some careful stalking, we suddenly found ourselves in the vicinity of the lions, and were greeted with ominous growlings. Cautiously advancing

and pushing the bushes aside, we saw in the gloom what we at first took to be a lion cub; closer inspection showed it to be the remains of the unfortunate worker which the man-eaters had evidently abandoned at our approach. The legs, one arm and half the body had been eaten, and it was the stiff fingers of the other arm trailing along the sand which had left the marks we had taken to be the trail of a wounded lion.

The lions got away and the Indian workers went on strike. Work on the Tsavo Railway came to a standstill and the killings continued night after night.

Soon after this Patterson called in a hunter named Whitehead who, on the night he arrived at Tsavo, was ambushed by a lion that clawed his back in the darkness. Whitehead's gun went off in the fracas and the lion switched its attack to Whitehead's askari, Abdullah. '*Eh, Bwana, Simba!*' (Oh, boss, lion!) was all the askari had time to say before he was dragged off and eaten.

The following night Patterson sat up in a very rickety machan, four metres (13 feet) from the ground. It was dark and the silence was absolute.

A deep long drawn sigh – sure sign of hunger – came up from the bushes and the rustling commenced again as [the lion] cautiously advanced. In a moment or two a sudden stop, followed by an angry growl, told me that my presence had been noticed and I began to fear that disappointment awaited me once more. But no; matters quickly took an unexpected turn. The hunter became the hunted; and instead of either making off or coming for the bait (a donkey) prepared for him, the lion began stealthily to stalk me! For about two hours he horrified me by slowly creeping round and round my crazy structure, gradually edging his way nearer and nearer. Every moment I expected him to rush it ... I began to feel distinctly 'creepy' and heartily repented my folly in having placed myself in such a dangerous position. I kept perfectly still, however, hardly daring even to blink my eyes; but the long continued strain was telling on my nerves ...[27]

Patterson then felt a blow behind the head, which terrified him beyond words. It was an owl but his involuntary start caused the lion to growl. It

now began to advance on the hunter. 'I could barely make out his form …
I took careful aim and pulled the trigger. The sound of the shot was at
once followed by a most terrific roar, and then I could hear him leaping
about in all directions.' The lion bounded off but was not far away when
Patterson heard it plunging about. He sent more shots after it and silence
returned. The first man-eater of Tsavo was dead and as Patterson shouted
the news from his machan hundreds of Indians in nearby camps yelled
'Mabarak! Mabarak!' (Saviour). The lion was an excellent specimen
measuring '9 feet 8 inches' (about three metres), which is about the
maximum for a lion.

It is interesting that Patterson lured one of the notorious pair by using a
donkey as bait and the second one by using a goat. In other words, like man-
eating tigers, some man-eating lions may vary their diet.

In Zimbabwe a pride of lions specialised in cyclists. Prides have been
known to prefer to tackle giraffes and there's a pride in East Africa that
specialises in killing elephants. Another lion population has adopted the
strange habit of sleeping in trees. Such specialisations – whether for climbing
trees or man-eating – are handed down for generations.

A healthy lion that has become a man-eater would need a minimum of
40 victims a year in order to stay alive. In Malawi one was known to have
eaten 14 people in a month, which would work out at approximately 168 a
year. But many people killed by lions are not eaten and man-eaters do not
always get the chance to eat a victim completely. Ionides mentions one that
ate a fat woman and then ate a warthog 'for dessert'. Ionides, who shot 40
lions in his day (of which more than half were man-eaters), shot this one as
it slept off its meal. Individual lions have killed as many as three people in a
single night and fed off them. A person who has never seen a wild lion will
find it difficult to appreciate how enormously powerful they are. To a cat
powerful enough to kill a buffalo, a man is small fry; lions have been known
to carry victims for a couple of kilometres without rest. One judiciously
placed bite – usually in the head or neck – kills instantly, as does a swipe of
its great pad, which can break an ox's neck. Lions have leapt over and even
through thorn fences, carrying victims in their jaws.

Patterson gives a vivid account of the strength of the lion in his Tsa.

The lion managed to get its head in below the canvas, seized a man by the foot and pulled him out [of the tent]. In desperation the unfortunate water-carrier clutched hold of a heavy box in a vain attempt to prevent himself being carried off, and dragged it with him until he was forced to let go by its being stopped by the side of the tent. He then caught hold of a tent rope and clung tightly to it until it broke. As soon as the lion managed to get him clear of the tent, he sprang at his throat and after a few vicious shakes the poor bhisti's [water-carrier's] agonizing cries were silenced forever. The brute then seized him in his mouth, like a huge cat with a mouse, and ran up and down the boma looking for a weak spot to break out. This he presently found and plunged into, dragging his victim with him and leaving shreds of torn cloth and flesh as ghastly evidence of his passage through the thorns.

Patterson describes how this lion showed complete disdain for fire and human shouts, since he ate his meal in the light of the camp fires, leaving only the skull, jaws, a few large bones and two fingers.

Man-eaters, unless harried, leave little behind. When children are their victims, the lion eats all except the skull cap, which is licked clean. All other bones are usually eaten. In the case of adults, skull and jaws are usually left, as are the soles of the feet or boots (usually with the feet still in them) and bones such as femurs and the hips. The meat is cleaned from these larger bones by the cat's rasp-like tongue.

Quite as chilling as the Tsavo episode is the story behind the man-eaters of Chirundu just below Kariba Dam. It was revived in 2001 when 'Ganyana', in the professional hunters' magazine *African Sporting Gazette* (now *African Hunting Gazette*), gave a graphic description. The setting is the 30-kilometre-wide (18-mile) floodplain on the Zambezi where, even today, man-eaters take their toll. I was near there, upstream in Kariba Gorge, in July 1999 and in the night heard lions in the hills. I learned the next day that a 19-year-old English tourist from Luton had left his tent open and had been woken by a lion; he ran from his tent and was pulled down by 12 lions, which began to eat him. The game guard, who had only a side arm, chased the lions off by driving a Land Rover at them.

In 1936/37 the present suspension bridge across the river carrying the A1 route from Harare to Lusaka was built. There was a custom among the locals in the vicinity of Chirundu Hill of leaving the dead outside the villages 'to be buried by the hyaenas', which, of course, also attracted lions. According to Ganyana the situation was compounded in those days by the custom of even tying up aged people and criminals who had become a burden and leaving them in a bone yard for the 'demons'. All lions were believed to be spirits that were bullet proof and must be appeased, not hunted. Lions that eat antelope were good spirits while man-eaters were demons.

During the summer of 1936, while labourers cut a path to the site from nearby Chirundu Hill, there had been plenty of lion incidents but no workers were killed. Then in May 1937 a surveyor who had tried shooting a lion was mauled and died of septicaemia. A nightmare followed.

The bridge builders had just moved in. On 3 May the BSAP[28] drafted Trooper Hewlett and a constable to the project. On their first night in camp the constable was taken by a lion and Hewlett, hearing the lion eating, lit a hurricane lamp and, without taking a gun, stepped outside. He too was eaten. A week later, when a lion and lioness took a surveyor, fear began to grip the camp. That same night workers managed to fight off a lion by using axes and spades. Thorn fences were thrown up and each dawn revealed the spoor of lions that had circled the camp during the night, seeking a way in. On 15 May a lion found a weak point and snatched a night watchman. Two days later a black-maned lion took a man. The next day half the workers left. On 20 May skilled and semi-skilled workers recruited from the currently depressed mines in Johannesburg arrived. Many were semi-urbanised and had no clue about the wilds. Ganyana says, 'The lions had a field day and by the end of the week there were 17 dead.'

Three professional hunters were brought in and offered a £10 bounty for each lion killed. By the end of May one had been eaten, a second mauled and was dying of septicaemia and the third was dying from malaria. The head of a nearby Seventh Day Adventist mission, Dr Frazer, calculated that if he killed the man-eaters the locals would stop believing in demons and turn to his church. He looked after his hospital during the day and spent the night sitting against a baobab tree to obviate being attacked from behind. He sat there uttering the cries of a dying man. He had no lamp and, with so little visibility, he had to wait until the lion was within 10 metres (33 feet) before firing. A problem was that hyaenas, expecting to snatch a meal, would approach him and, not wanting to make a noise, he had to swing at them with his rifle butt. They retreated.

'In the attacks on the labourers it had been noted that all the killings could be attributed to ... a very huge black-maned lion and a much slimmer beast with a limp.' The slim lion had been seen with a female and it was feared they would raise more man-eaters. In the first three nights Frazer shot three man-eaters but the killings went on. On the fourth night Frazer, not surprisingly, dozed off and was woken by a lion grabbing his boot and dragging him away. He managed to reach out and grab his rifle. He fired but missed. The lion retreated.

Frazer took a couple of days off, only to hear the black-maned lion had eaten the bridge engineer. The locals were now convinced that Nyaminyami – the river god – was behind it all and that killing the lions was merely making things worse. They took to sleeping in the baobab trees while the Johannesburg artisans dug ditches and placed iron girders over the top, 30 centimetres (one foot) apart. Nightly they cowered as lions barely an arm's length above their heads tried to drag the girders apart.

A lion was shot on the girders and troopers in the baobab trees shot two more dead. A jobless Scots prospector, Jock, arrived with a pump-action weapon and was offered £20 a lion tail and £100 for the black-maned or his mate. In two weeks Jock collected nine bounties 'but nearly a score of men had been eaten in the same period'. On 14 June the black-maned lion killed a man who was securing the gate for the night and the next day Jock, accompanied by a police trooper, followed its tracks for 35 kilometres (22 miles). They found the remains of an old woman and decided to camp on the trail to intercept the lion, assuming it would return to Chirundu. But it was already nearly at Chirundu. Even as they waited the black-maned lion killed and ate two men five kilometres (three miles) from the camp. It then made the odd mistake of sleeping under a nearby tree where, with a single shot, Jock killed it. By now he'd made as much money as he would have done in two years of prospecting, so he upped and left.

On 15 June Frazer came back 'determined to prove to the Batokas [the local people] that God would triumph and their river demon and his feline cohorts could not stop the bridge let alone the road'. On 16 June Frazer, on his motorcycle, caught sight of a lioness stalking a labourer and shouted a warning. He managed to fire a shot, giving the man a chance to scale a very inadequate tree. The lioness and a male began circling the tree and trying to claw the man out of it. Frazer killed her with one shot but the male came for him. Strangely it didn't move nearly as fast as he expected. When the lion was 10 metres (33 feet) away Frazer dropped him. He found the lion had an old but serious injury to a back leg – this was the notorious companion of the black-maned lion.

Great celebrations followed. Thirty lions had been killed and for days nobody was eaten. Workers became lax about their defences and more lions moved in from outside. Before the bridge was completed and the road to Zambia finished, 17 more men were to die and 11 more lions.

Ganyana says, 'The story does not completely end in 1938. Every year thereafter travellers on the road ended up as meals for passing lions.'[29]

Guggisberg points out how prompt action can on occasion save a man-eater's prey. The victim might remain alive for some time after being carried off. However, there was a case involving a priest in German East Africa who called – in vain – for 15 minutes while literally being eaten alive. He tells of a man who stood by helplessly when a villager was dragged screaming into the bush by a man-eater. He and some volunteers advanced on the lion, which, with determined charges, drove them back time and time again. All the time the victim moaned for help or screamed when the harried lion fed. Next day his abandoned body was found intact except for a thigh and calf.

It has often been said that a lion's victims feel nothing. David Livingstone, who was attacked by a lion in Botswana, described it thus:

... growling horribly close to my ear, he shook me as a terrier does a rat. The shock produced a stupor ... a sort of dreaminess in which there was no sense of pain or feeling of terror, though quite conscious of all that was happening. It was like what patients partially under the influence of chloroform describe, who see all the operation, but feel not the knife ... This singular condition was not the result of any mental process. The shake annihilated fear and allowed no sense of horror in looking round at the beast.[30]

Guggisberg quotes the Hungarian naturalist Kittenberger who was badly mauled in Tanzania as saying he felt 'no pain at all'. Others have repeated similar sensations. On the other hand C. Cronje Wilmot, a Namaqualand tsetse control officer, who was mauled and wounded 23 times in one attack, records feeling intense pain. Arnold Weinholt and Petrus Jacobs who were both attacked at different times recall terrible pain – 'like having nine-inch nails driven into you', said Weinholt.

A great deal of man-eating on the African continent is done by prides of lions rather than solitary lions. The Njombe man-eaters numbered 15, the Ankole man-eaters even more. The Tsavo killers, including the notorious pair, numbered eight.

The Njombe man-eaters, shot out in 1947 by George Rushby, were slightly smaller than average and their pelts were 'glossier and more luxuriant than those of lean, hard-working game-hunting lions'[31]. These lions, referred to in some records as the 'Ubena man-eaters', operated in the vicinity of the northern tip of Lake Malawi. They first made an appearance in 1932 and by the beginning of World War II were moving about in three or four small prides. In the game area under Rushby's administration they killed 96 people in 1941, 67 in 1942 and then another 86 before their reign of terror ended. During this period, records Rushby, they were killing at a heavier rate in a second area and at a lower rate in the third. 'The renowned man-eaters of Tsavo were small fry in comparison.'

Rushby was transferred to Mbeya in the Southern Province of Tanzania in 1946 and almost immediately received a telegram from W. Wenban-Smith, the Njombe District Commissioner. It read: 'I beg you to apply earliest attention to man-eaters. Conditions in this district pathetic.' Along the short Njombe section of the Great North Road 17 road workers had been eaten. The villagers had evolved 'a negative form of defence' by drawing into larger communities and abandoning the smaller villages. But the human toll did not decline and incredibly, during the 14 years of man-eating, not a single lion had been shot in the Njombe area.

An incident typical of the Njombe district at the time was when a lion rushed into Rujewa village, bowling people over as it went, and grabbed a woman as her husband stood frozen with shock. Without apparent effort it carried her in its jaws to a group of lions waiting on the perimeter of the village. They ate the woman in a thicket. The husband, armed with an antique rifle, was one of the few brave enough to go after the lions, but as the party drew near the thicket he came face to face with a lioness that was carrying his wife's leg. He was so shaken that he could not fire and the lioness walked off.

The man-eaters were adept at killing humans and usually did so by breaking their victim's necks with single bites.

Rushby tried every ruse imaginable to kill the lions, but each one failed, including a series of cunning traps. Because of the already strong local suspicions regarding magic, Rushby realised the importance of quick success. The problem with traps was that they had to be baited with the meat that the lions like best – human meat. But, even if some flesh could be found, it was difficult to gauge where to set the traps, knowing that the lions would wander off a dozen kilometres (seven miles) in any direction by the next day. Rushby had his first opportunity when a messenger brought news that lions had attacked the village of Mambego, 80 kilometres (50 miles) from where he had anticipated them striking. Two villagers had been taken. Rushby, tired from three futile hunts, raced to Mambego and followed the spoor of a lioness, which he shot with four bullets. She did not necessarily need four bullets; it was just that this one 'had to be dead' said Rushby. Three more man-eaters were bagged soon after, but the toll of human life did not appear to drop; nevertheless the four dead man-eaters encouraged tribesmen to take up the hunt and massed hunts began. These had an immediate effect upon the death toll. It rose. Villagers, firing wildly, killed no lions but managed to kill three of their own numbers.

By 1947 the lion's human toll was markedly falling, except in one area where the lions appeared to be making one last stand. Rushby, splitting his best helpers into pairs, combed the bush and shot a male and female. It seemed to be all over, when suddenly a woman was eaten. Two more lionesses were flushed out and shot.

In all 15 man-eaters were shot in the Njombe district, two were injured (probably mortally) and five other lions – probably not man-eaters – were shot. The man-eaters had been responsible for what Rushby described as 'without doubt the greatest and most sustained record of man-eating ever known in Africa' – in modern times at least. The hunt had lasted 15 months and in as many years successive generations of killers had eaten an estimated 1 500 people.

In Africa there is a firm belief among tourists and even professional hunters that lions will never attack a person in a car. The belief has largely grown up with the advent of game reserves where people can sit in their cars, with open windows, within touching distance of lions, or even sit in the middle of a pride in an open bush vehicle. The lions ignore vehicles and their passengers and sometimes use vehicles as a means of ambushing antelope. The petrol fumes mask the predators' scent.

In March 1962 the theory received a setback when Frederick van Wyk and Ronald Holloway were attacked as they slept in their car less than a kilometre south of the Chirundu Bridge over the Zambezi, between Kariba Dam and their home town Lusaka. They were severely mauled as they fought the lion inside the car. They finally managed to slam the door on its body, causing it to retreat. The incident is not unique. T. Murray Smith was arriving with the Maharajah of Jodpur in an open truck near Lake Manyara, Tanzania, when a lion sprang onto the bonnet and smashed the windscreen. The Maharajah shot it through the brain at point-blank range. Robert Caputo mentions how the American lion expert Craig Packer, rounding a corner in a minivan with some tourists, ran up against a pair of Tsavo lions mating. The male immediately charged the van and smashed two of the windows. Nobody was hurt. Lions sometimes jump onto cars and peer at the occupants through the windscreen. It is difficult to say what their motive is. Probably curiosity.

Westerners try to frighten themselves with such fictitious horrors as vampire bats or werewolves, but not even the top horror writers can dream up something to equal the real-life horrors suffered by Africans who are victims of the *watuSimba* – lycanthropy. It is a form of black magic in which people take on the shape of animals. It is found in various forms up and down the length of tropical Africa but, for some reason it is and always has been particularly prevalent in the Central Province of Tanzania.

In 1920 the police in the Singida district combed the bush and villages for the killers of more than 200 people. Scores of clawed bodies, thought at first to be victims of man-eaters, were found to have been stabbed and then clawed. W. Hichens, who shot the real man-eaters, described how he was stalking a lion when he came across a youth wearing a lion skin. The youth, drugged to a point of insanity, wore gloves to which lion claws were attached and carried long stabbing knives. Even where genuine man-eaters were about, people paid protection money to witchdoctors, believing them to be in control. Taylor refers to the same outbreak of lycanthropy and says there were actually 11 man-eating lions and that the witchdoctors took advantage of their presence. Those 'in the know' were able to hire the lion-men to settle old scores and then the relatives of the victims would be approached and they, in turn, could hire the killers for a revenge killing. Over a period some of the lion-men were caught and hanged by the colonial authorities.

In 1946 things came to a head again when, a little further south nearer Singida village, 30 locals were murdered by *watuSimba*. One victim, a woman, managed to run for her life and described to the authorities how she had been attacked by a youth wearing a skin. When she had fully recovered she changed her story and said she had been clawed by a real lion.

In January of the following year 53 Africans were rounded up by the police and eight of them were charged with running the lion-men ring. They appeared in Dodoma court. Because the lion-men (the actual killers in the field) were still under their masters' spells, the killings continued and, before the month was out, 10 more people died.

There seemed little doubt that the witchdoctors had also attempted to train real lions and hyaenas to be man-eaters and in 1947 a lioness, her teeth neatly filed to points, was shot in the district. In March and April a couple of dozen more people were murdered. By June the death toll of that year – despite the arrests – was 103. By then 29 of the arrested people had been sentenced to death but it was not until 1948 that the murders ceased. Since then there have been other outbreaks. In 1958, according to Bulpin (quoting Rushby), 21 lion-men victims were reported.

During the Dodoma trial a great deal of light was thrown upon lycanthropy. Some lion-men were hired out for 40 shillings a killing and were in turn 'sub-let' to others to cover the original costs. A woman said in evidence that her husband had been kidnapped by witchdoctors who drugged him and trained him to go about wearing a lion mask, with his body covered in baboon skins. He carried two long knives and on occasions cut meat from his victims and ate it.

The court was told how children were either kidnapped or sold to witchdoctors, who kept them in dark underground grain stores where they were unable to stand upright. They gradually developed a crouching walk and were never again capable of walking erect. All of them were driven to insanity. Their wrists were broken and their hands were tied against their forearms to simulate pads of animals. The tendons in their legs were cut to give them a particular gait. The court heard how a 15-year-old girl, kidnapped at the age of eight, was hired out as a killer at 30 shillings a time. Some of the lion-people lived on a diet of meat and lived in a lair like animals; they even copulated like animals (two were women). Almost every night they slunk out of their den in search of random victims.

Some victims might have later been consumed by real man-eaters; a five-year-old girl, snatched from her mother by a Singida lion-man, was found when only her skull, teeth and a few other parts were left. The witchdoctors – two of them women – were hanged for this particular killing, but the lion-man himself was never discovered.

I have found no record of lycanthropy after 1958 though it is possible that the occasional outbreak still occurs in remote areas of East Africa where the darker side of witchcraft occasionally manifests itself.

Solutions to the conflict between lions and humans are hard to come by. After millennia and hundreds of thousands of deaths, there still is no convincingly effective answer to man-eating lions, beyond eradicating them, as the Russians once planned to do to end the wolves–humans conflict. But to do that would surely be to emasculate Africa. Why not then eradicate elephants and hippos to alleviate crop damage? Why not wipe out all wildlife, leaving humans a free hand to plough and pave the continent? Fortunately, to go by the Ugandan survey referred to in Chapter Two, only a third of people living in lion country want that solution. Nearly a third felt people should learn how to behave in lion country.

Basic to any future strategy is to conserve the lions' natural prey species. If ungulates are overhunted then, naturally, lions will turn to livestock and humans.

The 2009 FAO report makes the point that several countries allow for the community or individuals acting on their own to kill problem lions. The paper cites the republics of Cameroon, the Central African Republic, Côte d'Ivoire, Mali, Mozambique, Niger, Senegal, Tanzania, Zambia and Zimbabwe:

> In all 10 countries there is at least one law article related to the defence of human life and property from wildlife attacks; the principle, whatever category the culprit animal comes from and whether protected or non-protected; when a culprit animal is killed, the case must be reported to the wildlife authority with slight differences between countries in terms

of delay to report: immediately in Niger; within three days in Cameroon; within 14 days in Zambia; and differences exist among the countries in terms of beneficiaries from the meat or trophies from the animals killed: in Cameroon and Senegal the victims benefit; in Niger and in Zambia the state does.

As far as stock losses are concerned farmers have the responsibility to protect their stock as best they can, especially at night when they are placed inside lion-proof kraals. For those who can afford it, electric fencing is very effective and such fences are necessary for communities living near the reserves. In Zululand rangers from some of the protected areas will help neighbouring communities strengthen their stockades.

It is equally important that wildlife authorities ensure that farmers who lose stock to lions or families that lose breadwinners are quickly compensated. This is being done here and there but the authorities – in Zambia for instance – claim farmers and local authorities abuse the system, and so the process of compensation is very slow and often becomes a matter of communal resentment. If anything, it might even further antagonise and incite communities to take revengeful action against lions, guilty or not.

Instances where lions break into homes are rare indeed but one wonders if this was far more common in the old days before the advent of the firearm. Some years ago I accompanied Revil Mason, professor of archaeology at the University of the Witwatersrand, to the ruins of a four-centuries-old abandoned Iron Age village 150 kilometres (93 miles) west of Johannesburg. Its foundations had recently been exposed by torrential rain. In the gap where the doorway would have been in the hut's circular foundations was a long black and shiny stone with a pronounced groove – the bottom runner of a sliding door. The huts had cavity walls at the front so that the door, during the day, could be slid back into the cavity rolling on tiny naturally-occurring ferricrete balls (ball-bearings!). At night the door would be rolled closed. Then a peg would be inserted from inside through the inner wall so that the door could not be pulled back from outside – an ancient but effective defence against man-eaters.

There are certain basic precautions that can be taken, apart from clearing the area around the village of long grass and of low bushes that might be used by lions for concealment. This is usually done as a matter of course to make it easier to spot snakes and particularly because of the threat of grass fires endangering thatched structures, yet even so I have seen Zimbabwean villages closely ringed by tall grass and scrub. Another precaution is to avoid walking alone in lion country – especially at night. When walking at night it helps to make a noise – shout and sing. But I imagine if there's a known man-eater around this might not be advisable.

In 2009 Mozambique established militia to seek out man-eaters just as a fire brigade is quickly deployed to fight fires wherever they occur. It is too early to say whether this is proving effective. In some countries, notably Zambia, village headmen are provided with the means of dealing with such occurrences: they appoint a village marksman and the headman has to hand regular reports in to the regional authorities.

Insofar as alleviating death in the bush goes, it seems the most effective route is to create, via schools and village headmen, a sustained campaign to educate people on how to avoid becoming a casualty, just as most urbanised countries have ongoing campaigns to educate children and adults on how to use the road safely. So many villagers' deaths in lion country are the result of a careless and often fatalistic attitude that if ever there was a 'highway code' for people living in lion country it should include obvious rules such as never walking home alone after dark, making lots of noise when walking after dark, never running from a lion, and, above all, avoiding reducing the lion's natural prey.

Sport hunters believe they are part of the solution and, whatever one's attitude is towards hunting (I am not a hunter myself), there is ample evidence that, where controlled trophy hunting is allowed on a sustainable basis, conservation scores. Paradoxically, responsible sport hunters can be the most practical of conservationists.

Organised lion hunting brings in $200 million a year into Africa according to the 2009 FAO report. Rolf D. Baldus, president of the CIC Tropical Game Commission[32], said at a World Forum on the Future of Sport Shooting (WFSA) congress in Nuremberg in 2011:

Wild lion populations outside national parks have a future only if rural people see a direct benefit from living with lions. Official and controlled hunting encourages the lion inhabited states to leave hunting blocks as wilderness and refrain from converting them into farmland with little biodiversity. Banning lion trophy hunting and preventing hunters taking home legally obtained trophies removes the economic as well as management and law enforcement incentives that are necessary for conservation ... [in Kenya] the lion has not been legally hunted for over thirty years and during that period the lion population size has crashed to roughly about 10% of the neighbouring Tanzanian lion population, which has been hunted all along the same period.

Bans clearly do not work and actually accelerate the extinction of species[33].

Baldus said all large cats that have been formally protected for decades are now even more endangered: the tiger, the snow leopard and the jaguar. He could have added the cheetah. In the 1970s there was a moratorium on hunting cheetahs and in Namibia – at the time it was the country with the most cheetahs – the population fell because sheep farmers who lost sheep to cheetahs began shooting them on sight and leaving their valueless bodies to rot in the veld. The ban was lifted and the cheetah population is now growing despite (or, rather, because of) the resumption of hunting them.

Namibia's Minister of Environment and Tourism, Netumbo Nandi-Ndaitwah, told the 2009 WFSA forum:

Wildlife has more than tripled in recent years, as hunting tourism has encouraged landowners to have game on their land. Wildlife has turned from a cost into an asset. This has been the case on farms and ranches, but more importantly many rural communities have formed their conservancies, and the income from wildlife now contributes to their livelihoods. Game is back on land where it became extinct a long time ago. And with the ungulates the predators return. Namibia is the number one cheetah country in Africa.[34]

5 THE LEOPARD

Nature, red in tooth and claw

– Alfred, Lord Tennyson

Unmolested in its natural habitat, *Panthera pardus* is the most graceful, beautiful and widely distributed of all the big cats and is found throughout Africa, from the Cape of Good Hope and including the jungles of Central Africa where the lion does not occur, and up to the shores of the Mediterranean. It is thinly distributed in Asia Minor and then is more densely distributed from India to the Chinese seaboard and down to Java. It is also found in Sri Lanka. When it comes to survival, it is probably the most successful of all wild felines.

Throughout this vast area the species remains the same, with only sub-specific differences, mainly in size and colouring that would be imperceptible to most people. The panther of India is the same species as the leopard of Africa and the 'black panther' is merely a melanistic form that is capable of throwing off normally spotted offspring. The so-called 'tiger' or 'tier' of South Africa is also the common-or-garden leopard.

The animal is inclined to be a little on the stocky side when conditions are really favourable, but never to the point that it loses its graceful appearance. It weighs on average 45 kilograms (99 pounds) but many males will weigh up 70 kilograms (155 pounds). In captivity leopards can reach almost 100 kilograms (220 pounds). The record length of a leopard is just short of three metres (almost 10 feet), which is not far off the record length for a lion, though a third of a leopard's length is tail.

The road to the Albert National Park between Lake Kivu and Lake Albert in East Africa is a winding road, which picks its way through damp, lush vegetation, the occasional banana plantation and clusters of beehive huts. On the right of the road and soaring over 4 500 metres (5 000 yards) above the jungle is Mount Mikeno, a volcanic peak that in the swirling mists usually shrouding its head broods like an unhappy ogre. Through glasses you can make out the spot where Carl Ethan Akeley was buried.

Akeley was an American by birth and an African by heart, and his special interest in Africa was its enormous variety of mammals. As a taxidermist and naturalist, the American made five prolonged visits to the continent to collect and to observe, and on his return to America he organised the mounting of some of the world's finest wildlife museum exhibits, including one tableau of an entire family of elephants. It has been said that his imaginative handling of museum exhibits ended the era where taxidermy was something akin to stuffing teddy bears.

Akeley died a natural death at the age of 62 in November 1926 but twice he had cheated death: once when an elephant badly mangled him and once, in 1896 on his first visit to Africa, when a wounded leopard ambushed him, sending his rifle flying. Akeley's fight with the leopard illustrates how, if a man keeps his head, he has more than a sporting chance when tackled by one of these animals.

Akeley was caught completely by surprise when the cat came at him and had time only to throw his arm up in front of his face. The leopard seized his arm in its teeth and began clawing at him with its front paws. Akeley, with his free hand, grabbed the cat round the throat and held it away from his body, his main concern being that the leopard might bring up its back legs and rip him down the middle; leopards occasionally use this tactic, although in most attacks they prefer to latch on with their front claws and then tear with their teeth. The taxidermist tightened his grip on the cat's throat and slowly worked his arm out of its mouth every time he felt its jaws relax. Soon only his fist was in its mouth and this he kept there so that the leopard could not bite his face and head. Akeley then deliberately fell on top of the animal and dug his knees into its rib cage and his elbows into the leopard's armpits, to force its flailing front claws apart. Slowly the cat went limp. By the time Akeley rose the leopard was dead. It had died from strangulation and its ribs were cracked from the pressure Akeley had exerted. Akeley's escape is by no means unique – wounded leopards, ferocious though they are, rarely manage to kill their human victims and usually end up running away.

The leopard, whether it is hunting along the nullahs of India or on the African veld, is something of a Jekyll and Hyde. Unmolested and in normal health, it is a shy, nervous animal with a very marked fear of man. It pursues mainly small prey and unlike the lion or tiger, both of which normally move out of a person's way with aplomb and dignity, the leopard will usually run, perhaps pausing to cast a quick glance over its shoulder. Should you make a sudden movement the cat will spring into the nearest thicket and flee like a startled hare. But when a leopard is wounded, trapped or cornered, it can be an entirely different animal. A wounded leopard is likely to attack the first man to come within striking distance. Colonel Stevenson-Hamilton described a wounded leopard at bay as 'the very incarnation of ferocity'[1] – its ears are laid back low against a flat-looking head, its teeth gleam between withdrawn and snarling lips, while its eyes, 'fixed with steady and sinister stare upon his enemy, and filled with dull, greenish red light, glare murderous hate. Even when you know his back to be broken, his appearance is so little assuring that you have qualms about approaching close to administer the *coup de grâce*.'

It is strange that a creature so well equipped in tooth and claw, so given to fierce attacks when wounded and so capable of lightning action should, at the same time, find it difficult to overpower a man (I am referring not to confirmed man-eaters but to the 'incidental' attackers such as freshly wounded ones). It is not as if the leopard lacks strength: its strength is one of its most astonishing characteristics. T. Murray Smith saw a '150 lb [68-kilogram] leopard kill a 90 lb (41-kilogram] antelope, and carry it in its jaws like a dog carrying a hare' and then climb up a tree with the buck in its jaws[2]. This feat is by no means unusual. Leopards frequently carry their prey into trees out of reach of hyaenas, jackals and lions and there is a record of one carrying a 90-kilogram

(200-pound) baby giraffe four metres (13 feet) up a tree. There are instances where it has dragged humans into its 'larder' in the branches of trees.

When tackling a man, the leopard appears to rely on fast claw work and repeated biting to overcome its victim – unlike a lion or tiger, which often kills by cuffing a victim or biting into the neck. The leopard's fear of man could be a mark of its intelligence and, along with its nocturnal habits, is one of the chief reasons it has survived within sight of large cities and even in suburban hills.

This apparent feeling on the part of the leopard that discretion is the better part of valour is often manifest when the cat is attacking a baboon troop and runs into a big male. I recall such an incident. The male baboon immediately attacked the stalking leopard and, screaming at the top of its lungs, it tore at the cat's neck and shoulders with its long canines. The leopard, spitting and snarling, rolled in the dust with the baboon and then withdrew and tried to 'box' the animal with open claws, but the baboon knew better and once again closed in and began biting. After perhaps a minute the big cat disengaged itself and fled ignominiously, leaving a badly torn baboon licking his wounds.

In the past many, if not most, people mauled by leopards died from infection. Gee states that the incidence of infection from leopard wounds (in India) was higher than with tiger's[3]. Penicillin has cut deaths from infection to less than 10 per cent of people mauled.

Going by the very inadequate statistics available from local authorities, wildlife bodies and (mainly) incidents reported in newspapers, there are probably a few hundred attacks a year in Africa. Again, relying only on anecdotal material, it seems that in most cases leopards lose out and there are many instances where they have been killed by hand.

In collecting data for *Man is the Prey*[4] I found not a single reported instance of man-eating in South Africa prior to when the book was published in 1968. I came across none afterwards – not until the 1990s when suddenly, in the Kruger Park, there was a change in behaviour. The first incident of which I am aware was in 1992 when a leopard entered a window (an extremely rare event) and dragged Thomas Rihlamfu, a game guard in the northern region, out of his sleeping quarters. It partly fed on him. A year or two went by and then a woman was ambushed and partly eaten as she walked home in Skukuza Camp's staff village – Skukuza, the sprawling 'capital' of Kruger, has a busy staff village that is almost suburban. Then a schoolboy – the son of a staff member – was killed near his home returning from school in the late afternoon. In each case it was a different leopard. In August 1998 a leopard killed a recently graduated ranger, Charles Swart (25), who was taking tourists on a night drive and had stopped for a smoke break on a bridge in the south of the park. It was 6.45 pm and dark and the tourists were standing 50 metres (55 yards) away when they heard the ranger's rifle clatter to the ground. In the torch light they saw a leopard standing over him. When two of the tourists ran shouting towards the scene, the leopard dragged its victim into the bush. The leopard was feeding on its victim when rangers arrived and shot it. It proved to be an old male in very poor condition. In its pelt were many bite and scratch wounds, indicating that it might have been involved in territorial fights with younger leopards.

A month later, just after sunrise, a large male leopard leapt at the windscreen of a utility vehicle near Hazyview just outside the Kruger Park's southwest border and jumped over the cab roof and into the back of the vehicle, which was loaded with labourers. Six had to be hospitalised and one had lost the flesh on his forehead, eyebrows and part of his cheeks. One of his companions managed to kill the leopard by stabbing it repeatedly with a small screwdriver.

This sudden spate of attacks in this specific region – leopards are found in many parts of South Africa – might have been because of the unknown numbers of Mozambicans killed and eaten in recent years while crossing illegally into South Africa via the Kruger Park at night. Lions and leopards were finding them easier prey than antelope, and the park's authorities issued a warning that habitual man-eating was becoming a problem. At first those crossing were refugees from the internecine wars in Mozambique, but more recent trespassers are in search of work or even 'just passing through to shop in South Africa' according to a senior ranger. A ranger one night was sent with trackers to capture a large party returning across the park to Mozambique; they had been spotted loaded with goods and moving east across the park at night. Laden as they were, the ranger was unable to keep up with them.

Dr Willem Gertenbach, the Kruger's former nature conservation manager, who is greatly concerned with the increase in man-eating, was quoted as saying, 'The problem is not the [predators] but the illegal immigrants. The big cats have not so much acquired the taste for human flesh but [have] developed an instinct that people on foot are much easier to stalk and catch than, say, an impala.'[5]

He said this was particularly true of older animals who found it difficult to hunt.

This was certainly aberrant behaviour for leopards in Southern Africa. In the space of four years in the 1960s I meticulously combed what records existed (mainly newspaper files) and found 32 cases of leopard attacks in South Africa and neighbouring Namibia, Zimbabwe and Mozambique. This does not mean, of course, that there were only 32 attacks in those years. There were undoubtedly many unrecorded[6]. What is significant is that, of the 32 reported attacks (some involving three or four people), none was fatal. Thirty-one people were mauled, most of them severely, while eight of the 32 survived unscratched. Of the 32 leopards, all had been provoked by being wounded or by being attacked by the victims' dogs. Ten leopards escaped and were not heard of again, 10 were shot, seven were speared, clubbed or axed to death and five were killed bare-handed. In four of the attacks the victims were able to punch the leopard on the nose and in all four of these instances the leopard broke off the engagement, in one of them only temporarily.

In the 1960s a 70-year-old Zimbabwean, Kudziburira, in the Sinoia district, took his dog and an axe to look for a leopard that had killed one of his goats. The dog flushed the leopard and was immediately killed. The cat then turned on the old man, who in his fright dropped his axe. The leopard bit into his left arm, which the man had thrown up to protect his face. Using his free hand, the man gripped the cat by the throat and held it there until he felt its jaws relaxing.

Then pulling his arm from its mouth he put both hands round the cat's neck and strangled it. Two months later, Castelo Branco Montero of Lourenço Marques (now Maputo), Mozambique, was attacked by a wounded leopard, which he managed to strangle, and not long afterwards Anselmo Gomes Matos strangled a leopard with his bare hands at Silva Porto just north of Namibia in Angola. In all these incidents the men were mauled[7]. In an incident in Kenya, Daniel M'Mburugu (73) was tending his crops outside the village of Kihatu near Mount Kenya when a leopard charged out of the long grass and, as he put up his arm to defend himself, it seized his wrist. He managed to get his hand down its throat and seize the root of its tongue, whereupon it began to choke. Villagers, hearing his screams and armed with pangas, rushed to his aid and killed it.

There are literally scores of such incidents on record, one of a man who is reputed to have killed two leopards by crashing their heads together. The man who is said to have performed this feat was Cottar, a Texan who became a professional hunter in East Africa and who, according to J.A. Hunter, killed three leopards bare-handed in his career[8]. (Cottar was later killed by a black rhinoceros in the most ridiculous manner: he was filming it charging for a female client and must have been unused to the view-finder, as his finger was still on the button when the rhino horned him.)

It is interesting that some hunters class the leopard as the most dangerous of all the big-game animals to hunt. Hunter called it 'the most dangerous game'. Ionides also considered it the most dangerous animal in the world and Rushby classed it as more dangerous when wounded than a wounded buffalo[9]. He described the leopard as a 'perfectly built killing machine' and said that as a target it was so small and so fast that it was most difficult to hit. To make things doubly difficult for the hunter, the leopard specialises, a little like the tiger, in short-range charges. Yet I have found no record of a hunter being killed by a leopard.

There is a theory that a female leopard will charge a man on sight if she has her cubs with her. Ted Reilly of Mlilwane Game Sanctuary in Swaziland told me how he once came across a leopard cub in the bush and, after observing it for some time, decided it was orphaned or abandoned. He picked it up. Even as he straightened up he could sense danger and, as he stood holding the bundle in his arms, he found himself looking into the eyes of the mother. Reilly, alone and unarmed, fairly jumped out of his skin. His involuntary movement caused the leopard to turn and flee. I have been told of other incidents where female leopards have abandoned their young under fraught circumstances. An Acholi game ranger in Queen Elizabeth National Park in Uganda was not so fortunate the day he cycled past a leopard cub. Guessing the mother would not be far away, he pedalled harder. The next thing he knew the mother was running behind him. She sprang onto his back where she remained firmly latched like a pillion passenger as the ranger put on an admirable burst of speed. The leopard, not terribly used to riding on a bicycle, fell off 200 metres (220 yards) further along. A similar incident befell Arian Suque of Dodoma, Tanzania, when a leopard with three cubs attacked him and pushed him off his bike. Suque fought the leopard and she ran off, but a minute later she came back for another round. Again Suque fought her and again she retreated. But this was an occasion when the leopard came out on top: she punctured the man's wheel and he had to walk 16 kilometres (10 miles) to hospital.

At the state opening of Kenya's parliament in 1963, Senator Godfrey Kipbury, a Maasai member of the Senate, made a grand entrance wearing a smelly, fresh leopard-skin hat. Forty-eight hours before, the senator had speared the leopard on his farm but was clawed in the process. Annually scores of leopards are speared, mainly because of their threat to livestock.

Although India, through the writings of such men as Jim Corbett, has received more attention regarding its man-eating leopards, Africa also has a history. Throughout its range the leopard, when it does turn man-eater, goes mainly for children or sick adults. Ionides says a leopard around the village of Masaguru on the Ruvuma River, in the notorious Southern Province of Tanzania, preyed only upon 'children and small women'. It was known to have killed 26 yet not one victim was eaten. Not even a bite was taken from them and when eventually it was shot it was found to be in good shape[10].

Rushby surmised that leopards eat humans merely for variety. He points out that, even as man-eaters, they still continue to kill and eat monkeys and baboons as well. In fact, says Rushby, there cannot be much difference between human meat and monkey meat and therefore there is no reason for the leopard to become addicted to human meat[11]. Rushby was senior game ranger in the Njombe district in the Southern Province and he recorded 'at least fifteen people a year' falling prey to leopards during the 1950s. In recent times both Mozambique and Tanzania record the occasional death by leopard.

Most of Africa's man-eating leopards have been reported in Central Africa where they have caused entire villages to be abandoned. Some of the man-eaters are crippled or enfeebled by old age, such as one that killed 22 people in northern Mozambique. It was too weak even to carry its victims off and would tear chunks out of them and then limp away into the night.

Ionides described the depredations of a man-eater that haunted Ruponda in Tanzania's Southern Province in 1950 and which might have been forced into man-eating because of the ill-fated British Groundnut Scheme. Workers had been clearing the bush for kilometres around and the leopard's natural prey had entirely disappeared. The leopard began by killing a labourer but, before it could eat him, it was beaten off by villagers. That same night, 10 kilometres (six miles) away, it ate a baby after stealing it from its bed. Two days later it hid behind some scrub and watched a mother teaching her toddler to walk; then when the mother went indoors for a few seconds the leopard snatched up the child and later ate it. Trackers found that the leopard must have crouched behind the bush for some time waiting for a chance to spring. Two more children were taken near Ruponda before Ionides got to the village, and then the leopard struck a fifth child 10 kilometres away. Eighteen children were taken by the same leopard in a few months; the youngest was a six-month-old baby and the oldest a nine-year-old girl. Eventually the leopard was caught in a trap.

In India there have been many notorious man-eaters. One was the Panar leopard, which is supposed to have eaten 400 people before it was shot in the mid 20th century. There was also the man-eating leopard of Rudraprayag of which Jim Corbett wrote in his book of the same title, which ate 125 people during roughly the same period[12]. The man-eaters of Bihar are said to have eaten 300 people between 1949 and 1960. There is a host of others, such as the

Gummalapur man-eater that was shot by Kenneth Anderson after it had eaten 42 people, that have plagued the wild and beautiful valleys of central and northern India.

It seems that individual man-eating leopards in India kill a significantly greater number of victims than their counterparts in Africa. One reason could be that the man-eaters of India appear to survive a great deal longer than the man-eaters of Africa; the Indian rural dweller is less equipped and less persistent when pursuing man-eaters than Africans, who were in any event assisted by the well-armed colonialists, who remained entrenched in Africa long after the colonialists had departed India. Jim Corbett, who shot both the Rudraprayag leopard and the Panar leopard, puts the high incidence of man-eating down to the way Hindus, in times of plague or famine when there is no time to burn their dead as they normally do, put pieces of charcoal into the corpses' mouths and leave them in the bush so leopards, always partial to carrion, acquire a taste for human flesh.

The whole character of a man-eating leopard differs from that of a mauler. Man-eaters show no ill-temper but instead hunt with extraordinary calm and cunning. In India, as in Africa, most of them specialise in children. Gee mentions how leopards usually hang about on the outskirts of villages, in the hope of knocking down stray livestock or village dogs, and so become familiar with the ways of men, though they rarely lose their caution[13]. Only a few become contemptuous of man – the man-eater of Panar was one of them.

When, in 1910, Jim Corbett was called upon by the Indian government to hunt down the Panar man-eater, he made straight away for the area, which was not very far from where he lived at Nianital in northern India. Questions were being asked in the British House of Commons about this man-eater, since it was picking over the same area as the infamous tigress of Champawat – between the two cats 836 rural people were consumed. It is significant that, until Corbett stepped in, no other hunter had heeded the government's appeal for somebody to kill the animal. The locals' reaction, as always, was to barricade themselves in at night – and even during the day when they felt it necessary – and, as a result, the Panar man-eater often tore down doors or burrowed into grass roofs to get at occupants.

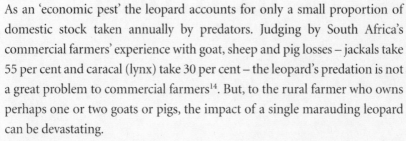

As an 'economic pest' the leopard accounts for only a small proportion of domestic stock taken annually by predators. Judging by South Africa's commercial farmers' experience with goat, sheep and pig losses – jackals take 55 per cent and caracal (lynx) take 30 per cent – the leopard's predation is not a great problem to commercial farmers[14]. But, to the rural farmer who owns perhaps one or two goats or pigs, the impact of a single marauding leopard can be devastating.

Beyond ensuring that the leopard's prey species remain in plentiful supply, there is little that can be done to avoid the occasional leopard attack.

6 THE ELEPHANT

The Elephant is a gentleman.

– Rudyard Kipling, 'Oonts'

Of all large animals the elephant is perhaps the most loved in the eyes of visitors and tourists, and probably the most hated among many of Africa's rural communities. The 2009 FAO paper 'Human-wildlife conflict in Africa' reported that the antipathy towards elephants 'goes beyond that expressed for any other wildlife'. It said that people living in Central Africa 'fear and detest' elephants; that farmers in Zimbabwe display 'ingrained hostility' to elephants. '[Elephants] are the focus of all local animosity toward wildlife' and rural Ugandans 'complain bitterly about elephants – except where they have been eradicated'[1].

But there's another side to the story – one that needs to be understood and addressed with urgency. First, it is an obvious moral duty for educated people to ensure the survival of the African elephant. Yet it is quite possible that today's infants will witness, before the century is out, the pathetic sight of the last heavily guarded elephant left in Africa, not because of what *they* are likely to do to the remaining elephants but because of what we and our forebears have allowed. But, to ensure the elephants' survival, it is necessary to alter the perceptions of millions of people who live among them. Those of us who have been with wild elephants feel the privilege of having watched the biggest land mammal on Earth, and many of us feel a distinct emotional attachment to them, though thousands will wonder what we are talking about. We understand the importance of biodiversity and the elephant's role – most rural dwellers do not. We have to understand their grievances and ensure that they derive tangible benefits from living among elephants. That is the challenge that conservationists have barely begun to recognise.

Dr Gay Bradshaw, psychologist and ecologist at Oregon State University who is involved in the university's environmental sciences programme concerned with human-elephant conflict (HEC), says, 'Everybody pretty much agrees that the relationship between elephants and people has dramatically changed. What we are seeing today is extraordinary. Where for centuries humans and elephants lived in relatively peaceful coexistence, there is now hostility and violence.' Bradshaw and her colleagues, in a 2005 article in the science journal *Nature*, titled 'Elephant Breakdown', suggested that elephants are displaying increased animosity. They are behaving in a way never before encountered because they are suffering a form of 'chronic stress' brought about by years of poaching, culling and ever-shrinking habitat. She wrote that stress 'has so disrupted the intricate web of familial and societal relations by which young elephants have traditionally been raised in the wild, and by which established elephant herds are governed, that what we are now witnessing is nothing less than a precipitous collapse of elephant culture'.

Charles Siebert, quoting, among others, Gay Bradshaw's concerns, suggested in the *New York Times* that human pressures on elephants in Africa and India were seriously disturbing the animals mentally. Siebert's articles ('An elephant crackup' and 'Are we driving elephants crazy?') suggested that elephant behaviour was changing and that they had grown 'strange and violent in recent years' – neurotic would have been a better word. Researchers, he said, were blaming human encroachment on the elephants' way of life[2].

Bradshaw's observations brought to mind the fate of a neighbour of mine, a German expatriate who was visiting the Pilanesberg National Park north of Johannesburg with his five-year-old daughter. He stopped to watch a pair of sub-adult elephants. For some reason father and daughter were out of the car when one of a pair of elephants charged them. As far as can be made out, the father threw his daughter under a bush before running in the opposite direction, possibly to draw the tusker away from her. The ranger on the investigating team found the man's lungs 100 metres (109 yards) from his torso. The elephant had knelt on him, trampled him and tusked him, tearing him apart. It was then joined by the second elephant in attacking the man's empty car, rolling it over and over.

In many regions of Africa, HEC is resulting in an increasing human toll caused by elephants, as well as increasing crop damage. There is also evidence of an increasing toll of elephants themselves – mostly by Far Eastern ivory smugglers who hire African poachers and bribe African officials and government ministers. There is compelling evidence that because of human activities – ivory poaching, rapidly growing populations, habitat stress, capture drugging and relocating elephants from one region to another or even from country to country – elephant behaviour throughout Africa is indeed changing and elephants are showing signs of a societal breakdown.

The IUCN, recognising the increased tensions between elephants and humans – not just in Africa but in Asia too – has launched a worldwide project aimed at alleviating some of the suffering – on both sides. HEC poses serious challenges to wildlife managers, local communities, conservationists worldwide and to the IUCN's African Elephant Specialist Group and its Asian counterpart.

The African bush elephant, as it is correctly called – the largest of all land mammals – can weigh up to 10 tonnes and can stand well over three metres (10 feet) at the shoulder. One killed in Mucuso, southeast Angola, in 1974 is claimed to have weighed 12.24 tonnes – the largest land animal known to be killed by a human[3]. American-Hungarian hunter J.J. Fenykoevi shot one 60 kilometres (37 miles) from Mucuso in 1955 whose skin alone is said to have weighed two tonnes. The animal weighed more than 10 tonnes and was '12ft 6ins' (almost four metres) at the shoulder[4]. It is on permanent exhibition at the Smithsonian Natural History Museum in Washington D.C. with Africa's smallest mammal, the pygmy shrew, sitting on its toenail.

The African elephant is found from the Nile Valley down to the south of the continent and is at home in forest, swamp, desert or the savanna. Elephants have been seen high on Mount Kilimanjaro in Tanzania and can scale slopes that would force a man onto his hands and knees.

Between 1900 and 1984 Africa's elephant population was reduced by 93 per cent and by the end of the 1990s was found in only five per cent of the continent[5]. Its numbers had fallen from 1.3 million in the early 1970s to about

450 000 in 2008[6]. Some argue the population may now be as low as 300 000, but that estimate comes from those opposed to culling elephants – culling even where the elephants' concentrated population is causing habitat destruction. In view of the fact that there are probably in excess of 200 000 in Southern Africa (south of the line of the Zambezi/Cunene rivers), I would put the figure for Africa at nearer 400 000. The recent sharp decline in numbers has mainly been due to poaching by ivory hunters working for Far Eastern crime syndicates. The elephants annually lose many thousands of their number to poachers, scores of poachers are killed in the process and at least one hundred rangers lose their lives each year protecting the elephants[7].

Far from diminishing, the illicit ivory trade appears to be increasing.

The ferocity and strength of an angry African elephant can hardly be exaggerated. In the 1960s a friend, Tony Ferrar, then a post-graduate in zoology, was working as a research officer in Zimbabwe's Gonarezhou National Park. He was driving a girlfriend through the reserve when he saw a lone cow elephant disappearing below a rise with her four- to five-year-old calf. Leaving the young woman in the vehicle to look after his small dog, he set off unarmed to check the herd (he admits he was trying to impress the young woman). He approached within five metres (over 16 feet) of one of the females who was peacefully browsing the mopane scrub and was unconcerned by his presence. It was not unusual for him to approach that close.

Suddenly Ferrar's dog, having escaped from the vehicle, came up to him, saw the elephant and rushed at it barking. The cow got a fright and charged the dog – and the dog ran behind Ferrar's legs for protection. Ferrar had but a split second to think. There was no tree big enough to dodge behind or climb. He had only one recourse – to run for his life. But he knew it was impossible to outrun an elephant, which can reach a speed of 35 kilometres per hour (22 mph) when it puts its mind to it.

Ferrar hazily recalls falling a couple of times and at one time flying through the air with the wind on his face. More vividly he recalls how it all ended – he was on his back his face inches from the screaming elephant's forehead. Her tusks were speared deep into the ground on either side of his chest, which prevented her lowering her head any further to crush the life out of him.

'I was determined to remain calm,' Ferrar said. 'I slithered out from under her head and stood up facing towards her backside, which was sticking up in the air.

'I then began running back the way I had come. I felt rickety.' The adrenaline was not enough to sustain him for more than a few metres and he had to sit down next to a tree. He watched the elephant withdraw her tusks and to his enormous relief she rushed off, still screaming, in the direction she had been facing.

Ferrar whistled to his friend who was out of sight 100 metres away. He thought he might have broken his back. His horrified girlfriend found him shaken and bloody. She had never driven a Land Rover before, but raced off in the vehicle to get help. Moments later she was back – to tear a branch off a tree and put it in the road so that she would recognise the spot on her return.

After a while Ferrar tugged at his shirt tail and was dismayed to find a fist-sized hole through the front of it. Gingerly he examined himself and found a tusk hole in his lower stomach wall. There was very little blood. He rested few a few minutes, drew a deep breath and, examining himself further, discovered a large hole between his legs where he had been tusked through the perineum. It later transpired that this had forced his pelvic girdle apart, breaking it in four places. He had obviously been tusked from behind, which would account for his unscheduled flight. Miraculously it had missed his more complicated areas and had pushed through the folds of his fortuitously empty intestines.

Apart from what he describes as some interesting scars that he can't show people, Ferrar is with us still, wiry and fit and living in Barberton, Mpumalanga.[8]

W. Robert Foran left us with graphic account of an elephant's temper and its enormous strength. Foran was one of the last of the 'old-school' ivory hunters. He carried a .256 Mannlicher-Schönauer that most hunters would consider too light for elephant. He tells of the time he was in the Zoka Forest in Uganda – scene of many elephant hunts in the first half of the 20th century

– with his gun bearer, Hamisi Bin Baraka, who was also one of the old school. The two men were keeping a sharp lookout for buffalo when they were charged by a bull elephant. A shot to the brain in such circumstances would have been risky, as the critical area is the size of the palm of a hand and the animal's enormous head was moving from side to side. A heart shot would have been absorbed or deflected by the hanging trunk. Foran aimed into the chest cavity, bringing the elephant momentarily to its knees. But a .256 has little stopping power against something the size of a bus. Before the elephant could rise, Foran put a second bullet between its eyes. The bull, screaming with rage, stood up and continued to charge. Foran had no time to grab the heavier rifle from Bin Baraka, who, for some reason, had not fired. A second later the elephant hurled Foran into a thorn tree. Bruised and almost shirtless and badly torn by the needle-like thorns, he scrambled down the tree. Then he heard a scream of agony from Bin Baraka:

> I do not know what actually happened but I think he must have turned to run for a safe refuge – most abnormal behavior on his part. Even the spare cartridges, carried in slots in his shirtfront, were bent and twisted almost double. The angry beast had left behind not a human body, only a pulped mass of flesh and broken bones.

Foran never again hunted elephant.[9]

According to Brian Handwerk on a National Geographic Channel programme in July 2009, the African bush elephant (*Loxodonta africana*) and the Asian elephant (*Elephas maximus*) are currently killing 500 people a year[10]. It's as good a guess as any. He said, 'Elephants are being pushed into smaller and smaller places and increasingly they are pushing back.'

Kenya's heavily poached elephant numbers are beginning to recover. This is despite that country's past unhappy record for profligate poaching and corruption among conservation officials, involving the exporting of illicit ivory to the Far East. In Kenya's largest reserve, the 22 000-square-kilometre (8 500-square-mile) Tsavo National Park (roughly the size of Belgium or Massachusetts), more than 11 000 elephants were counted in 2010, reflecting an increase of 1 300 in three years. South Africa's similar-sized Kruger Park has 14 000 elephants – about double its estimated carrying capacity (a figure that was arrived at in the 1970s but is being hotly debated). The removal of the fence between the Kruger and Mozambique might reduce some pressure, though elephants that were drugged and transported to the Mozambique side soon found their way home. I have heard that some have since become established.

Botswana, a country the size of France but with a human population of just over two million, is also said to be overpopulated by elephants. In 2003 this mainly desert republic on South Africa's northwest border had an estimated 123 000 elephants, from a population of about 8 000 animals in 1960[11]. Game hunter Ron Thomson put Botswana's elephant population in excess of 150 000 in 2006[12]. I think the number is now generally accepted as 160 000 – most of them being in the far north of Botswana (the Okavango Delta – the world's biggest inland delta) and migrating back and forth across the Caprivi and Zimbabwe. Some are showing signs of slowly returning northwards to their former habitats in previously war-torn Angola. The position is less clear to the east in Botswana's Tuli Block, which straddles the confluence of the Limpopo and Shashe rivers where Botswana, South Africa and Zimbabwe come together. The Tuli Block has, in parts, been devastated by elephant overpopulation. Botswana has eschewed elephant culling and allows very limited hunting.

Over to the west in Namibia, there were 4 800 elephant in 1980. There are now 20 000 and HEC incidents are increasing. Namibia is yet another country that continues to control its wildlife centrally, allowing landowners very limited rights when it comes to commercial exploitation. Namibian commercial farmers in the Kamanjab area northwest of Outjo are losing patience with expanding herds of elephants that are reclaiming their previous migration routes and moving back into their former habitats on which commercial farms are now situated[13].

Elephants in the former Kaokoland were virtually wiped out by the South African apartheid government and its military officers in the 1970s and 1980s, who used to shoot them with rapid-firing guns from military helicopters. But, since Namibia's independence in 1990, conservation measures by non-governmental organisations and the Namibian government have helped the elephants recover.

The former Kaokoland and Damaraland, now incorporated into the Cunene and Erongo regions in northwestern Namibia, are regarded as Namibia's last wilderness with freely roaming elephants, black rhinos and giraffes in spectacular scenery. Tourism is an important revenue source for the rural communities in these regions. In the Cunene region, farmer Helmke von Bach claimed 950 elephants were moving 'from the communal areas to our farms to get water because virtually every water hole in the communal land is occupied by people and the elephants are driven away'[14]. Speaking at the 2008 annual congress of the Livestock Producers Organisation, he said the government had reduced its provision of subsidised diesel fuel to rural communities for generators to draw water out of boreholes; as a result the waterholes had dried up and elephants had destroyed farm fences, gates and zinc reservoirs, and even ripped up water pipes to get at water. Elephant cows were tusking the sides of water tanks so that their calves could drink.

He ended on a surprisingly tolerant note: 'We must find an amicable solution for everyone, elephants, farmers and for tourism.'

Von Bach afterwards told *The Namibian* that farmers had formed conservancies to protect wildlife but had little say over game management on their farms. They proposed translocating 100 elephants to Angola at their own cost, but 'again the government did not want it'.

The Namibian and Botswana governments allow trophy elephant hunting on a limited scale: hunters pay up to $65 000 for a two-week safari, plus $450 a day for bringing along non-hunting friends. Hunters generally see trophy hunting as a means of bringing wealth to communities. In fact, in many instances this is becoming the only access locals have to wealth. Nobody is suggesting that controlled hunting will reduce elephant numbers.

Jeremy Anderson believes there are 60 000 surplus elephants in Southern Africa (that is, over and above the carrying capacity of the areas they occupy). Many riverine forests have been irrecoverably damaged in the region. The Tuli Block's ecosystem has been irrevocably 'rewritten' by too many elephants just as happened in Tsavo when, half a century ago, it became overpopulated and the culling of 5 000 elephants was ruled out. Eventually 6 000 died of malnutrition. In Cameroon's Waza National Park the destruction of *Acacia seyal* by elephants is endangering the survival of the giraffe, which relies on the acacias. In Chobe National Park, Botswana, there is concern about the survival of the Chobe's unique bushbuck (*Tragelaphus scriptus ornatus*) as the riverine forest is destroyed by elephants. In the Caprivi region of Namibia, there is concern about populations of roan, sable and tsessebe because of tree destruction. A similar phenomenon was observed in the Sebungwe region in Zimbabwe, where all three species have been in decline for a number of years, coinciding with an increase in the elephant population and consequent major structural changes in habitats.

Angola's elephants were slaughtered in their hundreds (maybe thousands) by South African troops and by the Angolan anti-government forces throughout the 1970s and 1980s during the Angolan civil war. The rebel army was greatly financed by ivory exports clandestinely organised by the South African nationalist government. An unknown number of elephants that survived these two decades of slaughter were mortally injured stepping on landmines. It is hoped there will be a natural northward movement from Namibia's Caprivi and Botswana to refill the current vacuum in Angola.

The situation in Tanzania, custodians of a quarter of Africa's elephants, is going decidedly against the elephant. From 2006 to 2009, at least 30 000 elephant were killed in the Selous Game Reserve and in the corridor between the two, nearly all by poachers. There are now about 100 000 elephants left scattered over Tanzania, two thirds of which are in the Selous region. Safaritalk[15], a website forum of mostly scientists and others voluntarily monitoring the wildlife situation in Africa, believes that, not only are supposedly anti-poaching patrols involved in the poaching and smuggling, 'but so are some of those high up in Tanzania's Wildlife Division'. It says volumes that all the big consignments of illegal ivory (that is, consignments of over one tonne) shipped out of Tanzania have been discovered only when they arrived in the Far East – never when leaving Tanzania. There have been only 10 successful prosecutions since 2006. Even if the Wildlife Division were zealous in its approach to ivory smuggling, judging by the government's meagre funding for conservation and even that donated from overseas, the division is unable to meet its conservation obligations. Safaritalk identified 31 wildlife corridors between Tanzania's protected areas still remaining open – 'but at the current rate of habitat change and land conversion these corridors have less than five years remaining before they disappear'. The corridors are being destroyed by rapid agricultural expansion, unplanned land use, 'unsustainable resource extraction (including "bushmeat") and road construction'.

The resultant increasing isolation of protected areas – they become islands in the midst of agriculture – will have serious implications for economic development and is likely to increase tensions between people and elephants. Tanzania, whose population is set to double in less than 20 years, has, according to Safaritalk, once more agreed to involve communities in its conservation planning and to see they get a share in any income from wildlife in their areas – an essential move if it is serious about conserving what is left. The Wildlife Division says it is working on a new management plan. 'Nonetheless,' says Safaritalk, 'the level of illegal killing of elephant in Selous [game reserve]-Mikumi [national park], which contains a major part of the country's elephant population … continues to increase.' Regulations to provide the operational basis for Tanzania's new Wildlife Conservation Act of 2009 were still being 'finalized' in 2011. New and harsher penalties for ivory poaching and smuggling are promised (up to 30 years) and the provision of additional powers to law enforcement personnel. A copy of the draft regulations, requested from the Wildlife Division, was not supplied to the Safaritalk panel. Safaritalk quotes a conclusion of the Elephant Trade Information Service (ETIS)[16] that the prevalence of large-scale ivory seizures only after the ivory leaves Tanzania 'indicates the involvement of active and entrenched organized criminal syndicates that are well-organised, financed, linked to trade networks and engaging in collusion and corruption.' Enforcement officials concurred that they 'faced a challenge of dealing with organized criminal elements involved in ivory trade within Tanzania, as well as the high possibility of collusion by individuals from agencies that fight smuggling'. Seizures between 1989 and 2009 amounted to more than 44 tonnes of ivory – that's a third of all illicit ivory seized globally – and Tanzania was Africa's biggest culprit. Safaritalk says it is questionable whether Tanzania is financially capable of committing itself to sustainable management and the protection of elephant. In the meanwhile, illegal activity continues unabated.

Wildlife, because of 'ecotourism' (enjoying the wilds, viewing wildlife, hiking in the bush, wildlife photography and hunting), is in parts of Africa the biggest cash crop and, properly managed, is a self-sustaining high-employment industry – and the African elephant is the star attraction. But it is difficult for rural Africans, harassed as they are by elephants, to appreciate the elephant's economic value, especially as so few receive any palpable benefit from it.

Although in many regions compensation for crop losses is obtainable, it is a laborious process that is open to abuse by farmers and officials – and there is no compensation for the permanent anxiety of living with marauding elephants as neighbours[17]. This makes it difficult, to say the least, to talk to families about the sustainable industry of hunting and tourism and its benefit to the national economy – especially if they have lost their crop, or a relative has been trampled or tusked to death, or when children are afraid to walk to school because of elephants – and when, in any event, they have no interest whatsoever in game reserves. In Kenya's Trans-Mara district elephants have developed a taste for village food; as a result, the women have to cook meals in daylight because elephant move around at night sniffing for food and will even push over dwellings to get at it[18].

In Mashonaland Central Province in Zimbabwe in 2011, villagers from Chimbuwe, Mukumbura and Kaitano began taking refuge in two local schools at night feeling 'terrorised' by a herd of 25 elephants, one of which had trampled a 16-year-old boy to death after flinging him into the air[19].

A month later a mother and her daughter were trampled and tusked. The elephants had broken out of a conservancy and villagers had thrown stones at them to drive them back[20].

The worst type of marauding is when elephants raid food stores during the dry months following the main crop harvest. The loss of this stored food is far worse than the raiding of crops still in the fields, because so much damage can be done to a concentrated food source in such a short space of time. Crops plundered in the fields can at least be replanted if it is not too late in the season. Stored food cannot be replaced until the next season.

How does one stop a five-tonne marauder? Wilderness Safaris, a company with 60 luxury safari camps in various countries in Southern Africa, has found that chilli hedges make effective barriers. Russel Friedman says, 'Elephants cannot tolerate chilli and will turn around when confronted by these plants.'[21] The company assists communities living near its concession areas to plant such hedges and to dig 'tank trap' trenches to check marauders. Some communities use chilli-smeared ropes to deter elephants. Some have tried using, with moderate success, the recorded sound of angry bee swarms. Another effective device is used in the Kruger Park to protect landmark trees and vulnerable infrastructure: they circle them with a bed of sharp rocks. Kenya Wildlife Service (KWS) prefers stout fences and deep ditches to protect croplands.

When it comes to conflict between people and wildlife, no species is causing more trauma than the elephant. Apart from crop damage, Kenya's elephants are responsible for three-quarters of the deaths caused by wild animals[22]. In Tanzania's Rombo district (which incorporates a large part of Mount Kilimanjaro) an average of 20 people are killed annually by elephants.

The 2009 FAO paper reports that in some semi-arid rural farming areas of Zimbabwe and Kenya elephant damage to food crops accounts for 75 to 90 per cent of all incidents by large mammals. Outside the Kakum National Park in Ghana, about two thirds of all farms that are susceptible to crop raiding are annually devastated. It estimates that as many as 300 households lose up to two thirds of their crops annually to elephants alone. The report cranks out equally disturbing statistics from throughout Africa: at the periphery of Djona hunting zone in North Benin elephants destroyed 50 out of an estimated total of 150 hectares (370 acres) in 2002, representing a loss of 61 tonnes of crops. Eighty per cent of people questioned had registered claims for damage every year from 1999. In Mali 1 000 hectares (2 500 acres) a year are demolished by elephants. In some areas entire families have abandoned their traditional fields in the face of elephant raids. Around the Bénoué National Park in Cameroon each family loses on an annual basis about a third of its crops[23].

The World Wildlife Fund (WWF) says, in order to reduce HEC, scientists and wardens must use cost-effective strategies and have a good understanding of, not just the elephant, but the people and the terrain as well. So many authorities conclude that the aim should be to transform elephants from a liability to an asset for communities, but first we have to increase human understanding and tolerance of elephants and so improve the animal's conservation status. The aim is to find land uses that are compatible with elephants in the vicinity (game watching and hunting being two such uses) coupled with affordable barriers (electrified fences, trenches, etc.). It seems in India this is better understood and accepted than in Africa, largely because the elephant is regarded by many as a deity and has been part of farming, war and ceremony for millennia. It is very much an Indian icon with cultural status. In Africa, generally, the elephant is valued by most rural people for its ivory and meat and respected only for its awesome size. Reconciliation is going to be difficult.

In some countries many villages are inside the reserves or inside the corridors used by elephants migrating from one protected area to another. In the Tsavo region – the entire protected area comprises 45 000 square kilometres (17 000 square miles) including Tsavo National Park – there are about 500 incidents a year of elephants trampling crops, on occasion wiping out a community's entire food supply. They sometimes break open huts and kill the inhabitants or they attack the farmers who try to scare them off.

A newspaper report in Kenya in July 2011 revealed a lot about the situation[24].

In 1969 Kenya's elephant population was 167 000. Within 25 years it was down to 16 000. Now its numbers have recovered a little to about 30 000. But since the 1980s Kenya's human population has doubled to 39 million. So, despite the drop in the numbers of problem elephants, the current upward trend in elephant and human populations is a recipe for future problems. What is happening in Zimbabwe is unclear. Once-carefully conserved areas – many recently seized from whites – are being raided by mobs with the blessing of their country's dysfunctional government. There are stories of hunters from Europe and the United States paying officials thousands of dollars to turn a blind eye to hunting excesses, discarding 'inferior' animals that they have shot until they find a trophy that satisfies them. For the time being the truth is hard to find. Zimbabwe's government claimed in 2008 that the country had 100 000 elephants and that elephants were destroying crops on a large scale. Others claim officials were inflating the figures because in February 2008 the Convention on International Trade in Endangered Species (CITES) was going to decide whether to accede to the request by Zimbabwe, Botswana and South Africa to resume selling ivory. Zimbabwe, like neighbouring South Africa, has enormous stockpiles of ivory harvested from culling programmes and confiscated from poachers, which they wanted to sell either in bulk or as manufactured ornaments and jewellery. Since the 1980s Kenya has publicly incinerated huge stockpiles of ivory to demonstrate an end to ivory trading. By then it had precious few elephants left.

A powerful lobby – mostly concentrated outside Africa – insists that the 20-year moratorium on selling ivory has been responsible for the recovery of elephants.

Botswana was among those countries that wanted the ban on ivory lifted. South Africa, whose national parks have a potentially valuable stockpile of ivory and rhino horn from past culling operations, has cautiously backed the call for a partial and highly controlled lifting of the ban.

South Africa's elephant population is 20 000 and almost all its elephant are in protected areas, mostly in the Kruger Park. For this reason HEC is nowhere as bad as it is north of the Limpopo River. Nevertheless elephant numbers are a growing problem and people are killed from time to time. The Kruger Park's former head of conservation, Willem Gertenbach, suggests that 'the fatal attacks by elephants on human beings [in South Africa] might be triggered by stress brought on by [elephant] overpopulation'[25]. He said the park was struggling to cope with the impact its elephants were having on biodiversity – and on humans – and that culling was the only way to go. Habitat destruction caused by excess elephants will affect many other species, particularly the browsers such as black rhino, kudu, bushbuck and giraffe.

The authors of the 2009 FAO report calculated that elephant densities need to be held below about 0.5 animals per square kilometre to maintain existing woodland canopy cover. They say, 'This level is far lower than the densities currently occurring in many of the national parks and safari areas, which in 1991 were estimated to range from 0.25 to 2.12 animals per square kilometre.'[26]

Clearly elephant 'translocation' from overpopulated areas is insufficient to relieve pressure. The massive relocation of elephant communities since the 1980s always was, mathematically, a limited option. Yet if the elephant population continues to grow unchecked there will be, says Gertenbach, irreparable damage to habitats, ultimately resulting in a loss of biodiversity, which is fundamental to ecological stability. An alternative seems to be to inject female elephants (via a dart gun) with a contraceptive drug – a method known as immuno-contraception and described as 'safe, non-lethal, reversible and effective in stabilising elephant populations'. It is being used in the Kruger Park but there is concern about the long-term effect on the elephants' reproductive behaviour. And, while contraception will reduce population pressure in the long term, the current rate of habitat destruction will continue for many more years.

The question is whether to cull. One of those who are adamantly opposed to elephant culling is Iain Douglas-Hamilton, a leading elephant specialist and founder of the organisation Save the Elephants. He feels that, because corruption has traditionally surrounded the ivory trade, permitting even partial trade would trigger a renewed demand for ivory and a 'new holocaust' – especially as ruthless traders in the emerging Far Eastern economies have displayed an insatiable greed for ivory and rhino horn. Because of demand, the rewards for ivory and rhino horn are, in the eyes of some rural poor, enormous and worth taking the risk of being involved in fire fights with the authorities. Indeed many are shot by law enforcers when they offer armed resistance.

As mentioned earlier, elephants, normally placid creatures, are in many parts of Africa behaving increasingly out of character, and more incidents involving tourists and inadequately trained trail guides are to be expected. Such is the growth of ecotourism and the tourist's desire to walk in the wilds that some of the smaller reserves are taking on rangers whose reactions in emergencies are untested, and visitors themselves can do unexpected things.

In the Timbavati area on the western border of the Kruger Park a German tourist was killed when, with a party of six, she left the vehicle to approach an elephant herd. The guide accompanied them but for some reason did not take his rifle. They found themselves between a cow and her calf – a dire situation. The ranger told them to stand still, a golden rule in such a situation, but the woman lost her nerve and ran. The cow immediately chased her and trampled and tusked her to death.

In 2007 in Madikwe National Park a visitor was flung from the back of a safari vehicle and tusked through his thigh. The driver had switched off his engine while his passengers in the open vehicle watched some elephants – a routine practice for rangers when stopping to watch animals. The driver, fearful for the safety of the other passengers, drove off and the man had to hobble to an accompanying vehicle. He then waited five hours to be evacuated to receive medical attention. He sued the lodge that had supplied the vehicle and driver for R300 000. The lodge denied negligence and said visitors in any event signed an indemnity form declaring they knew the risks – again a routine in all safari lodges.

In 2003 Madikwe was known for its grumpy elephants, which had been relocated from other reserves. Game ranger Sam Nkomo was driving an Italian visitor, Raul Canetti, and his wife, in an open safari vehicle when he spotted a cow elephant 60 metres (66 yards) away. Nkomo switched off his engine as etiquette demands. Inexplicably the cow charged full bore at the vehicle. Nkomo tried to switch on the ignition but the key snapped off in the lock. The elephant hit the Land Rover head on. She spun the vehicle through

180 degrees and ran her tusks through the metal doors. In the process Nkomo's gun was flung from its cradle and Canetti was catapulted out. Scrambling to his feet, he ran. The elephant caught him and knelt on his face, doing appalling damage. Nkomo found a stick and began beating the elephant behind her ears, at which stage she ran off. Canetti survived.

In 2000 Wendy Martin (48), a British mother of three, survived after being gored by an elephant outside a game ranch in central Kenya while taking part in a bush jog with two friends and a game guard. An elephant unexpectedly appeared and the guide told the tourists to run, but without indicating in which direction. Wendy Martin fell and the elephant drove its tusks through her chest, abdomen, right thigh and calf. It knelt on her, crushing her pelvis. The lodge claimed that tourists were given fair warning and had signed indemnities. Martin, after a year in hospital and 16 operations was, eight years later, awarded £500 000 in damages[27].

More and more lodges, should it be found that their guides are under-trained or that their emergency procedures are inadequate, are likely to find that their indemnity forms offer them little protection.

In 2008 a group of six American tourists in the foothills of Mount Kenya were charged from behind by an elephant that nobody had noticed hidden behind a bush; a woman and her one-year-old daughter were trampled to death. Deaths caused by wild animals are so frequent (though rare among tourists), that in 2008 the Kenya Wildlife Service set the rate for deaths at 30 000 Kenya shillings (almost R3 000).

In 2010 American billionaire industrialist Tom Siebel, on safari with his family in the Serengeti in Tanzania, took a dawn walk within sight of the lodge in which he was staying. He was accompanied by a guard carrying a .470 double-barrel rifle – more than enough to fell an elephant. He had been warned in the routine way not to run if there was trouble because animals chase people who run. They came across a herd of elephants 200 metres (220 yards) away – mixed cows and calves. A female charged straight at them. The guard froze. He fired only when the elephant was four metres (13 feet) away – and completely missed. The elephants then tossed the guard 10 metres (33 feet) away and turned on Stiebel.

'… the animal continues up right in front of me, and I'm standing there … maybe 2 feet [60 centimetres] away, and it's just standing there. And I'll remember this instant until the day I die. And for three seconds … the animal is standing there; I'm standing there. I can smell it … the pungent odor … I can see the gray, the hair follicles … the eyeball, the trunk, the tusk, the foot – the whole thing. And I was like, "Okay, what are we going to do now?"

'And the animal then proceeds to kick my teeth in, basically. It knocked me to the ground with its trunk, it rolled me, punched me, put a tusk through my left thigh, gored it, then ripped it out sideways. It stepped on my leg, kicked my leg, broke six ribs and ripped up my shoulder … I remember every instant of it … trying to protect my head with my arms. I remember the blows to my lower extremities, and it just hurt so bad I couldn't believe it … Imagine what it's like taking an elephant tusk through the thigh … or having a 6-ton animal step on your leg … It just snaps … The pain was intolerable … And after a while I looked up … The dust is settled. The elephant's gone. Dead quiet in the Serengeti … The guide is over there 12 yards [11 metres] [away], curled up in a ball, wrapped around the rifle, playing dead … Basically what happened is I got served up. So I said [to the guard], "This might be a good time to reload." He was virtually unhurt.'

Siebel, his left thigh 'flayed wide open, my right foot was dangling on my leg, held on by two tendons and a flap of skin', was flown to Nairobi for preliminary treatment, and then came a 20-hour flight to San Jose (California) with only a 10-hour supply of morphine and an inadequate supply of water.

Siebel added: 'Once you get hurt you hear about all the other accidents on safari that nobody talks about.'[28]

In 2004, in Hluhluwe-Imfolozi Park in KwaZulu-Natal, a television cameraman, Christian Hohmann, committed the fatal error of running from an elephant cow. He and his colleagues were filming a TV documentary for German television on the life of a game ranger. They were on foot and accompanied by a game ranger. They came across an elephant feeding peacefully on the fringe of a sand forest. One of Hohmann's colleagues panicked and ran when a second elephant suddenly appeared out of the bush only metres away. Hohmann, still holding his camera, also panicked. He ran in the opposite direction and was swallowed up by a thicket. The elephant went after Hohmann but stopped next to the thicket. The game ranger assumed the charge was over, but Hohmann appears to have tripped over a termite mound, causing him to cry out. The elephant charged through the thicket and emerged, carrying Hohmann on her tusk, impaled through his back. She shook Hohmann off onto the ground. The cameraman tried to crawl away and, as the elephant went to trample him, the ranger got in a brain shot. The elephant dropped next to her dying victim.

A cause of many encounters is that many tourists in Africa feel cheated if they do not see the 'big five' – elephant, buffalo, rhino, lion and leopard. It is the bane of field guides, as it is usually pure luck if one sees all five and the demand puts great pressure on rangers, guides and trackers. It led tracker Laybert Magagula to try to flush out some elephants at Hectorspruit near the Kruger Park for tourists to see. He startled a cow and her young calf and the cow killed him instantly, tusking him in the head, chest, back and legs. Other elephants then trampled him.

There was a succession of HEC incidents in South Africa in 2004 that suggested flaws in ranger experience. In May that year a small group of hikers in a Zululand game reserve watched in horror as a young game ranger, Fortune Mkhize, was crushed to death and flung aside like a rag doll by an elephant that had caught the party by surprise. Mkhize's backup had time only to fire a 'warning shot' – but *after* Mkhize was killed. A few days later field ecologist Kay Hiscocks, attached to the Sabi Sand Private Game Reserve on the Kruger Park's southwestern flank, was trampled to death by a cow elephant while 'shooing' away a small group of elephants that had entered the camp. She was forced to run for her life. Three ineffectual shots were fired by staff members.

Deaths are becoming more and more commonplace as tourists and rangers are prepared to take greater chances with wild animals. The proliferation of privately owned game reserves throughout sub-Saharan Africa, which offer timeshare to urban dwellers, attracts clients who are often ignorant of the dangers. I witnessed a father in a private reserve getting out of his vehicle and, taking his small son by the hand, walking up to a lone bull elephant at a waterhole. Fortunately the elephant moved off.

Jeremy Anderson believes visitors and game rangers are inadvertently 'training elephants to attack'. Anderson, who has spent 40 years working in elephant country, points out you should not reverse your vehicle in the face of a mock charge, because it teaches the elephant to expect it and then they get ratty if people do not reverse. He believes Zimbabwe-trained rangers of the 1960s and 70s had elephants taped and were probably the finest rangers in Africa. They never retreated from an elephant's mock charge – not even when on foot. Anderson's point regarding 'training elephants to charge' is based on the fact that self-drive tourists and inexperienced rangers reverse their vehicles whenever an elephant flaps its ears or trumpets or takes a few steps forward. Anderson cites the case of elephants of Gonarezhou National Park in eastern Zimbabwe – a reserve under constant pressure from poachers – from which a number of elephants have been relocated to various reserves in Southern Africa. When relocated within Zimbabwe's borders, the elephants settled down quickly but when relocated to South African private and provincial reserves, where some of the younger rangers are easily intimidated by mock charges, the relocated Gonarezhou elephants assumed an uncharacteristic and belligerent mastery over vehicles that has led to tragedies.[29]

In a mock charge the elephant spreads its ears (ironically, to make itself appear larger). John Taylor describes the ears as 'like a square-rigger's sails'[30], since they can span a good five metres (over 16 feet), making the animal wider than a double-decker bus – in fact a bull can weigh more than a double-decker bus. In a full charge the elephant holds its ears back, pressed against the sides of its head. It often curls its trunk under its head. In a mock charge the trunk is waved about and the elephant might well sway its body as it shuffles forward – but then it will pull up. Richard Carrington[31] and others say the trunk is always tucked in when an elephant is charging in thick country, but may be held extended forward in open country.

Although Anderson does not give way to an elephant, he was once forced to run for his life during an elephant immobilisation project. He was using a (drug) dart gun at a very short range. As the dart smacked home, the elephant charged and Anderson's gun bearer lost his nerve and ran. Anderson chased after him, trying to retrieve the gun. The gun bearer, obviously feeling guilty, several times held out the rifle for Anderson to grab. But every time Anderson drew close the gun bearer, seeing how close the elephant was, accelerated. Anderson glanced behind to see the elephant lowering its head ready to impale him. At that moment a colleague, 50 metres (55 yards) away, fired and dropped the elephant, which crashed at Anderson's heels.

In Sabi Sabi, a private reserve bordering the Kruger Park where rangers go through extensive professional training, one can sit in an open vehicle within 10 paces of browsing elephants, which studiously ignore people in vehicles. An elephant in a nearby reserve came up behind a stationary open safari vehicle and placed its trunk on a woman's shoulder – the woman sensibly froze.

But once an elephant – in Africa or Asia – does turn rogue it can chalk up an enormous toll in an area where there might not be a weapon capable of killing it or a man brave enough to hunt it. In the 1950s a marauding elephant in northern Zululand killed 12 people over a short period, in what appears to have been fits of madness. It was never shot. Another, whose trunk was festering from a wound, caused many deaths in Maputaland near the border of KwaZulu-Natal and Mozambique. It sometimes rested its head on the roofs of huts at night, causing them to collapse and the inhabitants to run for their lives. Twenty-year-old Shanakeni Tembe told an inquest in Ingwavuma (near the KwaZulu-Natal/Swaziland border) how he had never seen an elephant in his life until one stepped out of the forest in front of him and his mother as they walked along a sand road. It turned out to be the one with the suppurating trunk. His mother ran and the elephant chased her, took her by the legs in its trunk and beat her to a pulp against the trees. Rogues like this have flattened huts and terrorised users of busy roads.

The Dabi killer elephant in Zimbabwe, which frequented the south bank of the Zambezi in the mid 20th century, was a typical case. Apart from crop raids, it would ambush its victims and destroy them – usually by beating them against trees and then, placing a forefoot on them, ripping off their limbs and scattering them. John Taylor eventually shot it while it was raiding a millet field[32].

Another common action on the part of a sorely provoked elephant is to toss its victim into trees or straight over its back. Many hunters have survived this sort of handling. Among them is T. Murray Smith who was tossed into the air by a rogue and fell through a tree, to find himself lying back at the elephant's feet. The animal thrust at him with its tusks, which dug into the ground on each side of the hunter. As in Ferrar's case, Murray Smith lived only because the elephant's firmly planted tusks prevented the tusker from crushing the life out of him with its forehead.

In December 1992 Daryl Balfour, a well-known South African wildlife photographer, survived a similar set of circumstances near Tshokwane, a popular tourist picnic site in the Kruger Park. He was photographing in a sitting position an elephant – a huge tusker called Tshokwane – in a mock charge. It had charged him before that day. But this time the bull did not stop. The elephant struck him in the small of his back and then tossed him some distance. It took hold of his ankle and hoisted him over its head, before flinging him onto his back. As he lay there, Balfour saw a tusk coming towards his face and dodged it but was knocked out by its glancing blow. He regained consciousness 90 minutes later – evidently the elephant's tusk had dug into the ground and so prevented his being crushed by the forehead.

'Perhaps the biggest lesson from the event,' he said, 'was that a mock charge can turn very serious in an instant. The only predictable thing about a wild animal is its unpredictability.'[33]

Some elephants will catch people in their trunks and then impale them on their tusks, while others have the strange habit of burying their victims, covering them with leaves. Some people have survived attacks by feigning death and then being buried in detritus by their attacker. Douglas Chadwick mentions an Asian elephant that placed its victim in a shallow hole and covered the body with mud[34].

Two hunters, Jim Sutherland[35] and Samaki Salmon, in unrelated incidents, went through the harrowing experience of being picked up by a charging elephant, tossed through the treetops, and landing on the ground near enough to their fallen rifles to pick them up and kill the elephant. Others pursued by elephants have distracted them by casting off items of clothing as they ran.

There is some wisdom in the advice offered by the old ivory hunters that if you stand stock-still when charged, the elephant might well miss you and thunder past. It might also lose sight of you and lose interest, since elephants are short-sighted and would battle to distinguish a bush from a human at 40 paces. Standing still has saved many lives – though we'll never know how many it has cost. Hunters who have written of their experiences maintain that even when a herd of elephants was bearing down on them they remained still, relying on the elephant's supposed instinct for going around any strange object. This theory is also not terribly reliable: Elizabeth Balneaves witnessed a full-blooded charge by a cow elephant, during which its intended victim leapt behind a rock. The elephant crashed head-on into the rock, shattering a tusk[36].

The African bull elephant is indeed placid but when in musth[37] and on the lookout for receptive females it can be unpredictable. According to those who know them, Asian bull elephants in musth are responsible for most of the elephant-related deaths among tamers and mahouts.

Basic to the problem of badly behaved elephants is that, in the early culling operations in the Kruger Park, calves were spared and put into enclosures; only after some years were they released into reserves. Not having been brought up among elders, they were seriously delinquent and when, for instance, they were relocated to Pilanesberg 150 kilometres (93 miles) north of Johannesburg they were killing not only rhinos (63 were killed according to Siebert)[38] but also people. When Pilanesberg began importing entire elephant families – captured in a single operation and immediately transferred – the reserve's existing juveniles calmed down, thus illustrating the importance of adults to the stability of elephant behaviour. Elephants, under normal circumstances, are disciplined by their elders. The herds are led by matriarchs and the youngsters, for their first eight years, never stray more than a few metres from their mothers. They enjoy the perfect life with cousins, aunts and grandmothers up to 70 years old. Males on maturity form their own small placid groups, rejoining the females only to mate. The female-dominated herds stay together and assist each other with births and, when one of their number dies, the herd displays what can only be described as deep sorrow.

Most African elephants when they turn rogue bear a legitimate grudge, after having been wounded by hunters or farmers or having had their legs or trunk ensnared and cut into by wire noose traps meant for smaller animals. In 2007 Malawi's game department decided to relocate 83 elephants to Majete Wildlife Reserve at the country's southeastern tip, after they had 'trampled to death at least 20 farmers'. Accompanying veterinarians found that seven out of 83 were suffering trunk amputations caused by snares; one had a deformed foot from a gin trap and one was blind in one eye from a bullet. Three were still dragging metal snares and several others bore scars from bullet wounds. Others were suffering natural injuries received in fights. Poachers using AK47s and farmers protecting their crops with inadequate firearms often leave injured elephants some of which, tormented by pain, turn rogue. It has been claimed that an occasional cause of aggressive behaviour among elephants is drunkenness brought about by an elephant draining a village liquor still, but stories of them becoming drunk from eating fermenting marula berries are certainly fictitious.

Rogues, according to Ivan Sanderson, do not just vent their spleen on humans; they also 'lash out at little, inoffensive animals and rip up palm trees'[39]. Female elephants, especially those with young, are by far the more likely to react aggressively. The South African hunter Ian McFarlane says, 'The bulls are good-natured fellows but I avoid ever messing with a herd of females.'[40]

Nearly always when an elephant puts on a show of aggression it is bluffing. Big as they are, elephants are no more courageous than antelope and under normal circumstances are no more disposed towards seeking trouble than any other creature. Iain Douglas-Hamilton in Tanzania photographed a full-grown bull elephant backing away from a screeching blacksmith plover protecting her nest[41].

It is interesting to see how similar the HEC situation is in India, with its more compacted human population and far fewer elephants – perhaps as few as 25 000. Chadwick estimates there are probably between 35 000 and 50 000 elephants in the whole of Asia[42]. There are various races of Asian elephant all belonging to a separate genus (*Elephas*) from the African elephant (*Loxodonta*). They are considerably smaller than *Loxodonta* and the female is nearly always tuskless.

The Asian Elephant Specialist Group of the IUCN says that in Jharkhand, the Indian state just east of Bangladesh, 300 people were killed by elephants between 2000 and 2004. From the start of the century until 2012, elephants had killed 605 people in Assam (northeastern India), 239 of them since 2001. Most countries that have Asian elephants are keen to conserve their dwindling numbers but face the growing problem of HEC.

In a widely publicised incident in the middle of 2011, two young wild elephants left their native forest 35 kilometres (22 miles) from the city of Mysore, entered the city and in a busy shopping street trampled a man to death and tried to kill a cow. One of the elephants entered the grounds of a women's college. Local schools had to close for the day. Forest rangers and officials from Mysore zoo, rather than shoot the marauders, tranquillised them and escorted them back to the forest.

A subsequent report in the *Lahore Times* said, 'Mysore, Hassan, Kodagu and Chamarajanagar have a large population of jumbos[43]. According to an estimate, the elephant population has doubled from 2,500 a few years back to 5,000'. But their habitat is shrinking. 'Naturally, the pachyderms raid villages in search of food and kill those who come in the way. People are even scared to cross thick forest areas during the day because of the movement of elephants.'

Using the term 'naturally' ('Naturally, the pachyderms ... kill those who come in the way') reveals a surprising fatalistic frame of mind. The report goes on:

Joe Heffernan, an elephant biologist, believes aggressive elephants – whether in Asia or Africa – may be suffering a mineral deficiency[44]. There's a theory that some crave salt, which might lead them to demolish huts in which people are cooking salty foods or storing salt.

Heffernan records an interview containing a poignant quote from a woman who watched her uncle trampled to death. She said that when she was younger 'the elephants were kinder', which suggests the man versus elephant conflict might have been less severe in the past. The report also mentions that the woman said something particularly enigmatic – 'My uncle was stepped on by the elephants and his body was swallowed up.' Did she mean that literally? Did she witness a bizarre facet of elephant behaviour – man-eating? Man-eating elephants have been known.

There's an intriguing account of the shooting of a bull elephant using muzzle-loading guns in the diary of Jacob van Reenen (1790–91)[45]. Van Reenen went overland along South Africa's Eastern Cape coast in search of survivors of a wrecked East Indiaman. The account is not only an interesting example of the discouraging tenacity and cunning of a wounded elephant, but also suggests a man-eating propensity.

In 1948 *Time* magazine carried this report:

Eleven years ago, Chang (an Asian elephant) was bundled into the Zurich zoo's elephant pit, a fat, ludicrous baby only ten months old. He had been bought as the future mate for Mandjullah, an older female. Rapidly he became the zoo's star attraction and the pride of his keeper, Hans Rietmann. When Mandjullah took the kids for a ride on her back, Chang trundled awkwardly behind, amiably accepting peanuts...

One day, Chang brusquely snatched a doll from the arms of a little girl. For this he was banished to his pit... Three years ago zoo keepers saw blood on the floor of the pit. In Chang's straw bed they found a bloodied human hand and toe.

The horrified keepers and police learned the unbelievable truth. Chang had devoured a young woman; he had swallowed her clothes, her hat, and even her large handbag.

Police identified the woman as Bertha Walt, a pretty young Zurich office worker. The night before she had carried some bread away from the dinner table, and apparently went to the zoo to feed Chang.

An elephant that can process in its stomach several hundred kilograms of coarse vegetation a day, including tree branches, should be able to chew and swallow a human, once it has dismembered the corpse. The most surprising factor is not the size of the meal, but the fact that it is meat and the elephant is a herbivore. According to hunters in Africa, an elephant will occasionally carry a victim around in its mouth, and there are stories of elephants dismembering victims and carrying a limb around in their mouths. It seems feasible that they might occasionally chew and swallow these limbs.

Richard Carrington mentions the 'Mandla' elephant that terrorised a district of that name near Jubbulpore in the Central Province of India, and which, in the early 1870s, was said to have eaten some of its 'numberless victims'. This, says Carrington categorically, 'is of course nonsense, as elephants are exclusively vegetarian in diet, but the superstition probably arose from the animal's habit of playing with the limbs of dismembered natives, and holding them in its mouth. The elephant was eventually shot.'[46] This 'Mandla' elephant is probably the same as the 'Mandala' elephant mentioned by Ivan Sanderson, who suggests the stories concerning its man-eating arose from its habit of carrying its victims in its mouth before tearing them apart[47].

7 THE HIPPOPOTAMUS

There is no animal I dislike more than the hippo.
– Samuel Blake, explorer

It was April and the Zambezi was still deep and swollen from the summer rains. The moon rode high and it picked out the quietly running river sliding like quicksilver between the shadows of the heavy vegetation on either bank. The high-pitched ping of a fruit bat hung on the still air and somewhere in the reeds a crocodile moved, sending ripples pulsing out of the blackness along the river's edge.

Then, faintly at first but growing steadily louder, came the rough whine of an outboard engine. Bryan Dempster and his two assistants, Joseph and Albaan, were returning from a successful crocodile hunt with three good skins aboard. It was not quite four in the morning.

Dempster turned the boat into a quiet pool where the river ate into the riverine vegetation. There was no warning: one moment the dinghy was heading across the smooth water leaving a perfectly straight, silver wake and the next moment it was flung clear out of the water and was rolling over in the air. Guns, the lamp, the crocodile skins and the three occupants fell from it; the engine, tearing uselessly at the air, screamed and then cut as it crashed back into the river. Dempster caught sight of a huge bull hippopotamus submerging. And then, as the hunter lay floating on his back, he saw the massive head reappear and the great ivory tusks glint in the moonlight as the hippo's jaws clamped over the boat and crushed it to matchwood.

Dempster knew that his only hope was to remain as still as possible: any movement or sound would give his presence away to the animal that now floated, eyes and nostrils just above the surface, only a few metres away. Even if the hippo missed him, the crocodiles might not. Silence again reigned, then suddenly Albaan began screaming. He couldn't swim, Dempster remembered. The man shouted and set up a frenzied splashing and Dempster knew that his assistant was doomed, as would he be if he reacted to the man's calls for help. He had to grit his teeth to keep himself from shouting. Once again the hunter saw the hippo's monstrous head emerge; as he saw the great jaws open and shut, Albaan's scream was cut short.

Death in the African bush comes in many different ways, but mostly suddenly and violently for animals and very often for humans. This is especially so along the rivers, which, beautiful though they are, have an undercurrent of menace.

Many people view Africa's hippopotamus as a comical, huggable animal and so often one sees it frolicking in cartoons, even in a tutu. But, for millions of people who live in close proximity to hippos, the animal is a curse. It is uniquely neurotic and extremely dangerous at close quarters. George W. Frame and Lory Herbison described it as 'a bellicose beast of murderous temperament'[1].

Robert Bruce White was more complimentary: 'To be sure, there are rogue hippos, but even in their violent moods they are amusing. And ordinarily hippos are peace-loving animals'[2]. German zoologist Professor Hans Klingel, who made a study of hippos in Uganda, said, 'In Africa, tales abound of unprovoked hippo attacks. Yet in all my years of research I have found hippos to be quite gentle creatures which, like many other species, attack only when molested, cornered, or injured.'[3]

Many will argue with his assessment.

There is no doubt that people living near rivers and lakes fear hippos far more than they fear the crocodile, which shares the same territory. Some authorities argue that of all the mammals it is the worst man-killer in Africa. While the crocodile is a menace in the water, at least on land it flees from an approaching person. The hippo is inclined to attack on land and water and, if you find yourself between a hippo and water, it is almost certain to attack.

In the past one used to come across little mounds of earth marking riverside graves – graves that were sooner or later erased by the inevitable floods. In most cases nobody knew the names of those who lay buried there, but one could guess how they had died – usually the victim of a hippo. Crocodiles seldom leave anything to bury.

Explorers David Livingstone, H.M. Stanley, Richard Burton, F.C. Selous, John Speke and Paul du Chaillu each had a frightening episode with hippos[4].

The hippo, despite its weight, can move with amazing agility underwater and even walk along the bottom for long distances (they can stay down for almost 10 minutes). From the air you can see their underwater pathways.

When a bull hippo opens its mouth – the biggest mouth of any land animal – it displays its forward-jutting lower teeth: two chunky 20-centimetre-long (eight-inch) spikes. These rub against its two enormous canines so that all four are extremely sharp. Its canines grow to 50 centimetres (20 inches) and the strength of its jaws is such that it has been seen to bite a full-grown crocodile in half. Colin Willock cites a case where a hippo bit holes in the side of a Land Rover[5].

Spencer Tyron, a professional hunter, while canoeing along the shore of Lake Rukwa, Tanzania, was thrown from his dugout by a bull hippo, which then, with one bite, removed his head and shoulders[6].

Hippopotamus amphibius shares with the 2.5-tonne white rhino the title of the world's third-heaviest land animal, after the African and the Asian elephants. These huge animals have no sense of humour, huge jaws, huge teeth and, in attack, absolutely no mercy.

It has long been a moot point which kills the most – the hippo or the crocodile. Philip Caputo says 'the hippopotamus kills more people in

Africa than any other animal'. He quotes somebody who has been running safaris for 25 years: '[Our rangers] have rarely had to fire over the heads of elephants and have never shot a lion, but they have had to kill six hippos [in defending clients].'[7]

Ironically, but perhaps typically, where the hippo has been exterminated, the local population suffers in an unexpected way. Hippos, because they use the same tracks over the years, always move away from the river in the direction of the river's flow. Thus, when the floods come and the river swells, the water gradually fingers out over the floodplain along the herringbone pattern formed by the hippo paths leading onto the floodplain. They also keep channels open through the reeds. Where hippos have been eradicated, villagers sow their crops right down to the river's edge, erasing the herringbone pattern. The result is that when the floods come they tear at the river bank and eventually wash away the ploughed land. Within a short time, where for centuries hippos and livestock grazed, the meadows and cropland are gone. Starvation follows... The hippo's revenge.

A growing number of 'front-line' battles are likely to be fought over issues ranging from competition for grazing – the hippo being a heavy grazer and, frequently, a raider of crops – and potable water. There are many communities throughout Africa who view hippos as vermin. Villagers have many methods of dealing with them, including, while the hippo are resting in their daytime resting places in the river bed, barricading them in until they starve. The hippo's role in keeping river courses open and alleviating flood damage – damage that not only leads to loss of topsoil but also to silted dams – goes unappreciated. In mineral-rich Southern Africa the scarcest mineral is water and there is a fear that climate change will decrease it even more, again leading to greater conflict with hippos and a terrible waste of bushmeat.

In January 2011 a HuntNetwork report illustrated the conflict between hippos and villagers and the lack of understanding regarding the vital role hippos play:

A total of 21 people have been killed by stray hippos on the shores of Lake Albert in Kibaale district in the last one year. The latest incident occurred last week, when Wilson Monday and another fisherman, who is currently hospitalised, were attacked by hippos as they returned from fishing ...

However, the district fisheries officer, Francis Gwazo, said the deaths were over two years.

'It is true that people have been killed, but not in a period of one year as alleged by the fishermen,' Gwazo said.

Enraged by the killings, the fishermen threatened to beat the Uganda Wildlife Authority officials from Ntoroko station, who argue that the hippos had to be protected.

Tom Okello Obbo, the conservation manager at Murchison Falls, said the Uganda Wild life Authority was planning to sensitise fishermen on how they can live in harmony with the animals. The hippos were important because they fertilised the water for fish breeding ... they were part of the aquatic life necessary for the continuation of the fishing business.[8]

Africa is populated with hippos from just north of Durban right up to the upper Nile and across to West Africa. Judging by the numbers of people killed in relatively well-developed South Africa – only about one tenth of the country has hippos, yet there are more than half a dozen deaths reported per year – the number for the less-developed parts of Africa must run into a few hundred. Derek Solomon, who operates safaris in the Mana Pools area of Zimbabwe and along the south Luangwa River in Zambia, guesses they kill between 100 and 200 people a year. I think his guess is very conservative.

Two thirds of the people in sub-Saharan Africa still have to use hippo-infested rivers and lakes, not only for travel and fishing – usually in flimsy canoes – but also for washing, bathing and drawing water. It takes engineering ability and capital to establish safe communal points for such activities, both of which are scarce commodities throughout rural Africa.

Attacks on boats are common and it is likely that territorial bulls mistake approaching boats for rivals. Kobie Kruger, the wife of a Kruger Park ranger, whose home is on a river ruled by tyrannical hippos, agrees:

> Hippos are aggressively territorial, and most hippo attacks in the water are
> the result of bulls defending their territories. Being rather dim-witted and
> habitually paranoid, a bull hippo perceives a boat as an intruder with dubious
> designs on the resident lady hippos.[9]

In the 1960s I was with ranger Tony Pooley in a metal outboard-driven
boat on the Pongola, not far south of the Mozambique border with
KwaZulu-Natal. Having just passed over the heads of a pod of a dozen
hippos, we stopped to watch them surface. A minute or so later a large
hippo, open-jawed, exploded from the water and lunged for the transom.
Pooley gunned the boat forward just as the hippo slammed its jaws shut
with a mighty smack. A few months later a hippo attacked the same boat
on a wide part of the river and sank it. The passengers had to swim for
their lives; two were killed by the hippo.

On Lake Malawi in May 2002 an irritated hippo overturned a craft three
kilometres (nearly two miles) offshore, drowning 12 of the 15 people aboard.

A story that illustrates the uncompromising nature of a hippo attack is
that of game guide Paul Templer who, aged 27 in March 2003, took six tourists
for a lazy autumn afternoon canoe excursion down the Zambezi. They were
drifting down the river not far from where it plunges over the Victoria Falls
into the dark chasm of the Batoka Gorge. They were only a kilometre upriver
from the hotel landing. The river above the falls is wide, dotted with islands
and quite a few elephants and buffalo.

Templer was paddling one of the canoes with Jochem and Gundi
Stahmann from Bremen, Germany, on board. Ben Sibanda (24) was paddling
Murielle Fischer and her fiancé Pierre Lagardère, while Evans Namasango
(22) paddled Nathalie Grassot and Marc Skorupka. All six were tourists from
Europe and most were on their first trip to Africa. Mike McNamara (31), a
freelance guide, acted as an outrider in a fast kayak canoe.

Templer went through his usual introductory speech about keeping a
safe distance, not splitting hippo groups and avoiding getting between
them and a deep water channel because this would block their escape route
and could provoke a charge. He told them not to dangle their hands in the

water because crocodiles might mistake them for fish, the crocodile's natural diet. And he explained how hippos are territorial and bad tempered and how they could sometimes bump canoes, pitching those on board into the river. But he reassured them, saying hippo are strictly vegetarian (they graze far and wide at night).

Templer is a well-built man who grew up in the wilds of Zimbabwe and underwent a rigorous training programme to qualify as a guide.

The Zambezi has its share of notorious rogue hippos and the guides who operate along the river keep each other informed about troublesome bulls. Templer was aware of one in his section of the river, but what he did not know was that it had moved its territory; as the flotilla negotiated a rocky bar they were entering its new territory. The first Templer knew of the bull's presence was the sound of a thunderclap as he saw Namasango's canoe flung into the air and Namasango falling out. The tourists watched in horror as the hippo opened its huge mouth and then disappeared. Templer shot his canoe over to his floundering assistant and tried to grab him. The hippo exploded from the water and in an instant closed its mouth over Templer's upper body. The ranger was headfirst in the hippo's mouth with his arms pinned to his sides. The hippo again submerged. The canoe capsized and the terrified Stahmanns fell into the river.

The hippo released Templer – 'It spat me out,' he told a reporter – and Templer, pushing himself off from its bristly lips, felt strangely calm. Nevertheless he was badly wounded, with deep bite wounds in his armpit and the middle of his back; he had also sustained head wounds when the teeth had grazed him. Covered in blood, Templer surfaced near Namasango and tried to haul the traumatised assistant to the bank, but the hippo now grasped Templer by the leg, and again he was dragged below. In his frantic struggle to get out of the hippo's jaws, Templer managed to extricate his leg, only to be caught by an arm. By punching the animal's snout, he again freed himself and surfaced. McNamara shot his kayak forward so that Templer could hold on to it and be towed to shore.

But the hippo attacked again and in an instant had Templer crossways in its jaws, his feet out one side and head the other. Its tusks snapped his ribs and, shaking Templer like a terrier with a rat, the hippo also smashed his left arm above the elbow. McNamara saw a long fountain of blood as an artery under Templer's arm was severed. Templer was frenziedly punching the hippo's thick hide and, miraculously, the hippo released him next to the kayak. McNamara managed to pull him to a small island, where Templer stood with his left arm shattered, his foot crushed and a lung clearly visible through his broken rib cage. His mind was still sharp and he scanned the scene for Namasango, only to see the hippo drag the man below. Namasango's body was recovered two days later.

The severed artery in Templer's armpit, because it was neatly cut, sealed itself but Templer lost his arm. He is now running canoe holidays on Lake Erie in North America, using a prosthetic arm specially adapted for paddling. Meanwhile the man-killing hippo, rather like the shark in Peter Benchley's *Jaws*, is still there watching the canoes go past[10].

The majority of hippo victims are killed after being flung from boats or dugout canoes. Two of the worst areas for hippo mishaps are the Okavango Delta in Botswana and the Murchison Falls in Uganda. In the case of the latter, the local people hunt crocodiles from dugouts and, as is so common in Africa, few people can swim (which, under African circumstances, is understandable).

In 1959 a young South African, Andries Steyn, was asked to shoot a rogue hippo that had been upsetting *mekoro* (dugouts) on the Okavango River. He shot the hippo from a boat, but the commotion excited a cow hippo, which emerged under Steyn's boat, throwing him out. The hippo dragged him under and he was never seen again.

Not all attacks are in rivers; quite a few are on river banks and even well away from rivers. Many a hunter, for instance, has learned the hard way that hippos are irritated by fire and will sometimes charge a camp fire, with disastrous results.

A typical example of the hippo's often irrational behaviour occurred a few years ago on the banks of the Pafuri River near the Makulika trading store in the extreme northeast of South Africa. A man was walking along a path with his wife, who had a child on her back. He saw a bull hippo and as a precaution he shouted at it, expecting it would plunge through the reeds into the river behind it. Instead the hippo rumbled up to the man's wife and, with two quick bites, severed the woman's leg and took a large piece out of her side. She died on the spot. Her baby was unhurt.

In the 1970s a visiting angler to Lake St Lucia in KwaZulu-Natal was walking along a public path in daylight when a hippo attacked him. He died of his wounds and later the same hippo ran amok in a camping site, causing people to take refuge on top of their cars.

In 1966 a hippo on the Limpopo River, near Musina (then known as Messina) on the South Africa–Zimbabwe border, taking exception to a noisy party on the river bank, charged out with mouth agape and bit one of the revellers clean through his torso, killing him. It was the third fatality on that section of the river in a year. In 1961 a child near Charters Creek, Zululand, was bitten in half by a hippo that had charged from the water.

In February 2002 a woman, watching her husband play golf at a resort just outside Hazyview in Mpumalanga, saw a baby hippo in the reeds across the fairway and went over to photograph it. As she bent down to focus, the mother burst from cover and killed her with one bite. The following year Janice Simpson, a South African bride on honeymoon in the Okavango Delta, was killed when a hippo attacked the canoe she and her husband were in. In a single bite it penetrated her heart and lungs. That same year a former Miss South Africa, Diana Tilden-Davis, encountered a hippo in the Delta. The hippo bit into her lower leg, which had to be amputated.

These were high-profile cases that were reported in the metropolitan newspapers, by virtue of the fact that the victims were mainly metropolitan people. But in between these attacks I was told of two deaths involving rural South Africans whose demise went unreported in the big city newspapers, but it makes one realise how common such incidents are. The frequency of attacks steps up during drought when rivers are shallow and hippos, neurotic at the best of times, are feeling insecure.

A most dangerous situation is when people are caught on hippo paths at night. Hippos leave the river at sundown to forage along the bank and often far beyond. Invariably, year after year, they use the same old track and when disturbed they will turn back down the track and race for the river, steadfastly refusing to be put off by any obstacle that might present itself. Many people have died because they did not jump out of the way fast enough.

8 THE RHINOCEROS

What man dare, I dare.
Approach thou like the rugged Russian bear,
The arm'd rhinoceros, or th' Hyrcan tiger;
Take any shape but that, and my firm nerves
Shall never tremble.

– William Shakespeare, *Macbeth*

Shakespeare, in this passage from *Macbeth*, had Macbeth avowing that he feared Banquo's ghost more than he would have feared facing the 'arm'd rhinoceros'. Not that the real Macbeth, King of Scotland in the 11th century, would have known much about the rhinoceros. The Indian rhino was barely known by Europeans and its crusty African cousin became known only centuries later.

Africa has two species of the world's five rhinoceroses, both marvellously Jurassic in appearance. Yet neither is much feared by those who know them. Whenever I see a rhinoceros I recall T. Murray Smith's words, 'It is a miracle that this prehistoric idiot still exists.'[1]

The 2 000- to 2 500-kilogram (4 400- to 5 500-pound) white rhino[2] (*Ceratotherium simum*) is a grazer, while the 1 500-kilogram (3 300-pound) black rhino (*Diceros bicornis*) is a browser and belongs to a separate genus. Both are short-sighted but the white – which has slightly better eyesight – is generally docile, though it has killed people on occasion. The black rhino is seriously myopic and, as a result, nervous and inclined to defend itself by attacking or at least putting on a threatening display. Its myopia is such that it can mistake a car for a mate; rhinos have been known to put on quite an enthusiastic mating performance until they detect a certain frigidity, when they may ram the car before moving off with their tail curled up.

Although the black rhino has killed fairly regularly over the years, its reputation as one of the most dangerous animals in the bush has been greatly exaggerated. Hunters have long argued over its position in 'the big five' – the five most dangerous and sought-after animals to hunt. Some argue, unconvincingly, that they would rather run into a lion or leopard, maybe even a buffalo or elephant – since at least these animals prefer flight to fight. When the black rhino suspects somebody is nearby, it tends to spin around and advance, hesitantly, towards the source of its irritation, stopping and listening through its swivelling funnel-like ears and sniffing the air with distended nostrils. If the person stays still it will saunter off. On the other hand it might decide to charge. Rhinos have been known to charge trucks and, on one occasion in Kenya, a locomotive, when it was killed on impact.

In *Man is the Prey* I wrote of a theory 'held dear by a surprising number of big-game hunters that one can side-step a charging black rhinoceros and that it will then go trundling past and eventually stop and begin browsing again'[3]. I have since found it is no theory. Werner von Albensleven, who hunted in Mozambique for many years, says, 'The black rhino can be side-stepped with comparative ease.'[4] Jim Feely, a ranger with wide experience but who is particularly knowledgeable regarding the two African rhinos, used to stand his ground when a black rhino charged him and, as it reached him, whack it across the nose with his rifle butt and so turn it[5]. I imagine that takes very precise timing and a very cool nerve.

C.A.W. Guggisberg, an East African wildlife writer, correctly states that a number of people who claim to have been charged by black rhinos have merely been the subject of 'an exploratory advance'. If the black rhino senses something suspicious, it will throw up his head and trot toward the source of its annoyance; it might trot around in a half-circle and test the wind. It will then stand for a while before retreating, turning from time to time to face the direction where it suspects somebody is standing. It is wise to assume that it is going to attack and look for a tree to climb. Occasionally a shout or violent action will cause the rhino to rush off in a state of high alarm. Then again, it might make him charge. No other animal is so magnificently unpredictable[6].

Most big-game hunters agree that the black rhinoceros is easily killed with a medium or heavy rifle. Often it can be effectively turned off its course during a charge with a shot over its head or into the ground ahead of it. It is said to be easily felled when it presents a head-on aspect. J.A. Hunter would allow them to charge to within 15 metres (16 yards) of his clients' cameras before felling them with a single shot.

The black rhino also has an acute sense of smell. If it detects a slight movement or catches a human scent, it may charge with lowered head, but it might well chicken out before reaching its target. If it does complete its charge, hooking its head right and left, it will often be satisfied with tossing a person into the air (sometimes as high as four metres [13 feet] according to Captain C.H. Stigand[7] who was once tossed to such an altitude). But just occasionally it will whip around and bore its victim into the ground, or even gather him up on the end of his horn and toss him again and again. Benjamin Eastwood, chief accountant for Uganda Railways in its pioneer days early last century, had a remarkable escape when he approached a rhinoceros that he thought he had shot dead. The 'dead' rhino rose to its feet and fell on him, cracking four of the man's ribs and breaking his right arm. Then it impaled him through his thigh and threw him high into the air. Twice more it tossed him. Eastwood was alone and lay groaning in the long grass. Had it not been for his assistants who saw vultures circling the spot, he would have died. His arm had to be amputated[8].

Ian Player, founder of the wilderness movement in Africa and a world authority on rhinoceroses, said, 'I have known several men to be killed by black rhino over the years and I doubt whether there is a game ranger in these parts who has not been charged by one. The only sensible thing to do when confronted by a charging rhino is find a tree and climb it – even four feet [1.2 metres] from the ground is usually safe enough.' He did not advise trying to sidestep a rhino but suggested, 'Sometimes, the best trick is to chuck your hat or bush jacket – or anything – in its way and hope it will take it out on that.'[9]

His successor as KwaZulu-Natal conservator, Nick Steele, had numerous bad encounters with black rhinos. He said many a time a black rhino gave visitors a thrill by dashing towards them in what appears to be a frightening charge, but if nothing further provoked it, 'it would suddenly brake and stand there blinking'. But it can be mean. Steele recounts how ranger Gordon Bailey rode into a black rhino in dense bush, dismounted and smacked his horse on the rump to make it run so that he could divert ranger Ken Willan who was riding 50 metres (55 yards) behind. Too late, Willan ran straight into it and was instantly thrown from his horse. Then began a nightmare game of hide and seek until the rhino gave up, but then it spotted Bailey's horse, which it charged and mortally gored. Willan's horse found its way home, but it too had been mortally injured[10].

Player could recall four deaths from the less aggressive white rhino around 1970, but since then I have heard of at least two more, one of which involved a ranger who was walking with his girlfriend in Ithala Game Reserve in KwaZulu-Natal. They were charged by a white rhino and the ranger, to divert the animal's attention from his companion, ran off to the side and paid for it with his life.

There have been a few incidents involving tourists and black rhinos, including a woman who ran and fell face-down in soft muddy ground. The rhino ran over her, doing little damage. Another involved a rhino that charged a group of tourists and picked on a man who was running away. (Tourists are routinely and gravely warned *never* to run from a wild animal, no matter how big it is, unless the ranger orders it. He or she will do this only when there is no alternative and when the ranger feels he or she can distract the animal and down it.) He ran in a wide circle, which took him back through the throng of his companions who, wide-eyed, realised two things: firstly, that the rhino had disappeared and, secondly, that the man was not aware that he was running between them.

The black rhino was and is still considered to be a serious trophy and for this reason has been shot to extinction in most of its range in Africa. By 1994 the IUCN's Rhino Specialist Group said the black rhino's numbers were down to 2 300 in the wild. Today there are probably 700 in South Africa divided between Zululand and the Kruger Park[11]. The black rhino became extinct in the Kruger Park during the 1930s. It was reintroduced from the 1960s and today there are possibly as many as 350 in the park[12], which can easily sustain another 2 000.

Wilderness Trails, which were inspired by Player, where groups of up to eight tourists are accompanied by two armed escorts, were pioneered in the 1960s in Zululand's provincially run reserves. While Player and the Natal Parks Board (now Ezemvelo KwaZulu-Natal Wildlife) felt it was safe enough for people to walk inside game reserves where lions and elephants and other potentially dangerous animals existed, the National Parks Board (now SANParks) was for many years reluctant to allow walks. Since the Kruger Park introduced five-day trails about 30 years ago, thousands of tourists have safely walked there, but there have been incidents. In 2001 a party from a car rental company was on the Wolhuter Trail in the south of the park. They had been watching a small herd of peacefully grazing white rhino mothers and their calves when a bull, from some distance away, suddenly charged. The two rangers quickly moved the tourists behind a tree and tried to chase the animal off, but when it continued to charge a ranger had to shoot it. It was the second rhino attack on tourists in three years. In 1999 a white rhino had been fatally shot by park rangers after charging tourists on the same trail.

In 2004 a tourist was seriously injured in the south of the park near Byamiti, in an incident involving three white rhinos. Tracker Elias Chauke was lifted clear of the ground by a charging rhino and carried along, wedged between the rhino's two horns. As the rhino stormed past the lead guide, Dumisani Zwane, it received a smack on the head from the butt of Zwane's rifle. It dropped Chauke, who suffered a broken hand and three broken ribs. The other two rhinos advanced on the bewildered group and one of them gored a man in the buttocks and legs. It appeared that the hikers had unwittingly trapped the three rhinos in a loop on the Byamiti River and, in a panic, the animals charged through them.

Jeremy Anderson feels that rangers and trail guides tend to teach white rhinos to behave badly – just as they do with elephants – 'by retreating every time the animal snorts'. He was with a ranger in Zululand who began retreating as soon as a white rhino moved towards him. Anderson told him to stand his ground and they watched as the rhino passed within two metres (seven feet), sniffing the trail and totally uninterested in them. The ranger had misread the situation. Curiously, Anderson believes the white rhino is more dangerous than the black. While the black will charge and probably lose interest, the white will 'pursue you' he says. His wife, Liz, was chased 'round and round' by a belligerent white rhino before managing to hide inside a thicket[13]. I experienced a charge by a female white rhino with a calf. I stepped behind a tree but was torn away from it by a panicked tourist who hugged the tree. The two rhinos passed within a few metres and gave me not a glance. They were running blindly through our group and not at any particular target. Anderson believes they will behave aggressively only once in 100 encounters.

The slaughter of Africa's rhinos is yet another sad tale of mindless killing in Africa. John Hunter admitted without regret to having killed more than 1 600 rhinoceros (mostly black), some for 'sport' and some on contract to governments to clear land for human habitation[14]. In Kenya he shot 300 in 1947 and 500 the following year to prepare land for settling the Wakamba. The land proved to be unsuitable.

Poachers are taking a steady toll wherever rhinos exist. Because of the near extinction of Asia's three rhino species, pressure by Asian criminal syndicates on the two African species is annually stepping up, even though the Chinese regard the horns of Africa's rhino as inferior to those of Asia.

The rhino-poaching situation in South Africa epitomises the growing severity of the war being fought along the 'front line' between those living outside protected areas and the animals and their custodians within. In 2007, 13 white rhino fell to poachers in South Africa, the poachers being paid by Far Eastern crime syndicates. Many of the criminals behind the poaching are Vietnamese nationals. A year later the number of South African rhinos killed rose to 100. In 2010 South Africa's national parks and

reserves lost 333 – 10 of which were the endangered b...
448 were killed, 19 of which were black. More than half the rh...
killed in the Kruger National Park[15]. That year 20 suspected poachers were
killed and nine wounded in gun battles with rangers and the police – five
deaths more than the previous year. In 2011 the South African Army was
called in to patrol Kruger Park's border with Mozambique where most of
the action was concentrated. It failed to curb the poaching.

South Africa is targeted because its rhino population of 22 000 represents
about 90 per cent of Africa's total.

In January 2012 Kruger Park rangers, on one day, came across eight
dead rhinos – all had had their horns taken off by a chainsaw; some in
fact were still alive but immobilised by drugs darts. Rangers later met up
with a group of poachers who are said to have opened fire on them – two,
both Mozambicans, were killed. Some of the 379 poachers arrested in
2010 and 2011 are serving sentences of up to 16 years.

Dr Morné du Plessis, CEO of WWF South Africa, was quoted by news
agencies as saying, 'Rhino poaching is being conducted by sophisticated
international criminal syndicates that smuggle horns to Asia. It's not
enough to bust the little guy – investigators need to shut down the kingpins
organizing these criminal operations. Governments in Africa and Asia
must work together across borders to stop the illegal trade.'[16] The reports
also quoted Tom Milliken, TRAFFIC's rhino trade expert, who said that
rhino horn had gained popularity 'among wealthy Vietnamese elites and
business people to give as a gifts when currying political favour, or taking
as an antidote for overindulgence'[17.] TRAFFIC facilitated visits between
South African and Vietnamese government officials to discuss deepening
cooperation on law enforcement. By early 2012 little had been achieved.

Rhino horn, comprising compacted fibre, is considered to be a powerful
fever cure in the Far East and by some as an aphrodisiac. Powdered Asian
rhino horn has been listed as a fever cure in Chinese medical archives for
3 000 years. Until recently it was much coveted by Yemeni youth who
treasured elaborately carved dagger handles of rhino horn – nowadays they
are more interested in Harley Davidsons.

'We've always had subsistence poaching [for meat],' said George Hughes, a former head of the old Natal Parks Board. 'But serious poaching for large game by professionals selling rhino horn or ivory to Far Eastern syndicates is far more alarming.' He claims the fatal step was the international ban on rhino horn sales in 1977. 'It was like Prohibition in America in the 1930s. Prices shot up and so did poaching.'[18]

Former African army professionals with modern weapons are thought to be involved. In 2010 a Vietnamese national was caught on camera taking delivery of rhino horn outside the Vietnamese embassy in Pretoria. He was sentenced to 10 years.

Elephant- and rhino-poaching operations are commonplace in the game reserves of Tanzania, Kenya and Zambia, and in Zimbabwe the rhinos introduced over the years since the 1970s have largely been poached[19].

The other three rhino species are in the Far East: the Asiatic or Sumatran rhinoceros (*Didermocerus sumatrensis*), which has two horns; the Javanese rhinoceros (*Rhinoceros sondaicus*), which is one-horned; and the huge and more dangerous Indian rhinoceros (*Rhinoceros unicornis*). The Sumatran and Javanese are practically extinct and both are said to be short-tempered and aggressive; there are a few accounts of men being tossed by the latter.

The Indian rhinoceros with its single horn and heavily folded skin is every bit as crusty as the black rhino of Africa. Its method of attack is interesting, in that it tends to attack with its lower teeth, instead of its horn (as do the other Asian species). E.P. Gee, an authority on India's rhino, says that the animal is aggressive and 'annually kills a few people'[20]. Probably not many more than 600 survive today in their last strongholds in Assam, Bengal and Nepal.

There are ancient accounts of the two-tonne Indian rhinos being used in war by the kings of ancient India, as a sort of tank. This suggests that the Indian rhino is more tractable than it looks. The Indians are supposed to have lashed tridents to their horns. Was the war rhinoceros the start of the evolution of the modern-day tank?

9 THE BUFFALO

But this was Africa, and all things were ominous.

– Alan Wykes, *Snake Man*, 1960

Being hit by a charging buffalo is tantamount to being hit by a car, because the animal weighs about the same. Perhaps it would not be so bad if it were, like the rhinoceros (or like a car), satisfied with just knocking one down, but a buffalo will either hook a fallen person high into the air – some hunters have landed in the tops of thorn trees three to five metres (10 to 16 feet) above the ground, out of harm's way – or churn its victim into the ground by first going down on its knees and goring him almost to a pulp.

The African buffalo must have given the pioneer hunters with their inefficient weapons a pretty rough time, judging by their lurid accounts. In fact, the buffalo took a fairly heavy toll on them. The early explorers traded guns – mostly antique muzzle-loaders and deadly blunderbusses (deadly, that is, to the user) – with locals, in exchange for supplies, not realising that this would result in the wounding of many buffalo, which would then exact a human toll. There are stories of some individual animals – almost certainly wounded – killing a dozen and more people before being destroyed.

Although buffalo herds destroy crops throughout their range, the same animal might one day make up for all that. Conservationists and animal husbandry scientists see in the buffalo a potential beef animal that can be raised like ordinary stock but with many decided economic advantages. For example, it takes 11 years to improve the bushveld until it is fit for grazing cattle – even then it is necessary to wage a constant battle against bush encroachment and various tropical diseases that hit cattle in Africa. But with buffalo the veld need not be improved and, while cattle are only eight per cent efficient at turning Africa's grassveld into protein fit for human consumption (meat and milk), the buffalo is 40 per cent efficient. It is also disease-free, except for rinderpest, and can be culled at the rate of 25 per cent a year. Seventy-five per cent of the carcass is edible. It is astonishing that its potential as a food animal has not been fully realised by farmers in Africa. Half its trouble, possibly, is its dreadful reputation.

F.C. Selous, the Victorian hunter who ranged over sub-Saharan Africa, had some unhappy experiences with buffalo and as much as anybody helped establish the animal in the public mind as a ferocious beast bent on destroying humans. T. Murray Smith half a century later wrote, 'The buffalo is not only dangerous, he can be the most wantonly vicious animal in the wilds.'[1] Hunters, to this day – even with rifles far more powerful than in Murray Smith's day, even with soft-nosed bullets (these are used to stop a buffalo in a herd without ricocheting and wounding other animals), despite almost armour-piercing bullets for follow-up shots – are apt to see the African buffalo (or Cape buffalo) as a formidable foe.

One hunter wrote, 'Cape Buffalo are said to have killed more big game hunters than any other animal. Buffalo are thought to kill around 200 people every year, first they charge and then they gore their victims. An injured buffalo is incredibly dangerous.'[2]

According to Wikipedia, some hunters describe the buffalo as 'Black Death' or 'Widowmaker', widely regarded as 'a very dangerous animal, as it gores and kills over 200 people every year. Buffalo are sometimes reported to kill more people in Africa than any other animal, although the same claim is also made of hippos and crocodiles[3].

Graham Currin supplies more 'evidence', having witnessed a non-fatal but quite terrifying attack in the Serengeti (Tanzania) in 2005 where a companion was twice tossed in the air and then trampled and gored. The buffalo – a full-grown bull can weigh 800 kilograms (1 760 pounds) and more – then fell dead on top of him but fortunately the ground was soft and cushioned him. In the article 'No One Survives a Cape Buffalo Attack', he writes, 'They have been known to chase people up trees and then stay there for days eating around the tree waiting for them to come down, says native Kenyan Mlengu Mwachofi. They are also known to urinate on their tails and flick it into the tree to make you itch and scratch until you fall out. You do not always hear about them in the same breath as lions or crocodiles, but many say that Cape buffalo are responsible for more human deaths than any other African animal. They are rumored to have killed more big game hunters than any other creature.'[4]

As the buffalo is so widespread and as many are wounded when raiding crops or by lions, it is quite possible that wounded buffalo do kill 200 a year – but that can only be a guess. Under normal circumstances, unmolested, the African buffalo, *Syncerus caffer*, is as passive as a Friesland cow.

In many game reserves guides take tourists on foot quite close to buffalo. I have often watched tourists creep up to buffalo herds, their hearts in their mouths, their f-stops forgotten, but, as they see the animals' wet leathery noses and vacant bovine features, the tourists' reaction is sometimes one of disappointment. Buffalo, grazing or browsing in a herd, look and smell very much like a herd of rather large cattle. One or two in the herd might advance a few steps out of curiosity, nostrils flared and heads held high looking, literally, down their noses, but, if a tourist makes a sudden movement or if the herd catches wind of them, they will wheel around and trot off to what they consider a safer distance. The buffalo, alone or in a herd, is normally as nervous as an antelope. I have heard of only one instance – in a reserve adjacent to the Kruger Park – where a buffalo charged out from its herd and killed somebody.

Professional hunter John Taylor wrote:

> Men get queer ideas about buffalo. Most men without much experience seem to think that buffalo will attack without any provocation. There is a belief that buffalo will invariably whip around on feeling the lead and make a savage and determined charge. Well, all I can say is that I have never experienced either of these things and I have shot close to 1 200 buffalo … and have encountered a hundred times that many.[5]

Eric Noble, who was a game farmer on the Sabi in Zimbabwe in the 1960s, ranched several hundred buffalo as beef stock and maintained that they are more tractable than Afrikander cattle[6]. W. Robert Foran, despite asserting that the buffalo was the third-most dangerous big-game animal, also observed that the buffalo's 'reputation for inherent savagery in its general disposition is unwarranted'[7]. He records an incident, which, to say the least, underlines the docility of buffalo – if unmolested. In the Tana River region of Kenya, Foran and his assistant, Hamisi Bin Baraka (who was later killed by an elephant), spotted a magnificent bull behind a large herd of buffalo. Herd bulls, says Foran, place themselves on the upwind side of the herd, as it is normally from the downwind side that their one and only natural enemy, the lion, attacks. Foran and Bin Baraka tried for some hours to get around the herd without being detected, but late in the afternoon they found themselves back where they had started. Foran so badly wanted the trophy that he decided to risk what he calls a 'foolhardy action'. He and Bin Baraka began trotting toward the herd. The buffalo nearest them raised their heads but showed no inclination to run. They obviously had not caught the human scent yet. Foran and Bin Baraka, like a pair of rugby players, passed right through the herd, handing off any buffalo that got in the way. Once at the rear of the herd the hunter picked off the bull. Only then did the herd stampede.

A belief that dates back well into the 20th century is that a buffalo, when shot and wounded, will flee for a few hundred metres or even kilometres, and then double back along its tracks and wait in ambush for the pursuing hunter. It allows the hunter to pass it before charging from the rear. From this alleged habit the buffalo has earned itself an undeserved reputation for cunning. A wounded buffalo does in fact wait in concealment but, if it has ever purposely doubled back to wait in ambush, that must be counted as exceptional behaviour. When a buffalo is shot its first instinct is to run. A professional hunter during the first part of the 20th century, Owen McCallum, stated, 'A wounded buffalo will move on as you come up with [sic] it.' He once wounded a buffalo and five times got almost near enough for a shot, but each time the animal fled in the most determined manner. The buffalo's behaviour when it reaches thick bush may have given rise to the theory that it doubles back. Like most other wounded animals it will then rest, feeling relatively secure. The hunter following the blood spoor is at a dangerous disadvantage and might even run into the animal before he sees it. Hunters have died in such circumstances.

A problem is that, once the beast has made up its mind to charge, nothing short of death will stop its rush. The only exception to this seems to be when a herd is 'charging', or, more likely, stampeding toward the hunter. This infrequent situation is more tricky than desperate. Foran claims he prefers 'mass charges' to individual charges made by wounded animals[8]. It is his theory that the herd is not knowingly charging the source of danger, but is rather seeking a tactical advantage by rushing upwind. Even when a herd is running away from the hunter, it might suddenly wheel around and come straight at him. Foran says that a couple of bullets placed at their feet will often induce them to turn. There is an alternative measure – one used by Native Americans when faced by a stampede of bison: kill or down two or three in the same place. This tends to split the herd and send them glancing off in two directions. (Not that buffalo herds stampede quite as blindly as the movies would suggest the American buffalo [bison] does.)

Culling a herd of buffalo is not as dangerous as it might seem and, because of buffalo population explosions and meat production in many parts of Africa, culling is going on almost daily. John Taylor gives us an example of what it is like when he describes a night shoot in the Zambezi River valley where buffalo were destroying crops. He approached the herd to within 20 metres (22 yards) or so and, using a pair of doubles as well as a powerful hunting lamp, he opened fire on the herd.

My first shot slammed through the shoulder of a very big bull, dropping him instantly. They were still nearly all broadside onto me. At the shot they all swung and stood looking directly towards me. So my next shot was a frontal brain-shot; and I knew that most if not all subsequent shots would be similar. The second beast dropped in his tracks and I exchanged rifles. It was now a case of picking a target and firing just as quickly as I could, swinging on to another, firing, and exchanging rifles with my gunbearer. Both weapons were fitted with ejectors which slung out the fired shells, so that my bearer was usually able to have my second weapon ready when I needed it ... After my third shot the entire herd commenced edging towards me, jostling one another and crowding together ... Eventually I had the herd within ten yards of me, and still I continued to shoot. But now I took three or four paces backwards and away from them as Saduko whispered that a number of the buffalo were working up on my right. If I allowed them to get around too far they would get our wind. So, having taken up a new position, I swung around again and dropped another two from those in the center.

The alpha male then charged into the center of the pool of light and wheeled away with the herd, now in full flight, following on his heels. There were no wounded. But there were twenty-two dead buffaloes – all within a few yards from one another. This was at night, of course. Such a feat would probably not be possible in daylight.[9]

Although Taylor and people like Charles Goss, who shot two large bulls stone dead with a single .600 bullet, make buffalo-shooting look easy, a seemingly accurate shot – even a heart shot – may not stop a buffalo. John Burger, a South African hunter, once killed a large bull buffalo with a perfect heart shot using a .404 soft-nose. The bull, fortunately running away from and not toward the hunter covered '187 yard' (171 metres) before dropping dead. On opening the animal, Burger found its heart was just 'pulp'. An acquaintance of mine was killed by a buffalo that he and another hunter had hit 11 times. The first shot was a bad heart shot at 200 metres (220 yards). The buffalo turned around and looked for the hunters. Having good eyesight, it soon spotted them and charged full bore. It was then hit with the second barrel of the .270 (a favourite rifle among old-timers but, for hunting buffalo, a little risky). The buffalo showed no reaction and continued its charge as the bullet buried itself in its shoulder. The hunter swapped guns and rashly pumped off two brain shots, which he could hear ricocheting off the heavy boss that protects a great deal of the buffalo's head from the front. He then – at 100 metres (109 yards) – put a shot into the animal's right shoulder, and it went down for the first time. But in an instant it was up and charging again. He raked it with a sixth shot. His companion, who was carrying a .333, put the seventh shot in the animal's right shoulder, breaking it. The buffalo went down but again rose quickly and charged. Another shot hit the same shoulder and the buffalo stumbled but still came on. The hunter who had started it all tried a spinal shot through the neck and missed badly at about 20 metres (22 yards) and had yet another poor shot at about 15 metres (16 yards) but this shot brought the animal down again and it struggled to regain its feet. Then it came on again. The second hunter put a shot through its chest, which felled it instantly. It was a perfect frontal heart shot and the two men, both a little shaken, as the buffalo was lying a mere 10 paces away, shook hands. The first hunter walked over to his trophy and placed his foot on it for the camera. The buffalo lurched to its feet, knocked the man down, pummelled him into the ground killing him.[10]

One-armed George Gray did not allow his lack of an arm to hold him back – until the day he fluffed a shot at a charging buffalo. It killed him. His brother had been killed some time earlier by a lion – also following a poor shot.

T. Murray Smith described the damage inflicted on a 50-year old African, who had been gored and trampled 'literally into the ground' by buffalo. His intestines had spilled from a hole ripped in his stomach, every limb was broken, and one of his arms was all but severed from his body. The man's face was a pulp and his right hand still clutched his spear, the head of which was missing. The late Ken Beaton, chief warden of Queen Elizabeth Park, saw just how determined a buffalo can be when one charged his Land Rover, ripping off a door and gashing the body in a number of places.

There are on record several 'miraculous escapes' involving the buffalo. Once, a wounded buffalo, also in Queen Elizabeth Park, charged a mother and her child. The buffalo charged the woman first, hooked at her, and missed. It kept going and then caught up with the child, which it also tried to hook. Again it missed. It continued its flight until it was out of sight. Tobi Rochat of Acornhoek in the Lowveld of Mpumalanga described to me in 1966 how he was charged by a wounded buffalo. His gun bearer fled.

The buffalo rammed Rochat (who was in his 60s) into a *taaibos* ('tough bush') – a dense, springy type of shrub. Every time the buffalo tried to push the man into the ground, the bush absorbed the shock and Rochat bounced upright like a jumping jack. The buffalo gave up.

Alan Calenborne tells of a man who was tossed into the air and landed on top of the dense crown of a blackthorn tree (*Acacia mellifera*), which has densely packed hooked thorns as sharp as a cat's claws. It caused all concerned a great deal of pain and bloodshed and took considerable time to extricate him.

A friend walked past a sleeping buffalo and became aware of it only as it sprang to its feet and charged. He was flung into the air but the buffalo, fortunately, did not stop. I was told of a villager in Uganda who, riding a bicycle, was charged by a buffalo. He managed to bang his hat over the animal's eyes. The buffalo stopped to shake it off and the man got away. Normally it is impossible to avoid a charging buffalo since, unlike so many other animals, including the domestic bull, it keeps its eyes on you all the time and only at the last minute does it lower its head.

10 THE HYAENA

Like one, that on a lonesome road
Doth walk in fear and dread,
And having once turned round walks on,
And turns no more his head;
Because he knows, a frightful fiend
Doth close behind him tread.

– Samuel Taylor Coleridge, 'The Rime of the Ancient Mariner'

The man's face ended below his cheekbones: his nose, palate, upper teeth, tongue and almost his entire lower jaw were gone. Only his eyes and the upper part of his head remained intact. And yet he was alive and moderately healthy and had taught himself to swallow food. He had received one bite, just one snap, his friends explained, and that was all there was to it.

The hyaena had come during the night, as they always do, and had smelt food around the village. It had gone deep into the village until it had come to a hut where the smell of food was strongest, and there it had stopped (as its tracks indicated the next morning). It must have seen the men who were sleeping outside because the night was warm. It had loped forward to the nearest man and again paused indecisively two metres (seven feet) from him. Then it had moved silently forward until its nose was an inch from the man's face. It could smell the food around his mouth. The sleeping man, gradually becoming aware of the appalling odour of the animal's breath, opened his eyes. The hyaena clamped its terrible jaws over his mouth and nose and, with the ease of a man biting a biscuit, it bit cleanly through.

There are hundreds of Africans throughout the continent who have had their faces mutilated or limbs severed by the spotted hyaena (*Crocuta*

crocuta)[1], and I can think of three or four mutilated tourists around the world too.

Throughout Africa the hyaena, according to some, is a greater problem than the leopard, and in Mozambique some say it is an even greater problem than the lion.

Hyaenas are responsible for an annual loss of life caused either by outright man-eating or from its devastating 'hit-and-run' methods, which can cause lethal infection or cause a victim to bleed to death.

Because of the habit in parts of Central and East Africa in particular of leaving the dead and, in the quite recent past, the dying in the bush for predators to dispose of, a number of carnivorous animals have grown used to eating human meat. Many a man-eater began its career by acquiring a taste from the bodies of the unburied and, in the past, from eating the bodies of condemned criminals who were sometimes tied to trees. Some people leave their dead in the bush for superstitious reasons, but also as a practical way of disposing of them: the scavengers of the wilds are very thorough and very efficient; ecologically there can hardly be a 'greener' method for disposing of the dead.

In the Zambezi Valley, in Ethiopia and no doubt other areas, prostitution and Aids have produced a regular crop of abandoned babies and orphans for hyaenas to dispose of.

The 2009 FAO report on human-wildlife conflict records:

> In Sudan, because of the lack of proper housing children often have no choice but to sleep outside at night thus becoming vulnerable to nocturnal predators. A death census showed that in addition to being at risk to human trafficking, more than 280 orphans died in Nyamlell in 2006 because they did not have a safe place to sleep at night. Hyena attacks were shown to be the number one cause of death.[2]

It is noteworthy that in the Zambezi Valley man-eating hyaenas are found mainly between Kariba Dam and Mana Pools – two of Zimbabwe's prime tourist areas. This is where until the 1960s it was customary for some clans to leave their dead for hyaenas. Even though the then Rhodesian authorities (Rhodesia became Zimbabwe in 1980) tried to eradicate the custom, there has been a lapse in control in recent years. It is probable that the old slave routes along which the slave traders, over many centuries, left dead and dying captives for scavengers to eat have left a legacy of genetically predisposed man-eating hyaenas.

According to the 2009 FAO paper, spotted hyaena attacks on humans throughout Africa are considered to be common, with 'dozens of deaths reported each year'. Theodore Roosevelt, when in Uganda in 1908 and 1909, noted that spotted hyaenas regularly killed people in East Africa who were suffering from sleeping sickness as they slept outside[3]. There are frequent reports from throughout tropical Africa of hyaenas taking the sick and dying outside their huts and of hyaenas scavenging battlefields after various internecine wars – right up the present. A particular hot spot at any given time is along the Ruvuma Valley in Niassa (Mozambique), on the centuries-old Arab slave route. The World Wildlife Fund in 2004 reported that in the space of an unspecified year 35 Mozambicans were killed in Niassa by spotted hyaenas along a stretch of road just 20 kilometres (12 miles) long. The 2009 FAO report mentions, in the same (Niassa) province bordering Tanzania, hyaenas, in one year, attacking 52 people, 28 of whom died.

There is a great deal of difference in the habits of hit-and-run hyaenas that bite off a person's face or limb and a hyaena that kills in order to eat its victims. The former is behaving normally. In Africa both the spotted hyaena and the striped hyaena of North and northeast Africa have the habit of foraging around camp sites and on the outskirts of villages (rather like bears in parts of North America). Because of this they become used to people, though they remain wary of them. They are non-aggressive and, except in freak circumstances, would never attack a man who is awake. Hyaenas, although classically the scavengers of the bush, have recently been found to be far more predatory in nature than was supposed. In East Africa ethologist Hans Kruuk found that lions often reversed roles with hyaenas – lions followed hyaenas to feed off their kills[4]. But the hyaena's methods are far from bold. Frequently they enter camps at night, drawn irresistibly by the smell of meat, and they might steal and eat anything from a saddle or a pair of shoes to a tanned skin, a rifle stock (if it smells of blood) or even cooking pots. They snatch canned food and crunch the tins open in their jaws. The strength of their jaws is fascinating. They can leave teeth marks in forged steel and many Africans have had hunting spears chewed until they are unusable, merely because they forgot to clean the blood off the blade.

In many people's eyes there are few four-footed creatures quite so repulsive as the spotted hyaena, and certainly there is hardly a species so denigrated. You have to listen to them eating the bones of some carcass in the veld or hear their witch-like sniggering, giggling, moaning, shrieking and screaming with 'laughter' to appreciate the horror they can engender. They are enormously strong, with large heads and black, powerful jaws. Hyaenas will appear on the scene of a hunt, drawn by the sound of a rifle shot. Both spotted and striped hyaenas have been known to bite at the undersides of live cattle and eat their entrails as they fall to the ground; they are also said to patrol round the fence of cattle kraals and snatch off the muzzles of any inquisitive cattle that put their heads through the fence.

Although a normal hyaena will bite a sleeping man and might even snatch a newborn child and carry it off, there seems to be a definite difference between these opportunistic hyaenas and the man-eaters. In the Mlanje district of Malawi, there was a particularly bad period of man-eating, beginning in September 1955 when a man was killed and eaten on a well-beaten track between two villages. Fred Balestra, a local farmer, who later shot a pair of man-eaters in this district, was unable to find out whether the man had been asleep at the time of the attack, but he believes the killing was done by a single hyaena. It appeared that the killer shared its meal with four or five others and all that remained of the victim were a few shreds of clothing and a patch of blood[5].

This proved to be the first of a chain of killings that continued for several years. Balestra said the local people had known of previous episodes of man-eating involving hyaenas. They referred to the man-eaters as *lipwereri* and said they were bigger and stronger than the normal hyaena, which they called *fisi.* That these man-eaters were in fact bigger than normal was borne out by the weights of the two shot by Balestra, who found them to be 71 and 77 kilograms (156 and 170 pounds) respectively.

Seven days after the villager was killed, an old woman was dragged screaming from her hut at night by a hyaena that had broken through the straw door. The hyaena dropped her when a neighbour rushed up, but by then her arm was missing and she had been badly bitten around the neck. She died soon after the incident. The third and last killing that spring was a child of six who was killed while sleeping on a veranda. The hyaena killed her by biting her face off and then, along with other hyaenas, ate her entire body, leaving only the back of the head. Balestra believes that they left the head purely because they were disturbed by village dogs. The following year five people were taken and from then until 1962 the number fluctuated between five and eight each year, of whom about 70 per cent were children. In 1961 all six victims were children – four were eaten in January. It is noteworthy that all the attacks took place during the summer months when people sleep outside their huts. At one stage the government used an air-force plane to bomb the caves in which it was suspected the hyaenas were sleeping during the day, but the raid produced little effect and the killings continued over a belt of country 80 kilometres deep and 20 wide (50 by 12 miles).

Balestra, as the only man prepared to hunt the hyaenas, believed for a time he was up against lycanthropy: quite often victims would be taken from the midst of their sleeping families and yet nobody heard a thing. This was probably because they were seized by their faces and killed before they could utter a sound. Whatever the case, it also gave rise to fears of witchcraft and many witnesses were reluctant to give information. There are people in Africa who sincerely believe there are no wild hyaenas in the world – that they all belong to witchdoctors. This belief is furthered by the witchdoctors themselves, some of whom keep hyaenas as pets, rearing them from pups. Balestra says they go even further and, by a method that makes one blanch, they get them used to eating human flesh and then hire them out to settle scores. George Rushby, who worked as a game ranger in Central Africa for some years, shot hyaenas that had beads interwoven in their hair and some of them had mysterious patterns cut into their flesh. He also records finding a hyaena wearing khaki shorts. One shot by him was claimed by a witchdoctor as her lover and she gathered it up and carried the reeking animal away[6].

Tourists, from time to time, come up against hyaenas.

A fishing group was camped on the Zimbabwe side of the Zambezi downstream of Chirundu at New Year, 2004. They turned in at 9 pm but Di Patterson, finding it too hot to sleep inside her small tent, decided to sleep on the stretcher outside. She was aware of the threat of hyaenas…

She recalled:

> At ten to twelve I was jerked to wakefulness by the sound of scrunching bone and the most disgusting smell as a hyena bit into my face and hand and started dragging me. I screamed and screamed. It must have been only a few seconds before the brute, realizing that he'd bitten off more than he could chew, let me go and vanished into the night. As I knelt in the dirt, the blood pouring from my face, I realised that my hands and feet still worked and that I could still think so I must be all right!

She was quickly evacuated to Kariba, and then by MARS (Medical Air Rescue Service) to Harare hospital. She said afterwards with remarkable fortitude:

> I do believe that I am living proof that prayers are answered. From the moment that hyena let go everything was positive. I did lose my eye but the surgeon managed to reattach my eye-lid, which is a big plus for holding in a false eye, and still has hopes of finding tear ducts.
>
> After the first operation he thought he would have to do a couple of skin grafts, but during the second op, ten days later, he found that it wasn't necessary. The bone man managed to put my very graunched hand back together with skewers and I will probably get full movement back.

I really have no hang-ups about my injuries or disfigurement. I am still alive. My injuries could have been much more horrific.[7]

In August 2007 an eight-year-old Johannesburg girl, Christin Chalwin-Milton, was sleeping on a chair next to her tour group's camp fire at Third Bridge camp in Moremi Nature Reserve in Botswana. It was just after 11 pm when a hyaena crept up behind her and took her head in its jaws. Her father, Ralph Chalwin-Milton, stormed at the animal shouting, and scared it off. Christin's head was open from her eye to behind her left ear, which was missing. Chalwin-Milton found the ear and put it in ice.

The little girl was driven to Maun for primary care and then flown to Johannesburg where reconstructive surgery was carried out, but all her facial muscles and nerves, as well as her hearing and sight, were impaired.

Although the Chalwin-Miltons were aware of bush etiquette, Christin was the victim of those who were not. One rule is never to feed animals in the wild, but people leave meat outside the camp in the hope of attracting scavengers during the night – and this is one reason why animals such as hyaenas lose their natural fear of humans.

Four years earlier and in the same area, also late at night, a hyaena dragged an 11-year old American boy out of his tent and killed him. His mother in a nearby tent heard nothing until some workers raised the alarm after seeing the hyaenas dragging the boy's body into the bush.

As I was working on this book in June 2011, a 13-year-old schoolboy camping with his class in the Imfolozi section of the Hluhluwe-Imfolozi Park in KwaZulu-Natal had his face mutilated during the night. The boys had been warned about keeping food in their tents; although the sweets and chips in the tent were hardly food for a carnivore, it seems likely that those are what caused the hyaena to tear open the tent and bite the boy. The screams of his classmates scared the animal away.

One of the guests of the late Ted Steyn, chairman of the Northern Tuli Association in Botswana's Tuli Block, was dragged from her tent by a hyaena that had bitten into her shoulder. Her cries woke her husband who seized a rifle. He was unable to shoot the animal for fear of hitting his wife, so he used the rifle to club the animal, which fled. Fortunately the hyaena had not used the full force of its jaws and the woman recovered well.

Almost simultaneously there was a massive explosion in the open-sided kitchen at the other end of the camp, where another hyaena had bitten through one of the gas pipes; the gas leak was ignited by a pilot light under one of the paraffin-fuelled refrigerators, causing the gas tank to explode.

Some years ago Alan Calenborne was with his son Giles, then a schoolboy, on a field expedition in Botswana. Towards the end of the day they had some kilometres to walk before reaching their vehicle. The sun was low and they were following a game fence. It was then they noticed they were being followed by a hyaena. Calenborne, who was not armed, became wary of the animal as the distance between them decreased. Then there were two. Each time he turned the hyaenas had lessened the gap between them. He threw stones and stormed at the creatures, but they continued to follow. It grew darker and by now they were being tailed by five.

Eventually he and his son reached the Land Rover, but he has wondered ever since what might have happened had darkness fallen.

11 THE PRIMATES

**One, with a soul and a mighty brain …
the other, a wild caricature of ourselves.**

– Arthur Mee, 'The Animals Most Like Men',
The Children's Encyclopaedia

The *Concise Oxford Dictionary* is a sober little book. It squats there on my shelf, modest, quiet, unassuming, always willing to render what is asked of it; never more and rarely less. Except, that is, when you reach 'Gorilla'. Here it falls into the pit: 'Gorilla, n. Large powerful ferocious' it says. Large they are and powerful – but rarely ferocious, rarely a serious threat to humans.

Since World War II our knowledge of the ways of the great apes has increased enormously. The acceleration is mainly due to a realisation that, by studying the primates, we are studying a facet of ourselves. This in turn probably stems from a realisation that, if we are to discover where the human race is going, then it is best we find out from whence it came.

When you look through the whole gallery of modern apes and monkeys, it is the gorilla that most impresses, probably because of its size, and for this reason a great number of misconceptions have grown up around this enormous parody of man.

Sir Richard Owen, a 19th-century British biologist, succumbed to popular fiction when he wrote: 'Negroes when stealing through the shade of the tropical forest become sometimes aware of the proximity of one of these frightfully formidable apes by the sudden disappearance of one of their companions, who is hoisted up into the tree, uttering perhaps, a short, choking cry. In a few minutes he falls to the ground a strangled corpse.' This image of a massive, chest-beating, man-strangling ape persists today in many

145

people's minds. In fact the gorilla is a shy animal whose great displays of ferocity are a bluff, and unless it is driven beyond the point of endurance it will beat a noisy retreat when it sees a human. If its family is endangered it will charge repeatedly, beating its midriff with his open hands, but if a person makes a stand the gorilla will pull up short, scream with rage and frustration, and rush off into the undergrowth.

It is hard to believe that such a fierce-looking ape, which can weigh up to 500 kilograms (1 100 pounds) in the wilds (more in zoos), can be so scared. Could it be perhaps that the old explorers were right and that the gorilla *used* to be a dangerous animal, but now, after being persecuted by man and his gun, the last of the gorillas have learned they cannot win? According to recent observations of gorillas in the wild, they are scared of no other creatures, not even the leopard. There exist few reliable accounts of any dangerous acts perpetrated by gorillas and involving humans (apart from attacks by wounded or cornered animals). Its habitat shows that it is not a particularly adaptive animal. In fact, it is so specialised that it is doubtless doomed to extinction within a few generations.

Gorillas are found only in two parts of Africa: in the dense forests around Cameroon in West Africa (this race is known as the lowland gorilla – *Gorilla gorilla gorilla*) and in the dense, wet forests in the region of the Albert National Park between the misty Virunga volcanoes and the Ruwenzori Mountains in Central Africa. The latter area is the home of the *Gorilla gorilla beringei*, the mountain gorilla. The differences between the two races are negligible but 1 300 kilometres (800 miles) and probably many generations separate them.

In those damp mountain forests, where the last mountain gorillas feed upon bamboo shoots and other vegetation, a local game guide named Rubin, who was employed by the University of the Witwatersrand primate research unit in the mid 20th century, survived three potentially dangerous experiences with gorillas. It is an indication of the gorilla's geniality that this man, who for years was in almost daily contact with gorillas, experienced only three troublesome incidents. On one occasion he was following up the blood spoor of a wounded gorilla – the gorilla had been fighting a rival on and off for several days – when he suddenly found himself facing the animal. The enormous silver-back (as old bulls are called) came straight for him. Now Rubin knew the rules as well as any man: never run from a charging gorilla, but turn and face him and *he* will run. At the same time, Rubin could see that this gorilla was so badly wounded that he could not be counted upon to remember his side of the rules. So Rubin compromised: he began to dance wildly and loudly. The astonished gorilla stood rooted to the spot before turning and fleeing. On another occasion Rubin was watching from very close quarters a female gorilla that had been spurned by the local patriarch and was in a towering rage. She suddenly saw Rubin and charged up to him. Rubin, taken completely by surprise, struck her with his panga. The female bit him. Rubin then kicked her in the stomach. The gorilla retreated into the undergrowth. The same female threatened Rubin again two days later, but he shouted and the frustrated ape withdrew.

When a villager is wounded by a gorilla, he may be mocked on his return because it would be assumed he fled instead of standing his ground.

George Schaller, who spent practically two years living in gorilla territory in the Eastern Congo (Zaire) with the purpose of studying them, did not carry a gun until his wife, Kay, prevailed upon him. He ended up carrying a harmless starting gun, but never had cause to use it. Instead, he found his subject 'reserved and shy'[1]. Schaller said that on the rare occasions when gorillas do attack men they tend to bite and run. In one case a gorilla seized a hunter (who had just wounded it) by the knee and ankle and tore away his calf.

Fred G. Merfield, a hunter in West Africa, found the race of lowland gorillas there much the same as Schaller's gorillas: secretive and extremely nervous. These gorillas, protected since the 1930s, are still hunted by locals in the most ruthless manner. Merfield described some appalling hunts where gorillas are trapped and then speared until they resemble porcupines, and yet even then attacks were not common. Merfield, who put this theory to the test many times, says: 'Of course there are exceptions to this. If you happen to tread on a gorilla's toes in the forest, you can expect to be torn to pieces, but even then the gorilla will be more concerned with getting away than with killing you. His action will be to sweep you aside with his powerful arms and hands.'

This actually happened to Merfield.

Merfield claims that female gorillas 'are completely harmless'. He describes how hunters, having killed the bull, will gather around the female and beat her over the head with sticks 'and it is most pitiful to see them putting their arms over their heads to ward off the blows, making no attempt at retaliation'[2].

The extroverted chimpanzee – far stronger than a man – which roams a wide area of Africa's rainforests, is shy and decidedly nervous in the presence of man in the wilds. Apart from an astonishing but possibly not unique case of man-eating, it cannot fairly be counted as a dangerous animal.

In March 1957 in the Kasulu district of Tanzania a woman carrying a baby was attacked on a forest path by a large chimpanzee. The incident happened near the shore of the Lake Tanganyika north of Kigoma. The inquest papers carried the following evidence from the African woman: she was carrying the baby on her back when 'suddenly from the bush came a chimpanzee. We were in the bush and the village was far. I was tying up my faggots. I ran away and the chimpanzee hit me twice. He was about 4 feet [1.2 metres] tall. I fell down. Then it caught the child who was on my back. I made a great deal of noise and other women came. Then we saw the chimpanzee eating the child's ears, feet, hands and head.' Medical examination revealed five depressed fractures of the skull caused by the teeth, the scalp was missing and so were the hands and half of one foot. The coroner ruled that the child had died from misadventure and found that it had been 'eaten by some animal'[3].

Jane Goodall watched chimpanzees in Tanzania eating the flesh of monkeys that they had first killed. This local species, *Pan satyrus schweinfurthii*, the long-haired or eastern chimpanzee, is the popular one is zoos and circuses. It grows to almost the size of an average man, in weight if not in height, and its diet comprises fruit, plant shoots and occasionally eggs.

In 2002, in Gombe National Park, Tanzania, where Jane Goodall carried out her chimpanzee studies, a large male chimpanzee (*Pan troglodytes*), known as Frodo to those based at the nearby research station, killed a 14-month-old infant, having removed it from the back of a terrified 16-year-old girl who was walking along a public path with her mother. It took the toddler up a tree and fed on it. The 26-year-old chimpanzee was, to the chimp community he ruled, a mighty hunter. Jane Goodall, says he ruled 'with an iron fist'[4]. Chimps, as Goodall famously discovered, habitually hunt monkeys and baboons and eat them. An infant human being carried on its mother's back would be about the size of a big chimp's prey.

Allan Fallow in *National Geographic* commented on the report by Shadrack Kamenya, director of chimp research at Gombe Park, on the incident that appeared in *Pan Africa News*.

Around 11:20 on the morning of May 15, 2002, the wife of one of the park attendants was following a forested public footpath through the park near Lake Tanganyika's shore. Her destination: the Kasekela research camp ... Walking behind the woman was her 16-year-old niece, who carried her aunt's 14-month-old baby in a sling held firmly to her back.

The trio had just crossed a dry streambed when they surprised Frodo feeding on oil-palm fronds only 12 feet (4 meters) from the path. As the spouse of a park employee, the mother probably knew that park rules bar children under 12 from visiting the park, and she almost certainly was aware of the mortal danger posed by chimps. Her shock and terror must therefore have been unimaginably extreme as she watched the 121-pound (54-kilogram) Frodo draw near, wrest the baby girl from the niece's back, and disappear into the forest.

By the time help arrived from the research team, Frodo had scrambled up a tree and was holding the limp form of the baby, which he had begun to eat. Lacking the defensive support that the larger group would have lent him, Frodo was easily scared off, and the baby girl's dead body was recovered.

While representatives of the Tanzanian National Parks Department debated euthanizing Frodo, the Gombe research team weighed alternative courses of action and struggled to put his behavior into context. Pressed to clarify the circumstances surrounding the assault, Dr. Kamenya furnished the primatologists' perspective: What we see as murderous conduct, he explained, is standard for chimps in the wild. Characterizing Frodo's attack as the 'natural hunting behaviour of chimpanzees,' Dr. Kamenya pointed out that the animals regard human babies 'just as they view the young of other species such as colobus monkeys and baboons—as potential prey.

'This was not the first case of human babies being taken by chimps in the Gombe area,' Dr. Kamenya elaborated. (Abductions resulting in child deaths also occurred in 1987, 1984, and in the 1950s.) 'But it was the first within the park, and the first involving a habituated chimp of the research community.'

This is not to suggest that the Gombe region is the only one where such incidents have occurred. Other cases of chimpanzees seizing human infants were reported in the Congo in the 1950s and in Uganda in the 1990s.[5]

The only other potentially dangerous primate and the only other terrestrial primate apart from ourselves is the baboon but, by and large, even the biggest of them have the intelligence to give man a wide berth. In fact 'man' is the operative word, for some baboons – notably South Africa's chacma baboons (*Papio porcarius*) – are much less afraid of women and will even approach them, making threatening gestures. This same species has also learned to distinguish between gun-carrying men and unarmed men and will allow the latter to approach much closer than the former. If you are carrying a gun they will begin running, in their loping, four-legged gait, when you are still as much as 300 or 400 metres (328 or 437 yards) away. There are several cases recorded each year in South Africa of baboons attacking humans, but in almost every case the culprits are pet baboons. Attacks in the wild are very rare. My own experience of chacma baboons, with fangs every bit as impressive as a leopard's, is that they are, in the wilds, probably the least nervous of Africa's various baboon species but will, nevertheless, retreat if an unarmed man approaches within, say, 100 metres.

Chacma baboons along South Africa's Western Cape Coast, and especially the Cape Peninsula, are becoming less and less nervous of tourists –

especially as some inadvisably and illegally feed them. They raid houses when the inhabitants are away and have learned to break into cars and frequently enter parked cars whose windows are left open, in search of food. It seems a matter of time before somebody is attacked.

A large male baboon was shot by the police in the Cullinan district near Pretoria after people had complained that it had thrown stones at them and had repeatedly threatened them over a period of two years. The police discovered that this same baboon had, two years before, chased two girls, aged five and 13 respectively, over a cliff to their deaths[6]. In Sutherland in the Northern Cape it was reported that a labourer named Fred Visagie had practically all his clothes torn off by a big baboon that attacked him on the farm Rooiwal while he was looking after sheep[7]. The man was badly bruised and scratched. He claimed that as the baboon was attacking him the rest of the troop gathered around to watch. Two months later, in Fish Hoek on the Cape Peninsula, a pair of baboons terrorised a mother and her two children when they tried to break into their home. The mother told the police (who shot both animals in the garden) that the baboons had been banging on the doors and windows for some time. I wondered after reading the report whether the mother had not misinterpreted the baboons' intentions because the incident was reminiscent of an episode described by Eugène Marais in *My Friends the Baboons*. Marais, who lived for three years in a hut among a colony of baboons in the Waterberg Mountains in today's Limpopo Province, described how one night the baboon leaders came down and began banging at the windows. He saw their faces at the windows but he knew the troop well enough to realise that something was radically wrong. He went outside and they made off up the mountain, looking back and waiting to see if he was following. Marais did follow and they led him to the rocky outcrop where they slept at night and there, by the light of his lantern, Marais could sense something was wrong. He soon discovered what it was: eight babies had died. He carried their bodies down the mountainside to his hut and the mothers followed in silence. He took the corpses inside but it was clear that they were indeed dead and that they had died for want of good diet (there had been a famine). For hours the mothers waited but when they saw Marais could do nothing they turned and filed back up the mountain 'wailing mournfully'[8].

The yellow baboon, which is found from Zimbabwe north into Central Africa, has a similar record of rare attacks upon humans. P.J. Pretorius tells of a large, solitary male early last century, which killed and partly ate a small child. It operated at the side of a swamp in the Ruvuma River area of Tanzania and apparently rushed out at passing villagers (if they were alone) and disembowelled them with its fangs. Then it would break open the skull by using its teeth and eat the brains, leaving the rest of the body. The locals were so terrified of the animal that in the end they abandoned their village. As this was on a major Arab slave trail that had been in use for four centuries, it is possible that this was another instance of an animal reverting to a past habit, stemming from when wild animals came across dead and dying abandoned slaves and fed off them.

The biggest of Africa's baboons is the mandrill, *Mandrillus sphinx*, which has a face as fierce as it is colourful – sky-blue, red and orange. But, apart from one or two attacks by rogue males, they live in fear of man and are extremely difficult to approach.

Humans remain the most enigmatic and dangerous of the primates.

12 THE CROCODILE

A cruel crafty Crocodile

– Edmund Spenser, 'The Faerie Queen'

When describing a Nile journey in which he saw crocodiles close up for the first time, Winston Churchill wrote, 'I avow, with what regrets may be necessary, an active hatred of these brutes and a desire to kill them.' The old hunter W. Robert Foran got even more carried away and wrote: 'The loathsome and hideous crocodile ... no one should ever hesitate about killing crocodiles wherever a chance offers, because it is either already a killer many times over or a future destroyer of life.' Later, when he was discussing how he took pot shots at them from a Nile steamer: 'I felt neither the shame nor the remorse. The savage and cunning killers ought to be shot exactly as one would a mad dog.'[1]

Some amazing and highly unlikely legends have surrounded individual African man-eaters. A lurid example is Gustave, a crocodile that might still be living in the Ruzizi River at the northern end of Lake Tanganyika and was the subject of a National Geographic documentary around 2007[2]. Gustave seems to be the Chuck Norris of the crocodile world. Locals say he has killed 300 people, some for the sake of it – which makes him sound like a human – leaving the corpses uneaten. He is said to have eaten a dozen people in a day and still seemed hungry. He was apparently named by naturalist Patrice Faye who has been trying to hunt him down for years and who claims to have seen Gustave with three people in his jaws. Locals say he killed and ate an adult hippo. Bullet-scarred Gustave was last sighted in February 2008. Perhaps by now he has choked on an elephant.

The worldwide crocodile family comprises many species, from the alligator of America to the huge mugger crocodile of Asia and Australia. The crocodile saw the dinosaurs come and it saw them go. It has been around, more or less in the same shape and the same tough hide, for 170 million years. And since the genus *Homo* appeared around two million years or so ago, Africa's Nile crocodile has preyed on humans, uninterruptedly and legitimately, from the Nile to KwaZulu-Natal.

In neighbouring Mozambique, where predators of various species are stepping up attacks on humans, the crocodile is held to be the worst offender. Despite the official figure of 134 deaths a year Jeremy Anderson, who has been involved in quantifying the situation, believes the figure is more likely 300 – a figure that the 2009 FAO HWC report endorses[3]. The problem is there's no incentive to report deaths. In 2008, 30 people were taken along the north bank of the Zambezi in the Mutarara district, and the report says 'probably a similar number were taken along the south bank'. Another 100 were taken in the nearby Cahora Bassa Dam. The Niassa National Reserve in the far north of Mozambique reported in a 'partial survey' in 2007 that, 'despite low crocodile density' in the 39 years up to 2007, 57 people were known to have been killed – 40 of them in the last seven years.

The official reaction has been to declare war on the crocodile. In May 2010 Mozambique's Deputy Justice Minister, Alberto Nkutumula, announced an 'emergency plan to alleviate human-wildlife conflict'. The plan was initially to shoot over 130 crocodiles regarded as 'problematic' and collect 'thousands of crocodile eggs' – presumably for the crocodile leather market to hatch. He said the plan was based on the 'Strategy to Manage the Conflict between Humans and Wildlife' and that the crocodile was considered the most problematical animal. The plan would also ensure that people could draw clean water from wells and boreholes and so avoid going down to rivers and lakes.

The deeply embedded prejudice that surrounds the Nile crocodile might be due to the fact that, when it preys upon humans, it doesn't, in our eyes, fight fair, displaying a terrible indifference to whether it has caught a barbel or a human. Crocodiles can lurk undetected in close proximity to people and in the smallest waterhole. A fully grown croc can hide in a pool less than knee-deep and has the uncanny and ghost-like knack of quietly appearing and disappearing, even in waterways deep inside towns. An attack can last only seconds and can be made silently without leaving a clue – if there are no witnesses nobody will ever really know what happened to that person. Because of this, we can only guess how many deaths are due to crocodile attacks in Africa.

The 2009 FAO report on HWC said, 'An assessment of the scale of human deaths caused by wildlife species in Africa at the end of the seventies, concluded that the hippopotamus was responsible for more deaths than any other large animal in Africa. But, today, this "crown" seems to belong to the crocodile.'[4]

When you consider that crocodiles accounted for 11 people dying in 2003 in a small town near Polokwane (formerly Pietersburg) in northeastern South Africa[5] and 50 people taken annually along the Tana River in Kenya[6] you begin to get an inkling of the numbers that must be involved throughout Africa. In January 2010 Zimbabwe Parks and Wildlife Management confirmed that in the space of two weeks eight Zimbabweans – indigent men and women who had turned to poaching to catch fish to sell from door to door – had been killed by crocodiles in Lake Chivero close to Zimbabwe's capital, Harare[7]. The authority said their violent deaths failed to deter other poachers from continuing to wade waist-deep into the lake to spear fish. In 2005 Campfire Association Zimbabwe, nowadays a grossly under-funded Zimbabwean NGO whose aims are to promote the management of wildlife in communal areas and the wise use of wildlife resources, said in its annual report that crocodiles had taken a narrow lead over elephants as the most dangerous animals to humans in Zimbabwe. Crocodiles, it said, were known to have eaten 13 people in the first 10 months of 2005, whereas elephants had charged and trampled 12 to death.

Campfire's director, Charles Jonga, commented, 'Most of the time there is no recognition of that fact that communities are always on the front line of the battle between man and beast.'

What is happening along the shores of Lake Victoria in Uganda is particularly significant. Man-eating crocodiles were practically unknown throughout the 20th century. There was plenty of fish for both crocs and humans, and fishermen had no fear of the lake's reptiles, despite their unusually large size. But crocodiles are now exacting a steady toll on humans.

In June 2009 Uganda's *Sunday Monitor*, paraphrasing a report on the Lake Victoria situation by Thomas Aram, the District Environment Officer, reported:

> Climate change has made cultivation and growing of crops difficult for most farmers who depend on agriculture. As a result they have moved to the lake to practise fishing to earn a living. There used to be plenty of fish in the lake before the vagaries of weather came into force. Back then crocodiles had enough food and never hunted for human beings. People have now disturbed the ecosystem arousing the wrath of crocodiles. The reptiles have turned hostile to people making regular attacks.
>
> In the past month alone, crocodiles attacked fifteen people, three of whom were killed, and the rest escaped with serious injuries. In the last six years, 100 people were attacked by the man-eaters, fifty of whom were killed.[8]

It is interesting to note that man-eaters are not necessarily shot. The newspaper report mentions rather enigmatically,

> Isaka Nasiko, 20, was also attacked by a crocodile on April 17 at Kifu, Bugoto landing site [on Lake Victoria]. As Mr Leo Jazza, the district Vermin Control Officer explains, the body parts of Nasiko were recovered near the lake and buried. 'We captured the crocodile and took it to Murchison Falls,' Mr Jazza said. On May 3, at the same place, a 17-year-old boy was eaten up by a crocodile.

From 1999 to February 2004 crocodiles killed a minimum of 28 people and injured 57 others in the Jukumu Wildlife Management Area, an area no bigger than London and constituting 22 villages located in the northern buffer zone of Tanzania's Selous Game Reserve. In one village alone 11 people were taken within a year. In the Caprivi region of Namibia, 157 incidences of crocodile attacks on humans and cattle were recorded in 2005 in registered conservancies[9].

In July 2000 Tanzania announced it was to reduce its Nile crocodile population to 1 500 reptiles[10]. The decision came five years after a report by Clal Crocodile Farms Int. Ltd (CCF), which voluntarily conducted a two-month survey and interviews regarding predatory crocodiles in rural Tanzania from 10 December to 14 February the following year.

You have to wonder about the motive behind the survey, since it was carried out by a crocodile-skin trading company. Its stated aim was to clarify information on human mortality from crocodile attacks and the effect of crocodile populations in rural areas. It reported:

> Preliminary data analysis confirms information from previous surveys. Crocodile densities of around three per kilometer and more were recorded in protected areas in the Rufiji, Lake Rukwa and lower Pangani. A preponderance of very large individuals up to 20 feet (6m) were noted. The interviews with local people indicated that previous quantification of the problems of human mortality from crocodiles are underestimates and the scope of this problem in rural areas is quite shocking. For example the village of Mpanga on the upper Kilombero river with about 65 families lost 8 people (5 of them children) last year and an additional three people were taken in the last two months. Similar high levels were recorded from other villages and as far as we know, no other country in the world suffers similar crocodile fatalities.
>
> Detailed analysis of the data is in preparation. The causes of this appalling mortality arise in part from the widely dispersed but dense rural population along rivers and lakes. The government has disarmed local people and maintains extensive anti wildlife poaching units in each region so that the people fear the crocodiles and also fear to break the law and kill them. CCF has reached a comprehensive agreement with the Tanzanian Wildlife Management Authority to establish a proper Management Program for crocodiles in the count.

A 'preponderance of very large individuals up to 20 feet (6m)' is not possible for the Nile crocodile. It is to be hoped that the subsequent government decision to start shooting crocodiles was not based on advice from one of Africa's biggest exporters of reptile skins. Tanzania, despite the CCF report, is far from being the 'worst country in the world' for man-eating crocodiles, though they do pose serious problems there. Statistics provided by the Tanzanian Wildlife Department suggest that Tanzania's annual toll is in fact 10 times less than its southerly neighbour, Mozambique. The department says human deaths caused by crocodile attacks grew to over 400 in the 15-year period 1985 to 2000 – an average of over 26 a year – with 462 injured. However, in the 1990s, when man-killing increased in the Korogwe district, crocodiles killed 51 people in 52 months (from January 1990), of whom 18 were killed inside the first four months of 1992. This above-average spate of man-eating in the 1990s was ascribed to a 'human-induced reduction in fish'[11].

The highest at which the human toll from crocodile attacks has been put for the whole of the African continent is 20 000 a year[12]. That was in the 1960s and was as good a guess as any at the time. A more likely guesstimate of the annual toll is probably between 4 000 and 5 000 deaths each year, with 3 000 injured. But this might be an underestimate, because reliable statistics from most of West and Central Africa are non-existent. In some areas rural people used to – and maybe still do – dump their dead in rivers – and even their hopelessly sick as well. They would also dispose of deformed babies or the weaker of twins by feeding them to the crocodiles. This was outlawed in the mid 20th century in many countries but it is uncertain how effective such laws are in Africa's remote areas.

The 2009 FAO report on human-wildlife conflict reported:

Many deaths due to crocodiles go unrecorded because of the logistics involved for many people to get to a government office or because in remote areas, many births are not registered, so that the death of someone whose birth is not even recorded often escapes detection. There is a widely held belief that crocodiles which attack humans are not 'real' crocodiles but either creatures constructed by witches, so-called 'human crocodiles' or crocodiles controlled by a spirit following a curse.[13]

Crocodylus niloticus is one of nature's most successful creatures and its ecological role is important. Just as the elimination of the hippo has in parts wrecked river ecosystems and caused massive loss of agricultural land (the hippo's herringbone pattern of pathways helps alleviate the damaging impact of flood waters and keeps channels open through reed beds), so the crocodile plays a vital part in the regime of rivers. It maintains a balance between the barbel (catfish – the crocodile's preferred prey) and the all-important more edible freshwater fish (tilapia, etc.) on which millions of Africans depend for protein. Fish, not mammals, are the crocodile's staple diet.

The crocodile is a triumph of evolution. It enjoys a wide diet yet, when the rains fail, it is capable of aestivating for a year or more. It is wonderfully armour-plated and, until the advent of the high-velocity rifle, it was near to being bullet-proof. It has self-renewing teeth: most animals, when they lose their second teeth, are unable to follow their normal diet and so grow weak and die, but the crocodile's unique dentition allows it to eat the same diet for 60 years and more. Some zoologists suspect it might live at least as long as humans. Its strength is amazing: full-grown crocodiles, weighing around three-quarters of a tonne, have been known to pull rhinos and buffalo into the water and drown them.

One of the most controversial features of the crocodile is its length; Cherry Kearton did not help the argument much when he claimed to have seen a '27-footer' (8.4 metres) on the Semliki River in Uganda[14]. There is a 16-foot (nearly five-metre) crocodile in Maputo Museum that stands as high as a man's chest, which means Kearton's crocodile would have been higher than a horse, had the girth of a rhino and weighed just as much. Colonel Pitman, who in the 1930s shot a hundred of the biggest crocodiles he could find on Lake Victoria (from where the biggest crocodiles in Africa are supposed to come), found only three more than '14 feet' (4.3 metres) and those were only just over that measurement. Jack Bousfield of Lake Rukwa in Tanzania, who claims to have had a hand in killing 45 000 of them, says he never saw one over '18 feet' (5.5 metres). The biggest as far as I can make out was on the Semliki. It was shot by the Uganda Game Department in 1953 and was said to have measured '19 feet 9 inches' (6.17 metres).

According to acquaintances who breed the reptiles on crocodile farms, you can become quite attached to them. Of course there is always the danger that they might become attached to you. I must confess to feeling the way most people do about these reptiles: they have an infinite air of menace about them. The lipless smile of the crocodile hides nothing: he advertises all his crooked teeth even when his mouth is closed. He has an upper jaw that Robert Ruark admirably described as being like a spiked manhole cover[15], and his tremendous mouth is like a highly efficient rustless steel trap.

Many people believe a crocodile can sweep its prey off a river bank with its tail, which is a fallacy. What it can do is rocket out of the water onto a bank up to two metres high (nearly seven feet) to snatch an animal – or a person.

My first encounter with crocodiles was on a wide channel entering St Lucia Estuary in Zululand, where I counted 12 floating on the opposite bank and detected the presence of more in the reeds below where I was standing. An hour or so before I arrived a man had lowered himself into the channel to push a pontoon away from the bank. In two seconds there was a flurry of water and he was gone. Only one crocodile appeared to be involved, although several others were around; as crocodiles are inexplicably good-mannered over food and never fight each other, the crocodile that had seized the man was allowed to depart in peace with his struggling victim, who twice broke the surface and waved frantically to his horrified companions. He was never seen again.

The attitude of locals (and my own as well) towards crocodiles is odd. After a hot and tiring day in 1969 in the Zululand thornveld – I was attached to a rhino-capturing team – I would join my game-ranger companions in diving into a river, knowing there were crocodiles around. We'd be out of the water pretty smartly, but all the same it was a risky thing to do. An acquaintance did the same in a reserve abutting the Kruger National Park. He knew the pool was staked out by a large crocodile, but as he could see it on the bank some distance away he was unconcerned. He did not know that it had been joined by a second crocodile. In seconds he was seized by an arm and pulled under. The crocodile stripped all the muscle from his forearm, leaving just the bone – he reached out what was left of the arm to a colleague, allowing the other arm to dangle. This was then seized and severed. He survived the encounter.

There are undoubtedly some crocodiles that acquire a preference for man-eating; one of the worst cases was on the Kihange River in Central Africa where over some years 400 people were said to have taken by a 4.7-metre (over 15 foot) crocodile that was later shot by a hunter, Pieter Wessels. Wessels recalls a sobering conversation with a missionary schoolteacher who had just lost one of his pupils to a crocodile: 'Piet,' he said, 'he was the seventh this term.'

Most crocodiles would eat a human if they were hungry and, in populous areas, crocodile hunters frequently find human remains or trinkets such as beads or bangles inside crocodiles. Most of those killed are women and children, because it is mothers with their children who spend a great deal of time down at rivers drawing water or washing clothes. Many women are seized by the wrists as they bend over the water; a story that one hears throughout Africa, which could conceivably have happened, is about a woman who, on being seized by the wrists, immediately fainted. The crocodile dragged her under the surface and pushed her into its cavern beneath a river bank. Although the entrance to a crocodile's cave is underwater, the actual cave is above the water line. The woman regained consciousness and, seized with terror, she pummelled at the roof until it collapsed. When she appeared in her kraal that evening, the villagers were already mourning her death; it was some time before they accepted the fact that it was not her ghost that they were seeing.

In 1957 I was in the Black Umbulozi River area of Swaziland when I met a missionary doctor named Samuel Hynd who was looking for the mother of a six-year-old crocodile victim named Busisiwe Magagula. The mother had disappeared into the bush to mourn Busisiwe's death but in fact Busisiwe was still alive. Hynd told me that the child had been seized by a crocodile while she was playing in the river and dragged under the water. The mother, hearing other children shrieking, rushed down to the river, waded in and saw her child holding on to the reeds on the far bank. She crossed over and grasped the girl's hands, and only then noticed that the crocodile was still fastened to the leg (a crocodile, when its jaws snap shut, virtually locks its grip by slotting two of its lower teeth into holes in the upper jaw). The mother was clinging to her child when the reptile suddenly spun horizontally, tearing off the child's leg at the knee. The child's father, fortunately a police constable trained in first aid, made a tourniquet with his old police belt and began to carry the child, at a trot, in the direction of the mission hospital at Manzini (then Bremersdorp), which was 90 kilometres (56 miles) away. At some stage of the journey a farmer found him stumbling along and took the child to the hospital. She appeared to be dead. A doctor told me: 'I saw her carried in and it seemed certain that she would die of either shock, loss of blood or infection. I have seen too many crocodile victims to have any illusions. Miraculously Busisiwe survived. In fact within a week she was walking on crutches and we found her the most intelligent and cheerful child.' Eventually they found the mother, who refused to believe her child was alive until she arrived at the mission station and saw Busisiwe struggling on crutches towards her.

The story has a happier ending: when the story of Busisiwe appeared in the Johannesburg newspaper the *Star*, it brought in enough donations for the child's education; as her chances of marriage would probably have been nil, she would need a career. An artificial limb manufacturer guaranteed her a new leg for the rest of her life and went one step further: every time Busisiwe comes up to Johannesburg he buys her a new pair of shoes and socks and spends several hours matching the skin colour of the artificial leg to her other leg. Today Busisiwe Magagula is a very active mission nurse with important responsibilities at the Manzini mission.

Out of the water the crocodile is nervous of humans; as you walk along a river you see their dark shapes snaking down the banks to slide into the river – a scene older than the dinosaurs. Once they are in the water, their attitude changes and they float, watching with their eye-ridges and nostrils just above the surface, with not a ripple betraying their presence. Occasionally, especially towards dusk or very early in the morning when the light is bad, people step on crocodiles in the shallows, mistaking them for logs, but mostly in cases such as this it is the crocodile that gets the bigger fright. Explorer Alexander Barnes[16] stepped onto a crocodile at Fort Jameson. The reptile seized his foot but Barnes managed to throw an arm round a tree and hang on for his life. With his free hand he pointed his rifle down at the crocodile and pulled the trigger. The stricken crocodile let go and Barnes, after rubbing salt into his wounds to keep them from going septic, walked to hospital. In recalling the incident, T. Murray Smith mentions that Barnes was later killed in another stream – a stream of traffic in New York[17].

There is yet another misconception regarding crocodiles: some authorities claim crocodiles will never eat fresh meat. In fact they do and might even prefer fresh meat to old meat; certainly, when they catch a small antelope or dog, they lose no time in throwing their heads back and let it slide down their throats. This head action of feeding crocodiles is necessary because they have no conventional tongue, nor are they able to chew food. If they come across a carcass too big to swallow, they will line up at it in a most orderly fashion and then, when their turn comes, they will grip a piece of the carcass and spin horizontally until a piece is twisted off. If the carcass is too big for this type of treatment, they will leave it until it is putrefied. Some authorities claim they can swallow only small pieces of meat but this is not true: there have been several instances where sizeable dogs and even half the torso of a youth were removed from crocodiles' stomachs. One of the most horrifying collections of stomach contents taken from a single African crocodile was in East Africa and consisted of several lengthy porcupine quills, 11 heavy brass arm rings, three wire armlets, some wire anklets, a necklace, 14 human arm and leg bones, three human spinal columns, a length of fibre – the type used for tying up faggots – and 18 stones. Smooth stones are often found in the animals' bellies; nobody is sure whether they are swallowed to aid digestion, to act as ballast or merely because crocodiles feed on bottom fish such as barbel and scoop up stones accidentally.

Colonel Stevenson-Hamilton records a crocodile at Lujenda in Angola that took an average of two people a month. Stevenson-Hamilton asked the chief why, as he had a muzzle-loader, he did not shoot it. 'What!' said the chief, aghast at the thought, 'We can't afford to waste our gunpowder on crocodiles!'

Annually thousands of tourists take part in canoe safaris along Africa's waterways and, although fatal mishaps are uncommon, when they do occur they tend to get worldwide coverage and spark off unusually thorough official inquiries. They also bring home to people outside Africa the dreadful suddenness and horror of crocodile attacks.

Such was the case on 4 August 2003 when an American visitor, Jack Reeves, and his two daughters, Katy and Carrie, went for a short late afternoon canoe paddle in Mana Pools, a popular reserve on the Zambezi. Reeves and ranger A.J. Ferreira were in one canoe, while the two girls were with a professional hunter, Douglas Carlisle, in another. They were heading from Mucheni Camp to Nyamepi.

Ferreira later recounted the event:

> We were drifting downstream, when I observed a large crocodile a short distance from the bank of the river with only its head visible. I instructed that both canoes should head for the bank, so as to enable the crocodile to have free access to deep water. As the canoes moved closer to the bank and the crocodile, the crocodile submerged and disappeared.
>
> As we drifted into shallow water my canoe with Jack Reeves was slightly ahead of the second canoe containing Douglas Carlisle and Katy and Carrie Reeves.
>
> Without any warning the crocodile lunged from the water and attacked the second canoe. The canoe listed over, and as it started to right itself the crocodile whose head had remained out of the water snatched Katy Reeves from the canoe almost tipping the canoe over.

The crocodile with Katy Reeves in its jaws reappeared immediately and started to swim powerfully into deeper water. The crocodile then released Katy Reeves who struggled to the surface twice.

I had by this time turned my canoe, and was frantically paddling towards Katy Reeves. I drew close to the girl, and her father Jack Reeves was stretching out, in an attempt to grasp hold of his daughter, when the crocodile attacked her again pulling her under the water. In desperation I fired my hand gun into the water hoping that the concussion would force the crocodile to release Katy Reeves.

There was not further sign of either Katy Reeves or crocodile.

I continued my search of the river throughout the night of Monday until midday Wednesday.

Personnel from both the ZRP and National Parks were present when I located two large crocodiles. I shot both within 45 minutes of each other. Both crocodiles were dismembered by National Parks personnel and body parts of the late Katy Reeves were removed from the two.

The attack on the canoe is unprecedented ... The suddenness of the attack ... prevented any immediate reaction to save Katy Reeves.

In the last few years crocodiles have become a nuisance on Lake Kariba and a great deal of the problem is because those using leisure craft on the lake either deliberately feed the crocodiles, to entice them nearer, or accidentally encourage them by throwing scraps of food over the side. I have come across at least one instance where a crocodile pursued an inflatable craft, which managed to escape only by putting on a burst of speed.

The fact remains that attacks on canoes and people being taken in lakes and rivers are common – even very common. It can almost be equated to the instances of urban pedestrians being killed by cars. Attacks are usually the result of the casual – perhaps fatalistic – attitude of those who live in crocodile-infested areas. I can cite many cases of crocodiles taking people wading across streams and, once the victim disappeared, their companions resume wading across. Often, of course, they have no choice.

Attacks on tourists usually involve young people who take chances. But, considering the volumes of tourists canoeing down African rivers and on its lakes – especially on the crocodile-infested Zambezi where a few thousand visitors a year canoe and camp along its banks – the threat is not disproportionate to the adventure. I've known people who have spent years guiding tourists in crocodile waters without mishap. A golden rule is never take a chance and swim in Africa's tropical zone, even if the locals say it is safe and no matter how small the pool.

While shooting problem crocodiles is one solution, there is a simpler one, and that is to install pumps to bring water up to the villages which, of necessity, are usually some way back from the water. This would reduce the need for women and children to go down to the river or dam. Unfortunately when pumps are installed they are rarely maintained[18]. In Mozambique some regional authorities have fenced off a section of river from midstream so that crocodiles cannot access the bank.

13 THE SNAKES

That running brook of horror

– John Ruskin

When at the beginning of World War II Field Marshal Jan Smuts (then South Africa's prime minister) decided to send troops up to North Africa he asked for a supply of anti-snakebite kits. He knew of the notorious carpet adder (or saw-scaled viper) in that region and that troops would be operating in the bush. Four army volunteers were drafted for the duration of the war to the Komatipoort area on the Mozambique border to catch adders and milk them for the production of antivenin (antivenom serum). The men produced a steady supply and after the war a count was made of how many soldiers had been bitten in the five years that South Africans were 'up north'. There had been only four victims – the four snake-catchers at Komatipoort[1].

In Africa there are not much more than two dozen species of snakes that are potentially dangerous to humans. Aside from venomous species, there is also the non-poisonous but potentially dangerous rock python. Common though many of these species are, and deadly though some can be, they do not cause anywhere near the anxiety created by other dangerous mammals – yet annually they probably kill more than all other animals combined (apart from those killed by the malarial mosquito). There is no marked resentment towards them and never any suggestion that they should be exterminated. This is partly because snakes neither hunt one down nor do they ruin crops – quite the opposite; their staple diet is rodents that would otherwise devastate stored grain and crops in the field.

The dangerous species can be divided into four types:

- The elapids, comprising cobras and mambas;
- The adders (vipers); the puff adder accounts for most of Africa's fatal snakebites;
- The colubrids, including the back-fanged boomslang and twig snake;
- The constrictors – notably the rock python.

I was hesitant to include snakes in this book because, as I say, there is no resentment regarding them and Africa's rural communities have never petitioned against their presence.

Most cultures have an aversion to snakes and, if a snake enters their living space, most people's reaction is to kill it on sight, venomous or not. But it is interesting that the San people will pick up a poisonous snake and remove it from the camp so that children will not step on it. They do not see snakes as evil or in any way deserving of being slain without provocation[2].

Snakes are anatomically strange creatures. Most species are incapable of exerting themselves to any extent, since only the left lung has survived the evolutionary processes that were necessary to make a snake's anatomy what it is – just one long narrow rib cage. This remaining lung is so elongated that the rear end is almost non-functional. Nor do these animals have any antibodies in their blood – not in the normal sense anyway – and thus even an infective tick bite can kill a snake.

Thirty years ago I watched a newly caught four-metre-long (13-foot) black mamba in a glass pen rearing and striking at the glass pane separating it from those of us who were standing there. It struck with its mouth agape and we could see the mouth's black interior (from which this grey-coloured snake earns its title). B.J. Keyter, director of the now-defunct Transvaal Serpentarium, who had just paid a large amount for this magnificent reptile, was worried that the snake might damage its fangs and then it would be useless to milk for venom. To distract the snake Dennis Groves, the curator at the time, threw a white mouse into its pen. The mouse ran up to the rearing snake and bit it in the side. Two days later the mamba died of infection from the mouse bite. 'That's the trouble with snakes,' Keyter said afterwards. 'They're such delicate things.'[3]

Of the world's 3 000 kinds of snakes, only 300 have well-developed venom apparatus and of these 50 are sea snakes that rarely bother humans. Only about 150 species of land snakes can be regarded as potentially dangerous to man. Every continent bar the Antarctic has its serpent population, although some have considerably more than others. Western Europe, for instance, has only a dozen species, none of them really dangerous. Asia does not have the variety of venomous species that are found in Africa but because of other factors – and because of the presence of the huge king cobra, which is said to be the most venomous snake in the world – each year thousands of Asians are killed. India itself loses far more people through snakebite than Africa, which has 200 million fewer people in a landmass 10 times bigger. Australia, which is unique in having more deadly snakes than harmless ones, records only one or two lives lost a year.

It is impossible to estimate the annual death rate caused by snakes but in June 1963 the World Health Organization (WHO) issued the following statement: 'Forty thousand people are killed by snake bite every year according to conservative estimates … Most of the deaths, perhaps 70%, occur in Asia.'

In 2009 the WHO said envenoming[4] resulting from snakebites is a particularly important public health problem in rural areas of tropical and subtropical countries in Africa, Asia, Oceania and Latin America. A recent study estimates that annually at least 420 000 envenomings and 20 000 deaths occur worldwide from snakebite. It warns though that these figures may be as high as 1 841 000 envenomings and 94 000 deaths. The highest burden of snakebites is in three regions: South Asia, Southeast Asia and sub-Saharan Africa.[5]

Snakebite is primarily a problem of the poorer rural populations and affects mainly those involved in subsistence-farming activities. Poor access to health services in these settings and, in some instances, a scarcity of antivenin often leads to preventable deaths. Many victims fail to reach hospital in time or seek medical care after a considerable delay because they first seek treatment from traditional healers. Because most victims are young, the economic impact of snakebite can be considerable.[6]

Africa's annual toll can only be guesswork and the figure 20 000 is the one most mentioned over the last 40 years. If the WHO's maximum global estimate is sound, then 20 000 is plausible. There's certainly no reason for the African toll to have dropped, considering the human population has more than doubled and traditional remedies are still sought, despite the fact that they are useless. Even where victims are taken to hospital or to a doctor, antivenom treatment is often shockingly inappropriate, antivenom is often not available and the staff is insufficiently trained. Yet many envenomed victims survive.

In 2003 Dr Roger Blaylock analysed 333 patients admitted to Eshowe Hospital in KwaZulu-Natal with snakebite.

Forty-one out of the 333 were non-envenomed, 282 exhibited painful progressive swelling, seven showed progressive weakness and there were three cases of minor envenomations that were unclassifiable. Offending venomous snakes (brought in dead) included *Naja mossambica* (Mozambique spitting cobra), *Bitis arietans* (puff adder), *Atractaspis bibronii* (stiletto snake – also known as the burrowing adder), *Causus rhombeatus* (common night adder) and *Dendroaspis polylepis* (black mamba). Most bites occurred on the leg in the wet summer months during the first three decades of the patients' lives. The majority of patients used a first-aid measure.[7]

The paper describes some of the distressing symptoms but what is significant is that antivenin had to be administered to only 12 of the 282 patients who had definitely been bitten by venomous snakes. Five of the 12 developed an acute adverse reaction to the serum. And what is also noteworthy is the last four words of the paper's abstract: 'There was one death.' It illustrates the importance of having hospital staff trained in treating snakebite. I have no doubt that had those 282 victims been admitted to most other hospitals in Africa – even in South Africa – there would have been fewer survivors. In fact South Africa, with 12 lethal species, records only 10 to 12 deaths a year, and some toxicologists feel that most victims die because of poor medical technique. A number die of fright or shock, even in cases where the dose might have been sub-lethal. Panic-stricken victims have been found trying to drink milk from a cow's teats because they believed it helped neutralise the venom, while others have been found running until they drop because they thought that it would help. A number of deaths have been brought on because the victim drank alcohol, believing that it helps combat the venom. In fact it stimulates the heart and quickens the action of the venom.

A Nairobi safari firm instructs its employees to tell clients – if they are bitten on safari – that the snake was harmless. They are also told to say that the injection of antivenin is a precautionary measure and, presumably, if they apply a tourniquet (a once-routine technique but now unequivocally condemned) they pass it off as a practical joke. It sounds unnecessary and yet the idea is sound because the more a patient relaxes the slower the venom travels through the body. People have died from fright or autosuggestion after being bitten by a perfectly harmless snake. The first step in first aid is to reassure the victim and get him or her to relax and be still.

It is alarming sometimes to read the advice by professional hunters. Take T. Murray Smith who advised in the 1960s that puff adder bite wounds should be crisscrossed with a sharp knife or razor blade, that a tourniquet should be tied above and below the punctures and that the wound should be irrigated with permanganate[8]. In fact all three pieces of advice are dangerous. Permanganate has been carried all over Africa by hunters and explorers but it has long been proven worse than useless; cutting a snakebite wound would only help the poison enter the system more efficiently; and tying a tourniquet after an adder bite causes such terrible damage to the affected limb (gangrene) that it has to be amputated.

Africa's most lethal snake is the black mamba (*Dendroaspis polylepis*). I recall in the 1980s a man being bitten by one in what is now Mpumalanga Province on the northeastern side of South Africa. His wife drove him to the provincial hospital in Nelspruit, which was several minutes away from where he had been bitten, but found no doctor in charge. She was advised to take him to Komatipoort – 100 kilometres (60 miles) away – but the doctor on duty there said he did not know how to treat snakebite and advised the woman to take the now-unconscious man to his own doctor in Barberton another 130 kilometres (80 miles) away. The man died on the way.

Medical ignorance even today can be alarming. In May 2008 Michael Bester (74) was bitten twice on the inner thigh by a mamba he discovered in his house. He had flushed it out from behind the television set using an insecticide spray. He was taken to a doctor in Margate on the KwaZulu-Natal South Coast, who said he could not help and sent him, under his own steam, to Margate Hospital. The hospital admitted him but did not administer antivenin, for fear that he might be allergic. He died that night.

India is said to have the most lethal snake in the world – the king cobra – yet Africa's black mamba is every bit as dangerous. Its range extends from KwaZulu-Natal on South Africa's east coast to Ethiopia and across much of tropical Africa. It is the African species that gives its victims the least chance of survival. Unless help is at hand, death usually follows within the hour – three at most. Some victims die within 20 minutes. A full bite could inject 16 times the lethal dose and the victim dies of suffocation (the chest muscles collapse).

In 2008 a 28-year-old British student, Nathan Layton, who was studying to be a field guide, was attending a lecture at a college near the Kruger National Park at which a live black mamba was demonstrated to students. Layton was waving his arms about to encourage the snake to move when it suddenly reared and bit him on the finger. He snatched his hand away so fast he did not think the mamba had had time to inject venom. After the staff – all trained in first aid for snakebites – had examined the finger, the lecture continued[9]. After 20 minutes the student announced his vision was blurring and he quickly went into a coma, from which he never recovered. Less than three hours later he was dead.

Herpetologist and one-time curator of the Durban Snake Park and the Transvaal Serpentarium, Johan Marais, described an incident to me. Late one Saturday morning he was with an assistant, Crawford Coulsen, in the Valley of a Thousand Hills, about 50 kilometres (30 miles) from Durban. Coulsen was bitten in the calf by a large mamba and it took the man at least five seconds to shake the snake loose – long enough to have received many times more than a fatal dose. The pressure bandage in Marais' snakebite kit – so essential for slowing the effects of snakebite – was missing. He reassured Coulsen as best he could and got him to relax in the reclined passenger seat of his car. Marais (a one-time traffic policeman in Durban) then drove at up to 220 kilometres per hour (140 mph) on the N3. He was planning to take his assistant to Durban's Addington Hospital, where he was confident adequate help would be at hand.

After five minutes the victim's lips became numb. After 10 minutes his speech became slurred. Then he lost consciousness. As Marais neared the turnoff to Westville just outside Durban, he decided to chance the local hospital, but he found himself in solid Saturday morning shopping traffic.

He cut across the highway, heading back to the main road to Durban. Knowing Durban particularly well, he raced through its back streets, arriving at Addington about 30 minutes after the bite had been inflicted. He dragged Coulsen by his armpits across the pavement and straight into the hospital lift, since he knew the ICU was on the first floor. The sister on duty was slow in answering the bell and, when he told her the circumstances, she expressed doubt about whether the snake had been properly identified. She then told him there was no serum in the hospital.

At that moment a doctor arrived and put the victim, whose breathing was now barely discernible, in an oxygen tent. Four hours later he was sitting up talking, having made a full recovery. No serum had been used; his body had metabolised the venom[10].

The diurnal black mamba can grow in excess of four metres (over 13 feet) and is fortunately rare. Ironically, it is a 'threatened species' under the CITES agreement. It is not only Africa's largest venomous snake, but it is also the fastest, being able to glide gracefully along the ground at 15 to 20 kilometres an hour (9–12 mph) with the front third of its length raised. Like all snakes, it is nervous and will slide away on detecting the footfall of a human (snakes lack ears) or when approached within 40 metres (44 yards), but when cornered it is likely to inflict several bites in quick succession.

I recall an incident in 1958 at Ubombo in KwaZulu-Natal when a black mamba bit two girls repeatedly, both of whom died within an hour. A few years back a healthy Springbok rugby player, who had been bitten by a mamba, took the old-fashioned remedy – a bottle of brandy. He died within six hours. It was the brandy that probably killed in this case; he had only been scratched and a little common sense would probably have saved his life.

There are probably more yarns about this snake than any other. In some ways its reputation and its manner of striking a person high up in the body is reminiscent of the king cobra. A story you read and hear with monotonous regularity is about a farmer who was cutting back some scrub with a panga when he grabbed a black mamba instead of a branch. The snake bit his arm. On his next stroke the farmer severed the snake; on his next he severed his arm to save his life.

There is another more common mamba in Africa, the green mamba (*Dendroaspis angusticeps*), which was until 1946 considered to be the same species as the black. It is more arboreal than the black and, according to some, not quite as deadly. It is also less likely to attack. Nevertheless C.J.P. Ionides, a legendary snake catcher in Central Africa in the mid 20th century, recalled an incident in 1959 near Newala in the Southern Province of Tanzania: three men, three women and two children died after a green mamba got into their hut. Ionides later caught the snake. The only survivor, he said, was a baby[11]. The fact that Ionides caught some 3 000 green mambas within a few miles of Newala shows just how numerous they are. It also illustrates just how non-aggressive they must be, because so few people are bitten by them. Ionides sent a consignment of 50 to Dennis Groves, when the latter was curator of the Johannesburg Snake Park (later the Transvaal Serpentarium), who emptied the sack into a large glass pen. The snakes took to a bush about the height of a man, which became a wriggling mass of snakes. Later I watched Groves climb into the pen and duck under the bush to adjust something. Marais agrees that the green mamba is much less reactive than the nervous black mamba and has less toxic venom, but says its bite should be treated with the same respect as the black mamba's.

The mamba's venom attacks the nerves and, in the case of the black mamba, is quickly absorbed. The ordinary snakebite kit with its two vials of antivenin is pretty useless for a mamba bite, since a bite would need a dozen vials at least. Marais advises large amounts of antivenin injected immediately and intravenously by somebody who is trained to give such injections. Then a pressure bandage should be tightly applied (as with a sprained ankle), beginning by winding it around the bitten limb from the bite site towards the heart. Saliva should be prevented from blocking the throat and artificial respiration may be beneficial until the victim can be admitted to hospital. A splint on the bitten limb will keep it immobilised and minimise spread of venom.

Many people, believing cobra and mamba venom is transported through the blood, resort to using a tourniquet to inhibit it. These days tourniquets, unless applied by somebody with medical expertise, should not be used, no matter what snake is involved – in any event cobra and mamba venom is spread largely via the lymph glands and not the blood.

The biggest and most widespread killer in Africa (excluding man and the malarial mosquito) is the nocturnal puff adder (*Bitis arietans*). It avoids extreme desert conditions, dense forests and altitudes above 2 000 metres (2 187 yards). Most of the estimated 20 000 fatalities from snakebite in Africa are due to this thickset snake, which, sluggish though it is, strikes too fast for the eye to follow. Marais is sceptical about the puff adder's reputation. He says recent research indicates that the mortality rate for puff adder bite is quite low and that many of the previous serious bites in South Africa, especially in KwaZulu-Natal and Mpumalanga, that were attributed to the puff adder turned out to be Mozambique spitting cobra (*Naja mossambica*)[12].

Until the development of the high-speed camera, it was thought that the puff adder could strike backwards. In fact it can turn its head to strike forward at a speed that only a fast camera can capture. The species is normally sluggish and moves with a motion very much like that of a giant caterpillar, but when agitated it can move at speed in a typical winding serpentine manner. Puff adders are terrestrial but one was once found almost five metres (16 feet) up a tree and, like most snakes, they are good swimmers. They spend a great deal of time basking in the sun or keeping warm at night on bare patches of earth; since this is quite often on a footpath, barefooted children, who set up little vibration on the ground as they walk, are frequently bitten. Most victims are bitten below the knee.

The curved, needle-like fangs of a viper can be as much as 18 millimetres (three-quarters of an inch) long and are hinged; when the snake opens its mouth to strike, the teeth move forward so that they are pointing directly at the prey. In other words the prey is stabbed before the snake's mouth closes over the punctures and, usually, a large amount of venom is injected. The venom is powerfully cytotoxic (cell-destroying), haemotoxic (destroying blood vessels) and cardiotoxic (attacking the heart), causing severe pain and swelling in the bitten limb as well as haemorrhages and nausea. Death is normally from secondary effects, often kidney failure. Survivors usually suffer serious necrosis.

In cases of puff adder bites, the use of antivenin is essential. Untreated, the bite usually kills within a day, though I recall an 18-year-old student at the now-defunct Transvaal Serpentarium near Johannesburg dying within 10 minutes – the snake had bitten into her vein.

There are five other dangerous adders in Africa, one of which is the heavy, exceedingly thick 1.5-metre-long (five-foot) gaboon adder (*Bitis gabonica*). It has the most beautiful markings – rather like autumn leaves – and its habitat is the forest floor. It packs a tremendous bite, which contains both neurotoxin and haemotoxin in fair quantity. These four-kilogram (nine-pound) adders are much bigger and heavier than the puff adder (which is a third shorter and a third lighter) and have broad heads shaped like a shovel, the bulging sides containing the venom sacs.

Dennis Groves, while at the Transvaal Snake Park, was bitten on his little finger by a gaboon adder and, although he received large injections of polyvalent serum[13] within 30 seconds and was assisted by one of the world's leading authorities on snakebites within an hour, his life hung in the balance for 12 hours and his finger had to be amputated[14]. Fortunately this lethal animal is good-natured – Ionides actually used the word 'charming' – and very rarely bites people. An acquaintance in Zululand learned this one day when he sat on a log and opened up his sandwich pack. He felt something soft move beneath his feet and saw it was a gaboon adder. He lifted his feet and the gaboon slid slowly away. Usually a gaboon gives a good warning when you get too near – it emits something between a growl and a hollow hiss, which is very audible and unmistakable in meaning.

The saw-scaled or carpet viper (*Echis carinatus*) of the more northern countries of Africa, the burrowing adder (*Atractaspis bibronii*) and the berg adder (*Bitis atropos*) are each capable of very serious bites but, apart from the first-named, no fatalities have been recorded. The carpet viper was described by Ionides as unusually aggressive and he mentioned that all 311 he had handled tried in the most determined way to bite him[15].

Many authorities state that the genus *Echis*, to which the carpet viper belongs, results in more human deaths than even the puff adder[16]. I can find no numbers but as the genus *Echis* is found right across the barefoot world, from the West African coast (where the species *E. leucogaster* is found) to East and northeast Africa (*E. pyramidum*) and across the Middle East to India and Bangladesh (five species occur between North Africa and Bangladesh), this seems a fair assumption. Within Africa itself the puff adder, being far more widespread, is usually cited as the worst killer.

The carpet viper is unusually aggressive and strikes vigorously and often, but at least it gives fair warning by rubbing its scales together to produce a hissing sound.

Attesting to its notoriety, medical scientists were able to study 115 patients with envenomation caused by *E. leucogaster* in the savanna region of Nigeria 'where victims of this snake may occupy 10% of hospital beds'[17].

There is one more troublesome adder found almost throughout Africa barring the arid southwest – the ominous-sounding night adder (*Causus rhombeatus*). There are some interesting but very suspect stories about the night adder killing people. One that is often repeated concerns a farmer who was bitten and reputed to have sucked the wound to clear out the venom.

Because he had a sore throat (or a gum ulcer) the venom caused his throat to swell suddenly so that he choked to death. Apart from this, I have not come upon a case where the night adder has killed, but, with venom sacs that go along one third of its body, it has the potential. While some herpetologists say that an injection of antivenin can be more dangerous than the night adder's venom, Marais cites a case where a victim needed three days in hospital. He says the bite can cause serious, painful and quite alarming symptoms and must be taken seriously and medical aid sought[18] .

'It is much more pleasant to be bitten by a cobra [than, for instance, an adder],' a snake catcher once said in all seriousness and you can see what he means. The cobra's neurotoxin causes sleepiness, weakness, vomiting and partial paralysis within a fairly short time. The lungs collapse but the heart action, intensely accelerated, carries on and convulsions may precede death, which is usually from suffocation. Nerve poison usually attacks the anterior brain (medulla oblongata), which controls breathing. If the victim recovers, it is usually rapidly and there are rarely complications. An adder bite is extremely painful and can cause massive tissue damage, the effects of which can be manifest for years.

The yellow-and-black sea snake (*Pelamis platurus*), a cobra-like reptile with an oar-like tail, is perhaps the most ubiquitous, being found across the world. From time to time, offshore fishermen along the East African coast accidentally catch the snakes in their nets, but how many are bitten is unrecorded. Occasionally these snakes are washed up on beaches or even crawl ashore and traverse land for short distances, but I have found no instances of people being bitten inland. Most sea snakes prefer the shallows and estuaries but they can be found in mid-ocean.

Africa is unique in being the home of spitting cobras, the most notorious of which is the black-necked spitting cobra (*Naia nigricollis*), which can eject a fine aerosol of venom up to three metres (10 feet) in range. The effects are immediately painful and, if you have a scratch or a wound of some sort on the face, the venom can enter the body with possibly fatal results. The effect on the eyes is to cause an inflammation that might last days and can in extreme cases, if the eyes are rubbed, cause permanent blindness. In rural areas if someone is struck by cobra venom, the victim is placed on his/her back and has urine sprayed in his/her eyes. This is fine and probably quite dramatic and, while it usually works, plain water, milk, or any bland liquid will do just as well. The aim is to dilute the venom speedily.

The cobra's spitting action is so expert that it is uncanny. The snake rears, spreads its hood, opens and shuts its mouth and there it is: as quick as that. The spray is pushed out with tremendous force through the tiny holes in the end of tubular fangs and from a distance of two metres (seven feet) it just cannot miss. It can eject quantities of venom three to four times in a few seconds.

A snake that can almost rival the black-necked spitting cobra when it comes to spitting is the infamous and quite common rinkhals (*Hemachatus haemachatus*), a dull-black snake on the South African Highveld. When it rears you can see the high gloss on its underside and the one or two broad white bands across its throat that give it its name (rinkhals, directly translated from Afrikaans, means 'ring necklace'). Outside the Highveld it has creamy white bars across its back. This cobra-like snake is confined to Southern Africa and, like the black-necked spitting cobra, it has a highly toxic bite. Surprisingly, Marais asserts that as far as he is aware the rinkhals hasn't killed anybody for the last 50 years and maybe longer[19]. But the bite causes dramatic and painful reactions – as well as unconsciousness and could well kill a person weakened by some secondary illness. The snake is so common in Southern Africa that it is surprising that no deaths have been reported in recent years. (Death from snakebite is not a notifiable condition.)

But with all Africa's cobras – to which the rinkhals is related – providing you carry a snakebite kit, the chances of complete and rapid recovery, even after a full bite, are very good – and you do have a bit of time to find help. Dennis Groves was bitten many years ago at his home 20 kilometres (12 miles) from Johannesburg and, as his own supply of antivenin was discoloured and stale, he drove himself to Johannesburg General Hospital where they could not find any antivenin. He was beginning to feel dizzy. He was put into an ambulance and, with sirens wailing, was driven home and injected using the stale antivenin. He lost two bones in the back of his hand.

Africa's cobras, as far as their bites are concerned, appear to be less dangerous than the two larger cobras of Asia. Nevertheless the cobras are probably responsible for many hundreds of the fatal snakebite cases on the continent of Africa. In South Africa, specifically, the Cape cobra accounts for most snakebite deaths, according to Marais, who says 'Around 10 out of the dozen snakebite victims who die each year [in South Africa] are bitten by Cape cobras.' He says most of the deaths are because of ignorance, very often the victim relying on some inappropriate traditional remedy but, if you apply a pressure bandage and get to professional help within a few hours, recovery can be expected.

There has always been some controversy over the species of cobra that Cleopatra used in order to commit suicide. The odds are it was the asp – or Egyptian cobra as it is sometimes known (*Naja haje*) – which is found all the way down Africa. The asp would have been the logical choice, as it had deep religious connections in Ancient Egypt; another reason is that political prisoners were usually given the choice of being tortured to death or dying by the bite of an asp. This was an odd choice, as the bite of the asp is supposed to be relatively painless, if a little messy. Paintings of a beautiful Cleopatra lying composedly and serenely, with her hands clasped and her gown smoothed down and with her handmaidens draped around, are more fanciful than accurate: although Cleopatra would have quickly gone into a coma, death would have been preceded by violent convulsions, copious salivation and evacuation of the bowel and bladder.

Many years ago I accompanied members of the Herpetological Society on a veld expedition in the Highveld near Bronkhorstspruit, 80 kilometres (50 miles) east of Johannesburg, to capture snakes for the Transvaal Serpentarium. I was surprised to find a dozen schoolboys among the 20 or so members, and even more surprised at the number of snakes the boys captured in the space of one summer morning – about 15 as I recall. These included a magnificent snouted cobra (*Naja annulifera*) and a 1.4-metre-long (four foot seven inches) rinkhals, which greatly excited the Serpentarium as it was the longest recorded at the time. The boys also captured two night adders, which they carried inside their shirts. It was the capture of the rinkhals that was particularly interesting because the group sat around it in a circle, with their feet stretched out but just – and only just – out of range of the snake's strike. The snaked reared, spread its hood and sprayed its venom; those not wearing glasses or, in a few cases, goggles, shielded their eyes with their hands. When somebody behind the snake wanted to take a picture, he would lean forward and tap the rampant snake on the back of its hood and it would turn and strike, but its strike was surprising slow and easily avoided. It appeared to fall forward rather than lunge. I have noticed the same with the Indian king cobra and a black mamba. Fast as a mamba is along the ground, it is rather languid in striking. I was told your arm, used in a sideways chopping motion, can beat the mamba to the draw. In fact you can easily break the back of a rearing cobra by hitting it with a walking stick, should the need arise.

One of the few dangerous snakes of the colubrids in Africa is the boomslang (*Dispholidus typus*); until 1962 there was no antidote for its bite and any man who received a full bite was doomed to die a lingering death. It is interesting to note that Raymond L. Ditmars describes them as 'mildly poisonous'[20]. In fact most zoologists considered them absolutely harmless and up to about the mid 20th century they were kept by children as pets.

The boomslang (Afrikaans for tree snake) is a longish, slender, arboreal back-fanged snake with, for a snake, conspicuously large eyes. It can be olive, bright green, yellow or brown and shades in between. It is usually very difficult to provoke into striking and Ditmars' experience, where he describes half a dozen of them emerging from a box lashing and biting, is unusual indeed. Weight for weight, according to B.J. Keyter, their venom is the most potent of any snake in Africa[21] but, fortunately, the snake's fangs are set so far back it is difficult for the snake to latch onto a person. The venom needs a specific antivenin and a bite normally takes three to four days to kill.

An interesting case history is that of herpetologist Bert Mitchley who was bitten by a pet boomslang on his farm near Polokwane (formerly Pietersburg) in September 1961. Mitchley was bitten on the finger and the snake managed to hold on only for a second or two. He immediately motored the 300 kilometres (186 miles) to Pretoria General Hospital where the best toxicologists in the country worked on him. Nothing helped and within three days he was so black and blue from subcutaneous bleeding that he looked like a bad road accident case. He died on the fourth day.

Dennis Groves, greatly disturbed by Mitchley's death, appealed (partly through the *Star*, the Johannesburg newspaper for which I worked) for boomslangs to be sent to the Snake Park. He received nearly 100 and, knowing that if he were bitten he would die, immediately began a daily milking programme. Only after he had collected enough venom could antivenin be produced[22]. It is stored to this day at the South African Institute for Medical Research in Johannesburg, from where it can be flown to anywhere in Africa within a few hours – time enough to neutralise the venom. The reason for the rarity of the antivenin is the difficulty in getting supplies of boomslangs for milking, because those that are milked usually die in two or three weeks from lip canker.

There were men who emerged from the South American jungles a century or so ago with stories of anacondas 12 metres (40 feet) long. Some even claimed 30 metres (99 feet) long, which would have been so wide in girth people might have mistaken them for tube trains. When, a few years ago, the New York Zoological Society offered $5 000 for the first 10-metre (33-foot) specimen, the prize went unclaimed and remains so to this day; and thus the stories of giant anacondas died down. The fact remains that the biggest anaconda (belonging to the larger of two species, *Eunectes murinus*) ever collected was just short of six metres (20 feet) and nearly a metre (over three feet) in girth and weighed 107 kilograms (235 pounds). There are persistent stories of pythons (anacondas, boa constrictors and pythons belong to the family Boidae) in the Far East measuring 10 metres but I can find no authentication. Estimating a snake's length is extremely difficult. In 2004 a captive Burmese python was said to be more than 14 metres (46 feet) long and people who queued to see it were happy to accept its reported length. The British newspaper the *Guardian* sent journalist John Aglionby with a tape measure to measure it. He did – it was under seven metres (23 feet)[23].

As far as Africa's rock python is concerned – it rates among the longest and heaviest snakes on earth – it seems doubtful that any have exceeded six metres. The snake would find it difficult to kill an adult human, although there are authentic instances of this on record. One involved a Malawian man named Hurly, who was working in 1961 at the Alpine Mine in what is now Mpumalanga. One day he saw a python's tail sticking out of the bush and he grabbed it. The snake, which was longer than he had expected, threw two coils round him and began to constrict. Hurly fell to the ground and he and the snake rolled about for some time before the man managed to uncoil the reptile. He returned to the mine and, although shaken, showed no signs of damage. The following day he reported to the mine hospital with a severe headache. He was admitted and died the following day. An autopsy showed a ruptured spleen and kidneys.

Another case took place during the Easter weekend in 2009 near Malindi, Kenya. The BBC reported:

A Kenyan bit a python that had wrapped him in its coils and dragged him up a tree during a fierce three-hour struggle, police have told the BBC.

The serpent seized farm worker Ben Nyaumbe in the Malindi area of Kenya's Indian Ocean coast at the weekend.

Mr Nyaumbe bit the snake on the tip of the tail during the exhausting battle in the village of Sabaki.

Police rescued Mr Nyaumbe and captured the 13ft (4m) reptile, before taking it to a sanctuary but it later escaped.

The victim told police he managed to reach his mobile phone from his pocket to raise the alarm when the python momentarily eased its grip after hauling him up a tree on Saturday evening. Mr Nyaumbe used his shirt to smother the snake's head and prevent it from swallowing him.

His employer arrived with police and villagers, who tied the python with a rope and pulled them both down from the tree with a thud.

Peter Katam, superintendent of police in Malindi district, told the BBC News website: 'Two officers on patrol were called and they found this man was struggling with a snake on a tree.

'The snake had coiled his hands and was trying to swallow him but he struggled very hard. The officers and villagers managed to rescue him.'

Mr Nyaumbe told the *Daily Nation* newspaper how he resorted to desperate measures after the python, which had apparently been hunting livestock, encircled his upper body in its coils.

Supt Katam told the BBC the officers had wanted to shoot the snake but could not do so for fear of injuring Mr Nyaumbe.

He added: 'It's very mysterious, this ability to lift the man onto the tree. I've never heard of this before.'[24]

Jane Flanagan, a Johannesburg journalist, reporting from Johannesburg for the London *Daily Telegraph* in 2002, wrote of a 'six-metre' African rock python eating a 10-year-old boy near Durban – the first recorded man-eating incident for the species. She wrote:

For three hours other children hid up mango trees near the township of Lamontville, too terrified to flee, as the snake first trapped the 10-year-old and squeezed the life out of him, then swallowed him whole.

Police and snake experts found no trace of the child, or his clothing. They found nothing but flattened grass and a trail leading down to a stream.

The incident last week prompted widespread panic among the township's 50,000 residents and great fascination among herpetologists across the country.

Eleven-year-old Khaye Buthelezi, who saw the extraordinary attack, was persuaded to revisit the site on Saturday.

His eyes darting nervously for signs of the python, Khaye showed where his companion had been gathering fallen fruit when taken by the giant snake.

'The snake quickly wrapped itself around his body, pinning his arms to his side. He didn't cry or scream and neither did the rest of us – we didn't want the snake to come and take us as well,' Khaye said.

'The snake squeezed tighter and tighter around him until his eyes closed and his head fell back so I thought he was dead or had fainted. Then the snake's mouth opened very, very wide and started to swallow him from the head down – his clothes and everything. It all took about three hours because it was dark when we saw it slither away and we finally came down from the tree.'

Snake experts and the police followed the python's trail to a nearby stream, which the herpetologists said the snake would have used as an easy route to get away to digest its prey.

Craig Smith, the owner of a snake park in Durban, is one of those trying to find the python. 'The children I spoke to had excellent detail about the snake's markings and killing technique, which suggested that they were either reptile experts or had had the chance to watch something like this for a very long time,' he said. 'This will be the first time this species has been known to be a man-eater.'

He said the snake had probably just woken from its winter hibernation and was extremely hungry when the boy wandered into its path. 'We have never had a case of an African rock python eating a human, but they are very opportunistic eaters and the snake was obviously hungry enough to think it could cope with a child,' Mr Smith said.[25]

Johan Marais remembers the case well and recalls going out to the site 'to try to make sense of it':

Firstly, the snake was never found, which is most unusual as a large python with a large meal cannot move very far. The whole community went looking for the snake. The site is next to the Umlaas canal which was in flood at the time and the theory was that the snake had come out of the canal, up a steep concrete slope, caught and swallowed a young boy and then disappeared. The two friends who reported the missing boy gave quite meticulous accounts of the event but their accounts differed. Herpetologists who visited the site were very sceptical but never followed up to find out whether the boy had, by some other means, disappeared or perhaps drowned in the canal. Regarding the snake – the Southern African python (*Python natalensis*) reaches a maximum size of around 5.5 metres [18 feet] and such a snake would certainly be capable of eating a young boy. It easily consumes small antelope such as impala.

It is highly unlikely that any humans have been killed by pythons in South Africa and searches of the literature reveal only two or three deaths in Africa.[26]

Ugandan newspapers reported in 1951 that a 13-year-old boy had been swallowed but the python had been forced to disgorge the body. In 1973 another newspaper reported that a Portuguese soldier had been discovered in the stomach of a snake. In 1979, a 4.5-metre (15-foot) python tried to swallow a 13-year-old boy but after being hit by stones it regurgitated the body and retreated. The boy was 1.3 metres tall (four foot three inches) and weighed 45 kilograms (99 pounds).

The python, whose teeth are needle-sharp, can inflict terrible bite wounds. Ionides records a woman on the shores of Lake Victoria being 'thrown down by a python which savagely bit her causing her serious injury'[27]. A friend who was bitten on the hand by a python showed me his swollen spiked hand the next day. Judging by the damage of that one bite, several bites would indeed be serious.

In the 1960s I watched 18-year-old Dawie Field, who was then a slight young man, demonstrate how to catch a python. He selected a 4.5-metre python weighing 59 kilograms (130 pounds) at the Transvaal Serpentarium and provoked the snake into attacking him. At one point he fell into a swimming pool (on purpose) and, although the snake had three coils around him, one of them around his neck, Field never appeared to be in trouble.

When the snake began to constrict him, Field uncoiled it from the tail and the snake did not have the strength to resist. 'The secret,' said Field, 'is always to keep one hand free. I think if it had pinned both my arms I would have been in trouble.'

Anatomically, pythons differ from boa constrictors (*Constrictor constrictor*), by lacking a certain bone in the head, by living in a different environment – pythons prefer the bush and boas the forest – and by laying eggs where boas, being viviparous, produce live young. Both pythons and boas differ from other snakes by having vestigial pelvises and vestigial hind limbs and by possessing paired lungs.

The African or rock python (*Python sebae*) and the Southern African python (*P. natalensis*) used to be common south of the Sahara right down to the Eastern Cape, but pythons have not been seen south of KwaZulu-Natal in recent years and the two species are now considered 'endangered' and 'threatened' throughout their range[28]. Their main threats are the leather industry, where python skins are used for handbags and shoes, and traditional healers who use python fat as an ointment for various ailments; both pay high prices for pythons. Pythons are generally respected throughout Africa for their role in patrolling cane fields for cane rats (*Thryonomys* – known as grass cutters in West Africa). Young pythons live almost exclusively on rodents but when fully grown they can be a nuisance where livestock is concerned, taking anything up to the size of goats. In the wilds, the large ones eat warthogs, medium-sized antelope and even young crocodiles.

When you consider the world's array of highly venomous serpents, you cannot help wondering why nature equipped snakes with such powerful venom, when all they need it for is to paralyse or kill small creatures. Snake venom is certainly not for defence; it is far too slow acting for that. Even the faster-killing snakes are quite unable to immobilise an attacking animal quickly enough to save their own skins. Their venom, powerful though it is, is still pretty well useless against owls and eagles and birds such as the secretary bird, which kill snakes with impunity. I have watched a secretary bird in the Free State pick up and swallow three small snakes in one spot in a few seconds. Many snakes depend upon their hiss to warn approaching animals, but this often invites attacks; dogs, cats and several species of wild animals, particularly mongooses, will go for a rampant snake, killing it long before the effect of the snake's bite kills them. We can only wonder about the reason behind the evolution of a black mamba's or a gaboon adder's huge reservoir of venom – a mysterious cocktail of protein and enzymes – when its main diet is rodents. A fascinating conundrum.

It is a misapprehension that the African veld is crawling with snakes. There are certainly plenty about and, if you know where to probe for them, you can soon find some. On the other hand, I know people who have lived their lives in Africa and never seen a snake. Even in the most infested parts, you would be lucky to catch a glimpse of more than half a dozen a year unless you spent your time in the veld. Professional hunter J.A. Hunter, in a letter to Denis L. Lyell, said that he saw only about one snake a month on his safaris[29]. Yet John Hillaby, in his journey to Lake Rudolph on the border of Kenya and Ethiopia, passed through a particularly bad area when, it seems, the time of day and the temperatures were just right, since he saw several carpet vipers – particularly deadly reptiles – on each side of the track. He literally had to watch every step[30].

I have seen only four or five cobras in the bush in Africa and yet they are at least as common as, for instance, chaffinches in England. The thing about snakes is that they hide away and go into a state of lethargy when the weather is cool, and they hide in rock crevices when the weather is too warm: their temperature tolerance is very narrow indeed. The asp, for example, is found widely through most of Africa, but you would be hard-pressed to find anybody who has ever seen one. Oddly enough, the first one I saw was in 1971 in a garden in Parktown, a built-up suburb of Johannesburg. It was fully grown and had probably been driven from its habitat – a north-facing rock face and therefore warm in winter – 500 metres (550 yards) away, by the building of the M1 motorway.

When it comes to precautions against snakebites, the most fundamental is at least wear shoes, preferably boots. But telling this to barefoot Africa is like Marie Antoinette's apocryphal words asking why the bread-starved poor of Paris did not eat cake. Raymond L. Ditmars claimed that, if the rural people of India wore shoes, snakebite deaths would be halved. He said, once footwear became obligatory in India's cane fields the death toll from snakebite dropped dramatically[31]. Apart from the protection that thick leather shoes afford, they also set up a vibration that bare feet do not, which snakes lying on the path will detect and move off. I was told by a snake hunter that if, for some reason, you are crawling along the ground and you come nose to nose with a snake, blow gently in its face and it will move away.

As far as snakebite kits are concerned, there is a strong argument these days in favour of dispensing with them. After all, they are useless against the bite of a mamba – and with all other species of snakes there is time to reach a hospital and receive professional help.

It can be said of any snakebite (with the exception of the black mamba) that antivenin is unnecessary if an intensive care unit is within reach. Once on a life-support system, the body will metabolise the venom.

When you examine the evidence, the chances of being bitten by a snake are very small indeed. In South Africa – despite the numbers of people walking barefoot or bare-legged across the veld, despite 27 potentially dangerous species and 12 that have been known to kill – of the few thousand annual snakebite cases, nearly all are from non-venomous or only mildly venomous snakes or are 'dry bites', where no venom is injected. As mentioned earlier, Dr Roger Blaylock's findings at Eshowe Hospital in KwaZulu-Natal – one of South Africa's most snake-infested areas – put snakebite in perspective.

In spite of the bare legs, in spite the high snake population and in spite the lack of hospitals in areas where snakebite is frequent, only 10 to 12 people – out of a population of around 50 million – die from snakebites in a year in South Africa.

While South Africa is fortunate in having the best medical resources in Africa, the picture north of the Limpopo River is very different.

Johan Marais, who has written several books on snakes, including a book on snake identification and modern treatment methods[32], points out that 'very often a snake will strike but it does not put its mind to injecting venom'. 'Dry bites' are common. He says, 'We see a lot of dry bites among snake handlers. I have received three such bites – from a Cape cobra, a boomslang and a rinkhals.'[33] Marais, who has travelled the world in search of snakes, no longer carries a snakebite kit; he carries only a crepe (pressure) bandage in a general first-aid kit. All the same, he says antivenins today are fairly reliable and cover almost all the world's dangerous snakes. Throughout most of Africa, you can buy a polyvalent serum, which covers cobra and adder bites, with the exception the boomslang, which needs specific antivenin. A problem can arise in that a lot of people are allergic to antivenin.

It was S.K. Sutherland of the Commonwealth Serum Laboratories in Melbourne, Australia, who developed the now-universally used life-saving technique involving tightly bandaging the bitten limb. This has superseded the tourniquet as a means of impeding the spread of venom through the body. The trouble with the tourniquet was, that if applied for an adder bite (an adder's haemotoxic venom is a powerful coagulant), it would result in massive local damage and, frequently, gangrene. Even for the neurotoxic cobra bite, a tourniquet is only a marginally useful technique.

In dismissing the snakebite kit (as far as the layman is concerned), Marais points out that, in the case of a mamba bite, a victim would need 180 millilitres (six fluid ounces) of antivenin, whereas the standard kit has 20 millilitres (0.7 fluid ounces). And, for other kinds of bites, antivenin is a pretty crude remedy anyway, when a hospital or doctor is within reach.

The former Rhodesian Army, during the bush war of the 1970s, carried no snakebite kits at all. Instead it relied on cortisone. This was in the belief that it is best to subdue the symptoms and get the victim to hospital. The problem with this is that cortisone has to be injected intravenously and this requires skill. It can also have serious pharmacological effects. Marais believes village headmen and safari organisers should appoint at least one of their number to take a first-aid course with the Red Cross or St John Ambulance, which includes training in intravenous injections. He says that doctors on safari should also familiarise themselves with modern methods of snakebite treatment.

A recent theory is that electric shocks can break down venom. A South African snake park kept a cattle prodder for this purpose in its first-aid room. Some farmers carry battery extension leads just for this purpose – to apply electric shocks to the bite site.

Marais says the theory has no validity at all.

14 THE END OF THE GAME

Time is running out for us to solve the human-wildlife conflict
problem. Prejudices are deepening, patience evaporating.
As long as those with the power – political, knowledge,
economic and financial power – delay coming together to resolve
resource management problems the victims on the frontline will
continue to pay the costs. By 'victims' I mean all of us animals.

– Julie Clarke-Havemann, environmental analyst

The last third of the 20th century saw a widespread swing in public sentiment
towards a commitment to nature conservation – albeit mainly in the
West. There was an explosion of volcanic intensity in natural history
publications, a wonderful variety of spectacular television documentaries
and a spontaneously concerted worldwide media campaign to encourage
environmental awareness. But the 'green' sentiment has been slow in filtering
down to Africa's rural population, which has other priorities than looking
after wildlife – survival being one. The long-term benefits of achieving a
sustainable way of life incorporating wildlife are lost on them and on many
of their leaders.

The renewed concern about the direction of conservation in Africa is
being driven partly by worldwide sentiment, partly by scientific curiosity, but
not enough by the potential of economically uplifting rural Africa. Tourism
has become the 21st century's fastest-growing industry, and Africa is the
world's favourite destination for adventurous tourism. Game hunting,
particularly big-game hunting, is generating billions of dollars, but the
revenue does not always benefit those who live in wild Africa, with its stresses.
Instead it filters upwards. And the developed world's wildlife societies and

private donors, who annually pour millions of dollars into Africa believing it is going towards sustaining wildlife, are being deceived.

In 2007, a succinct evaluation of the challenge facing all who are involved in conservation in Africa was written by Mike Norton-Griffiths, a land-use economics researcher and a long-time resident of Kenya. His paper 'How Many Wildebeest Do You Need?' is about Kenya but has relevance throughout the continent. He was driven to writing it because of Kenya Wildlife Service's (KWS) top-down attitude when it comes to the management of wildlife. As he says of Kenya, 'the State is the sole owner and manager of wildlife'. He points out how those who live among wild animals have little chance to be heard and no opportunity to benefit economically from the animals they are expected to conserve. Indeed, if they shoot a problem animal, the penalties are severe.

Norton-Griffiths says the Kenyan system has failed conservation on three counts: its policies, its institutions and its market strategies:

The most important of the policy failures is the continuing ban on all consumptive utilisation of wildlife which not only restricts the opportunities for pastoral landowners to generate revenues from their wildlife resources but also largely disenfranchises 95% of the pastoral rangelands from any income-generating opportunities (tourist wildlife viewing is restricted to a mere 23 000 square kilometres [8 880 square miles] – 5% of the rangeland where wildlife are found).

Landowners not only have no rights regarding wildlife; they also receive no compensation for destruction and damage to life and property. The KWS 'acts solely as a regulatory and enforcement service rather than an enabling institution'. Europe's animal-rights groups and wildlife fans – 'protectionists' Norton-Griffiths calls them – are 'deeply at fault for [being] too focused, obsessed even, on topical single issues which rarely concern the economics of producing wildlife'[1]. These non-government organisations are largely unaware of market forces in determining land use and production decisions for pastoral landowners, and they are 'reticent'

(Norton-Griffiths' word) to criticise the Kenyan government's policy. Kenya is losing between US$20 million and US$40 million a year in potential hunting revenues[2].

But why should KWS worry? In one year it received as much as $400 million from European donors alone. The irony is plain: 'wildlife lovers' outside Africa are subsidising the decline in African wildlife.

Again Norton-Griffiths makes a point that is relevant throughout the sub-Saharan region:

> Equally glaring are the market failures for the provision of wildlife goods and services which can be laid squarely at the door of the tourism cartels. These cartels divert the major portion of all wildlife generated revenues away from the pastoral landowners to the service side of the industry (agents and the providers of transport and accommodation). In general terms landowners (which here includes private landowners, the KWS and country councils) see perhaps 5% at most of the total revenues generated by wildlife. The cartels also maintain strict barriers that prevent landowners becoming more directly involved in the tourism business (eg: by offering transport and accommodation) and thus capturing more of the potential revenues.[3]

Kenya, feeling deeply beholden to generous wildlife preservation groups in Europe and America, long ago began shaping its wildlife policies to please them. Since 1977 the country has received hundreds of millions of overseas dollars to perpetuate what Norton-Griffiths calls 'hopelessly inefficient and bloated state conservation monopolies aided and abetted by international conservation organisations which with their seemingly limitless resources, lack of accountability and hidden agendas, wield such power and influence over conservation policy'.

Since Kenya's no-hunting policy, dating back to 1977, well over a third of a century ago, it has lost two thirds of its wildlife. It has never had so little. Worried about the collapse of its elephant population through poaching, in July 1989 the KWS staged the burning of 12 tonnes of elephant tusks to demonstrate how it was, forever, dusting its hands of ivory sales and was hoping other nations would follow. President Daniel arap Moi, who ignited the pile, said the threatened demise of Kenya's elephants would be a devastating blow to the country's biggest foreign exchange earner – the tourist industry.

Lions too have been on the decline. There are now fewer than at any time in Kenya's history and there is concern about their viability. In next-door Tanzania lions are on the increase. After a drastic crash in the Selous Game Reserve's wildlife numbers due to poaching, unscrupulous hunters and corrupt wildlife administrators, the government banned all hunting from 1973 to 1978. Uganda did likewise. All except Kenya have since reinstated hunting, with positive results.

Pretoria University zoologist Peter A. Lindsey, in publishing the results of a 2007 survey for which hundreds of hunters and safari operators were interviewed, commented: 'Each of these bans resulted in an accelerated loss of wildlife due to the removal of incentives for conservation. Avoiding future [hunting] bans is thus vital for conservation.'[4]

Lindsey's survey found that in Europe the majority of experienced hunters still considered Kenya as the most desirable country for a hunting safari – if only hunting were allowed – but by default Tanzania has become the country of choice, followed by Mozambique and Zimbabwe. South Africa was the most favoured country among inexperienced or first-time safari hunters because it was considered safer. Experienced hunters were not bothered by political instability; in the first year of Zimbabwe's violent campaign against white farmers, when rampaging armed youths were involved in 'land grabs' and drove long-established farmers off their land, tourism, not surprisingly, plunged by 75 per cent, but hunting revenue showed only a 12 per cent drop.

Banning hunting does not bring about an increase in wildlife; it increases only one thing: rural poverty.

Overnight, lions, leopards, cheetahs, hyaenas and other predators become vermin in the eyes of livestock farmers. A vivid example was experienced in Namibia in the 1970s when a worldwide ban was placed on the importation of cheetahs and cheetah products such as skins and masks. Sheep farmers, who were losing stock to cheetahs, began shooting them on sight and leaving their now-worthless bodies to rot in the veld. When an alarming dip in cheetah numbers became apparent, the ban was lifted and cheetahs recovered. Any financial loss as a result of cheetahs' killing sheep was more than offset by the collection of hunting fees.

The controversy over whether hunting is a tool of conservation and an honourable source of revenue for rural people is certainly an emotive one. It has polarised all who are concerned about the future of Africa's wildlife. But in 2011, after days of intense debate, a thousand members at the IUCN assembly of the third World Conservation Congress confirmed a landmark recommendation 'that well-managed recreational hunting has a role in the managed sustainable consumptive use of wildlife populations'. In other words hunters are the allies of conservation. At the same time it condemned, along with the international hunting industry, 'canned hunting'. This is a notorious practice found mainly in South Africa where captive, specially bred lions are set loose in small enclosures so that hunters who are too timid to hunt in the wild can 'execute' them (that is what it amounts to) at close range. One estimate suggested 95 per cent of lions shot in South Africa were bred for that purpose. There are only 3 000 lions roaming free in South Africa and probably not more than 20 000 further north.

A former national park warden in Zimbabwe and hunter of considerable experience in Africa, Ron Thomson, believes hunting zones should be allowed under careful management inside national parks[5]. If we accept that culling is necessary and if the cost of culling is borne by the parks' administrations, there is an argument to be made for allowing professional hunters into designated blocks well away from areas accessible to the public. Revenue from hunting safaris will go a long way to covering the cost of culling. Pilanesberg National Park has done this successfully since it was established in 1979. In the 37 years prior to the 1994 moratorium on culling, the Kruger National Park shot 14 562 elephants. Many tonnes of meat were sold to the mines (for miners' compounds) but thousands of carcasses had to be left where the elephants died. The ivory is in storage, in case one day a legitimate market re-opens. The last elephant census, in 2005, put the

Kruger Park's population at 12 467, mostly concentrated in the central region[6]. The park's administration has said culling may again be necessary if more habitat destruction is to be avoided.

Thomson says the administration of national parks throughout Africa needs fewer scientists and more business-trained people 'with MBA degrees':

> Governments would become virtual 'sleeping' partners overseeing adherence to policy matters only. A third partner (of sorts) must comprise the rural African communities that live on the boundaries of Africa's national parks. These people – the communities out of which the poachers come – will accrue major benefits from the legal, consumptive and sustainable harvest [through controlled and licenced hunting in 'hunting zones'] of those wild animal populations within the national parks that can withstand such harvest – in return for stopping poaching.[7]

Dr David Mabunda, head of South Africa's National Parks, speaking at a film premiere in 2011, emphasised how recreational hunting was a legitimate part of ecotourism, but pointedly spoke of the need to eliminate bad hunting practices. He said South Africa's local hunters, who were largely biltong hunters, annually contributed nearly R1 billion to the economy. Foreign trophy hunters contributed another R1 billion. He alluded to the ongoing controversy regarding legitimate recreational hunting, which many South Africans want banned. The anti-hunting lobby believes photographic tourism could take its place. Mabunda acknowledged that photographic tourism was a 'massive' contributor towards the R70 billion that South Africa's tourist industry earns ('though no figures are yet available') but as a developing country he said it would be 'suicidal to want to make trade-offs between hunting and photographic ecotourism – we don't have the luxury of choice. We need both.'[8]

Tanzania's experience provides some insight into the wildlife crisis. Dr Rolf D. Baldus, the foremost authority on wildlife management issues in

Tanzania, has spent two decades campaigning to get the Tanzanian government to give communities outside the huge Selous Game Reserve the right to manage and benefit from their local wildlife[9]. The frustrated communities are given to bouts of seriously damaging poaching (for which they can hardly be blamed) and the lions, robbed of their natural prey, then turn their attention to cattle and humans. Baldus and his colleagues want to see the communities receive tangible benefits for acting as custodians of the wildlife around them and a fair share of the national income from tourism and hunting concessions. He has served as president of the Tropical Game Commission of the 84-nation International Council for Game and Wildlife Conservation (CIC) which, in close collaboration with the IUCN and the CBD[10], is dedicated to the sustainable use of wildlife. He says that between 1987 and 2003 the Tanzanian and German governments jointly agreed to implement the Selous Conservation Programme (SCP) which, after its agreed 18-year span, has now ended. The SCP was to ensure the long-term conservation and sustainable use of natural resources – in particular the initiative was aimed at the region that includes the Selous Game Reserve and its surrounding community-owned wildlife areas. The Selous Game Reserve – the biggest wildlife reserve in the world – is partly surrounded by wildlife conservation areas, which are owned by communities but from which the communities receive very little income. The reserve itself was created by the Germans when Tanzania was part of colonial German East Africa in 1896. The ecosystem – mostly miombo (*Brachystegia*) woodland and grassland – extends from the reserve itself 160 kilometres (100 miles) southwards down a wide corridor to the Ruvuma River. On the other side of the Ruvuma, on the Mozambique side, is the Niassa Game Reserve, which is almost as big. So here is a region well in excess of 100 000 square kilometres (39 000 square miles), potentially a huge international or 'transfrontier' park, which according to official promises should one day be under joint government and community management. While the Tanzanian government publicly professes agreement to joint management with neighbouring communities and a sharing of income, in practice it ignores them.

Over the years Germany has pumped several million euros into the Selous, yet the Tanzanian government, despite its pledges to the donors, who include the European Union, the WWF, USAID, the African Development Bank, the German Development Bank and the African Wildlife Foundation, has made no move to share its income from hunting and tourism with those in the community lands.

I have dwelt on East Africa for three reasons: first, it is one of the world's most exciting wild regions; second, it illustrates how the wealth from wildlife reserves is not trickling down to those along the front line, but is doing the opposite; and, third, because the Tanzanian situation reflects what is happening over a great deal of Africa.

Tanzania is perhaps the worst country in the world for human-wildlife conflict. This is where, every year, hundreds of lives are lost to wildlife and where thousands of hectares of cropland are smashed by elephants and hippos. Yet, ironically, wildlife presents the communities' best (and probably only) route towards creating a sustainable way of earning revenue, easing poverty and implementing more effective preventive measures against man-eaters and marauders.

Throughout East Africa international agreements have so often been crushed by lack of progress in benefit-sharing developments. As hope fades so, not surprisingly, communities are turning back to large-scale poaching, similar to what devastated the Selous during the 1980s when rampant poaching for illicit ivory, rhino horn and meat – involving corrupt government officials and politicians – did enormous damage to the game reserve's equilibrium. In the 1960s there were probably 3 000 black rhinos in the Selous. By 1990 many thought they had become extinct[11]. Elephants numbered between 120 000 and 140 000 before poaching extinguished three-quarters of them. In 2011 the WWF said almost two thirds of the ivory being smuggled out of Africa was coming from the Selous and Niassa reserves.

Baldus reported that in 1987 the management system of the Selous Game Reserve had 'more or less broken down'. There were two Land Rovers operational. 'Governance was the core problem. More than half of the poaching originated from the official staff, often on orders of superiors, higher authorities and politicians. With very few exceptions those responsible were never taken to court.' Nothing says more about the shallow level of commitment of Tanzania's government than, heavily subsidised though it is, it had only two vehicles patrolling an area of 54 600 square kilometres (21 081 square miles) – far bigger than Switzerland.

For many years Baldus has been involved in efforts to involve the buffer-zone communities around Selous and helping them manage their own wildlife and benefit financially from it. The Selous Conservation Programme was agreed to by the government in 1988. Its Wildlife Division was to administer the buffer zones in partnership with the Deutsche Gesellschaft für Technische Zusammenarbeit (which is a big donor) and the various district administrations and communities. The government did, initially, make an effort but, says Baldus:

> At the end of the Programme in 2003 the results were excellent: Overall level of management was satisfactory, trophy poaching was insignificant and an adequate, secure and long term financial basis was in place (US$2.8 million retention per year). Community involvement was well developed and practised around the Selous, however, only on a pilot basis. The paradigm shift had been accepted and further developed by the central Government as a national programme called Community Based Conservation (CBC), for conservation outside protected areas and for poverty alleviation within the Poverty Reduction Strategy. Its implementation beyond pilot status was delayed by the Wildlife Division, as it would have meant sharing power and revenue with the communities.[12]

Important decisions were taken without consent or even the involvement of stakeholders such as the districts and communities concerned, who were left out in the cold. A formal international agreement between the Tanzanian government and German donors regarding retaining half the income from the joint initiative for the administration of the Selous Game Reserve – which has been grossly undermanned – was in fact arbitrarily cut by two thirds in the first year. It was increased again in the financial year 2005/2006

– after the Ministry had been reminded of the existing international agreements – but it was still a third less than agreed to. Baldus says the funds are now insufficient for the proper operation of the reserve. 'Trophy poaching has shown a strong upward trend and the effectiveness of management is in jeopardy. The situation is further aggravated by a number of planned environmentally doubtful projects.'

What Baldus says is applicable to many other countries:

> Whether the involvement of communities and their receiving benefits from wildlife use on their land will in the long run maintain the survival of wildlife outside the protected areas is unknown. However, without an approach which takes into account the needs and rights of the communities in the wildlife areas, wildlife does not have much of a future. There are strong indications that the top wildlife bureaucracy would prefer to return to their traditional 'fences-and-fines-approach', which serves their own individual economic interests well.
>
> At the core of the problem lies the administration of the wildlife revenue which comes primarily from hunting (90%) in the Selous. All central decisions (quotas, allocation of blocks, revenues) are taken by the Director of Wildlife. There is a severe case of Bad Governance and no tender or similar procedures are followed for the allocation of hunting blocks. All efforts to induce transparency and initiate some debate towards introducing reform within the industry have been blocked in recent years. This action is supported by the major actors in the [Tanzanian] hunting industry as they thrive within the present system. The chairman of the Tanzania Hunting Operators Association has leased approximately half of the Selous area for more than thirty years now without ever having been required to compete for these blocks in a public tender. Instead, hunting blocks with an estimated market value of US$80 000 to $150 000 continue to be allocated at the discretion of the Director of Wildlife for an official annual fee of $7 500.

The Tanzanian authorities are 'unanimously in opposition to grant the communities any decision making', says Baldus, who maintains it is this opposition that is a major stumbling block in achieving community involvement. The long-term sustainability of the Selous region is dependent on the existing governance, but he adds if 'good governance cannot be installed into the management of the hunting industry the Selous could fall back into the anarchic state of the 1980s'. He says Tanzania's wildlife system has received significant support from foreign governments and non-governmental organisations in recent years and the donors have engaged in 'a constructive policy dialogue with the Ministry and the Wildlife Department over years. This resulted in many agreements, policies and promises, but in very little practical action on the side of the Government and no tangible improvement in governance.'

In recent years and after encouraging beginnings, Tanzania's Wildlife Division has been using donors' money 'mainly for endless participatory meetings, conferences, evaluations and studies which were … probably never intended to bring about any change'. The donors – and the communities – were always promised, even by the minister, that the agreed reforms would be implemented, but to no avail. Baldus then puts it bluntly: 'The most important single aspect of Governance in Africa is corruption.' He says there is a general agreement that four decades of voluntary funding have achieved very little towards self-sustaining economic growth and development. In Africa the governments keep 'hopes and illusions' alive while donors' money rewards those who benefit from bad governance and punishes those who want to reform. 'Bad Governance – or should I better say corruption – pays after all!'

He says little has changed since he wrote that report[13].

Charles E. Kay, professor in Political Science and senior research scientist with the Institute of Political Economy at Utah State University (his PhD is in Wildlife Ecology) supports Baldus' sentiments. He said that, when talking of banning hunting as a means of increasing wildlife numbers, you have to look at the wildlife situation in Kenya since 1977:

There is no sport hunting. There is no meat hunting and landowners, be they white or black, have no right to kill wildlife on their property. The ban is total and absolute there being no legal market in either game meat or wildlife products. Kenya outlawed all consumptive use of wildlife at the urging of animal-rights groups in an attempt to stop poaching, or so they said.

At the same time that Kenya prohibited hunting, the Kenya Rangeland Ecological Monitoring Unit began recording the numbers and distribution of livestock and wildlife, primarily large game species, throughout Kenya. This included national parks and other protected areas, black communal lands, and private property, mostly white-owned ranches. So has banning all consumptive use of wildlife worked? Absolutely not, instead it has been a spectacular failure. Since 1977, Kenya has lost sixty to seventy percent of all its large wildlife even in national parks. Moreover, it is predicted that most large mammals will be extinct in the next 10 to 20 years.[14]

The wildlife population crash is due to the increased poaching of what has become valueless game and because of the cost of having it around. A poor African farmer, whose cattle or forage and vegetable crops are consumed by wildlife, faces ruin and possibly starvation. Loss of cattle is particularly significant; cattle provide not only milk, meat, hide and manure (which when dried is used as fuel), but they are also the measure of a family's wealth and social standing.

Kay (an American and obviously addressing an American audience) said, 'You would be appalled at the number of local people injured or killed each year by lions, elephants, and other dangerous game. Children walking to school in rural Africa are all too routinely attacked by wild animals. No American parent would tolerate what goes on in Africa.'

There has been an ongoing effort by anti-hunting and animal rights groups to list the African lion under the US Endangered Species Act. This might well compound the problem. Baldus and others say that all large cats that have been formally protected (tigers, snow leopards and jaguars) have declined in number. Kay says Kenya's lion population has crashed to roughly 10 per cent of neighbouring Tanzania's lion population, which has been hunted (almost) all along. There is concern about the future of lions throughout Africa, but particularly in Kenya. In South Africa, where communities have the right to exploit wildlife on their own land and where communities can run hunting safaris, species across the board are improving in numbers and distribution. However, one must bear in mind that maybe as much as 95 per cent of those shot in South Africa by self-styled 'sport hunters' were bred for 'canned hunts'.

Baldus says:

> [Wild] lion populations outside national parks have a future only if rural people see a direct benefit of living with lions. Official and controlled hunting encourages the lion range states to leave hunting blocks as wilderness and refrain from converting them into pastoral rangeland and agricultural land with little biodiversity left. Banning lion trophy hunting or creating barriers for hunters to take home legally obtained trophies removes the economic as well as management and law enforcement incentives that are necessary for conservation. These counter balances were removed in Kenya that downgraded the lion to vermin, and led poor rural herdsmen to poison lions with easily obtainable insecticides. It is difficult to prevent retaliatory killings when livelihood strategies are threatened: the law is reluctant to impose stiff sentences that compromise poverty alleviation. Conservation authorities cannot defend their justification to conserve lions in such circumstances.[15]

The situation is not much better in Zambia, where the government long ago announced its intention to share the management and benefits of the country's wildlife resources with the communities living around reserves. The results have been dismal. It announced it had recognised the need to bring rural communities into the management of wildlife and the control of problem animals – 'to transfer power and decision-making processes (regarding wildlife management) into local communities and establish principles of local ownership of natural resources'[16]. But greed and a lack of vision have hampered what good intentions there were.

The Zambian government changed in September in 2011. The previous government established game-management areas (GMAs) in which rural dwellers are supposed to co-manage wildlife with the government-appointed Zambia Wildlife Authority (ZAWA also administers national parks) and they are supposed to benefit financially. Communities were said to be using the proceeds to construct clinics and schools, to improve roads and farming systems and to empower women through women's club facilities and initiatives. Local communities are supposed to have received 45 per cent of hunting fees (chiefs getting five per cent, ZAWA 40 per cent and the national treasury 10). That, at least, was the announced intention, but the money tended to evaporate long before it reached the villagers. Zambia remains a long way from sharing control with landowners.

Dr Paula A. White, director of the Zambia Lion Project of the Center for Tropical Research at the University of California, Los Angeles, says that rural communities in Zambia 'do benefit from wildlife – in several ways'. Photo lodges in the parks offer employment and lodge owners have to pay large sums to ZAWA (its board was peremptorily disbanded in 2011 by the new government) for lease fees for the land and for 'bed nights' and a long list of other things. Bordering many of the national parks are hunting blocks – this land is actually owned by chiefs but is leased to hunting operators by ZAWA[17]. Hunting lodges pay similar area fees and also steep licence fees to ZAWA for each animal hunted and for the hunting expedition itself to ZAWA. They also pay annual community pledges agreed upon between the operator and the chiefs. White says:

Although few communities 'own' hunting companies, I get annoyed at reports that claim that hunting provides only minimal revenue for local communities. In fact, hunting provides huge direct and indirect benefits for the villagers who live in the hunting blocks in the form of cash, meat, employment, and community projects. However, much of these benefits never reach the people, not because of the hunting operator but because either the ZAWA (which receives the funds initially) does not pass them on as they are supposed to – or the chiefs pocket them without sharing them with their own community. Some chiefs even take all the meat and sell it rather than give it to their own people.

Several years ago, Community Resource Boards (CRBs) were formed to try and rectify this problem. CRBs consist of 3–5 community members who presumably broker the funds and other assets due to the community to ensure that they are divided up fairly. Well, big surprise: many CRBs merely divide up the money amongst the 3–5 board members and then THEY pocket it! Everybody agrees that CRBs are a complete failure but no one has a better solution.

There have been a few attempts to have communities own photo lodges. Let me tell you firsthand, they are an absolute disaster. Groups like the Wildlife Conservation Society in Zambia will claim success for building community camps. In reality, the first of these camps were illegally placed in hunting blocks without permission. Lawsuits ensued. Eventually, the few that opened for business were run-down before they had seen their first guest. The material assets (beds, pots) quickly grew legs. What was left were bare minimum shelters that may appeal to backpackers or self-drive campers at best – both of which are very rare in Zambia.

The fact that these ventures are typically placed within hunting blocks – against the legal lease agreement of the hunting operator, means that visitors cannot legally tour the area as one is not allowed to 'self-drive' in a hunting block for obvious reasons. And you cannot hike (backpack) through a park or hunting block. Thus, the only community lodges with even a chance to work are located at the entrances to national parks, where guests must get a transfer. But most people coming this far to visit a park are not interested in sleeping in a low-budget, poorly appointed accommodation where they will not be able to do anything but sit in camp and sleep.

White, writing to me three months before the old government was ousted, feels that, even if there are rural community-owned lodges within parks (she doesn't know of any), they are unlikely to thrive because there is 'too much corruption, greed and an odd "jealousy-factor" [in Zambia] that is as puzzling as it is pervasive'. Without adequate external management, standards quickly slouch, equipment fails and assets walk. For this reason funding means 'perpetual support – an open wallet policy'. She is aware of countless good ideas, businesses of every kind, that *should* have worked 'but the goose that is laying the golden egg is always slaughtered in the end'.

She feels a policy of rural communities owning hunting concessions is even less likely to succeed. The mainstay of making a living as a hunting operator is being able to attract international clients successfully. Few rural Zambians are even interested in pursuing what would be required. Communities can be given 'shares', but all this really means is that they will be given more money by the foreign operator who otherwise runs and is responsible for the show.

If this sounds unduly harsh, consider the following: I am sitting in a hunting camp as I write. Last evening, the operator took his clients to another area for three days. In less than 24 hours I (as a visitor) have been approached for six handouts plus additional favours. First by the chief who asked for diesel for his car, then for meat (all for free). Then a motorbike rider whose bike needed fixing, gratis. Next came a string of four camp staff asking for money for various reasons. Ten minutes ago yet another person wanted time off to go home – despite the operator leaving explicit instructions that nobody leave camp or ask me for anything! It never ends. The Western World with its long history of donor aid has created this hand-out mentality, and this is its reward.

White says the operator in whose camp she was staying plans to make the local community the 'Zambian partner' in the next round of lease tenders for this hunting block. While this might increase his chances of receiving the bid and the community might perhaps get a bit more capital, she believes nothing else is likely to change.

Years ago she asked an educated (bachelor's degree) Zambian man why the 'average' Zambian did not aspire to improve his lot in life by opening a small enterprise. 'I shall never forget his sadly resolute face as he replied very matter-of-factly, "Zambian people do not expect very much." Here, rural people do not even think about tomorrow. It is all about getting through today.' She wonders how, 'against that stark reality do we encourage [rural dwellers] to care about conserving lions? Or to not want to kill that elephant that in one night destroyed their entire crop? Or to care whether or not the pillowcase in room number 3 [at the lodge] is clean – when in fact there is no longer a pillowcase in room 3?'

Yet, if the advanced world feels responsibility towards helping to preserve sustainably what is left of Africa's unparalleled wildlife, it has no option but to help Africa's thinking population to see its situation holistically. Traditional rural dwellers in Africa are really no different from the peasants of Europe and the British Isles that I knew as a boy. I was, after the age of five, brought up in a rural environment and helped in the hay making, potato picking and mucking out pigsties, working with poorly educated farm hands. They grumbled about their lot and looked to the government for anything they could scrounge, rather than taking any initiative themselves – and they, like the Zambian, did not expect very much. There was no ambition and no desire to work any harder than the minimum they could get away with.

Fortunately, perhaps, it is not the rural people that conservationists have to convert. They first have to convert an even more difficult, medium-term thinking, self-interested crowd – the politicians.

Dale Lewis, conservation scientist for the Wildlife Conservation Society in Zambia – the WCS works in close collaboration with ZAWA as technical adviser for Community-Based Natural Resource Management (CBNRM)[18] – spotlighted a crucial synergy that should have been obvious as a strategy for HWC-stressed regions right across Africa. He pointed out how healthy livestock can reduce poaching. In parts of Zambia the decline in wildlife can be traced to the sudden reduction of funds for vaccinating chickens and for financing cattle dips. As disease reduced livestock, the landowners fell back on bushmeat, and so both resources went into decline.

At the 2003 World Parks Congress in Durban Lewis pointed out that more than two thirds of Zambia's wildlife – spread over almost 300 000 square kilometres (115 000 square miles) – is on community-owned land. When in the late 1980s the Zambian government found it was impossible to police such a vast area, it turned to the communities – hence the National Conservation Strategy of 1985. The communities were to receive a share of safari-hunting revenues as part of the new community-based wildlife management strategy. The programme was given the clumsy title Administrative Management Design for Game Management Areas (ADMADE) and was to be guided by Community Resource Boards (CRBs), made up of democratically elected leaders.

The leaders received powers and responsibilities to manage wildlife by using their own local scouts. In exchange CRBs receive 45 per cent of revenue generated from their wildlife resources (hunting licences and fees). These revenues also went towards community improvements. Manifestly it isn't working. Lewis says:

> Despite these advancements a significant percentage of households residing in these wildlife areas have remained poor and frequently experience seasonal shortages of food. Many [communities] adopted coping strategies that are not compatible with wildlife production, such as snaring or poisoning of waterholes. Not only did these practices prove difficult to control by law enforcement but they also accounted for significant loss of wildlife.[19]

The WCS, working with the Zambian wildlife authorities, found in the game-depleted Luangwa Valley – the valley has four national parks – communities that kept chickens or cattle might have the answer. The communities were prone to frequent outbreaks of stock diseases that annually wiped out a considerable percentage of their livestock. They were then forced to turn to poaching. On average households owned at any given time between 10 and 20 chickens – an important source of protein for the family's diet, but Newcastle disease annually killed off up to 90 per cent. It was much the same with cattle-owning households. They too were seasonally hit by diseases – especially after overseas donors in the mid 1990s ran out of money to subsidise cattle dips and vaccines. The government showed no interest in stepping in with financial aid. As diseases returned, so the people began indiscriminate poaching. The greater the epidemics, the more the communities poached.

'The significance of this simple relationship was not fully appreciated until recently,' said Lewis at the 2003 World Parks Congress.

> Our research then turned to chicken husbandry, and we suggested that poultry production could increase three to four-fold by vaccinating against Newcastle disease and by reducing mortality of young chickens using simple enclosures to reduce predation. We estimated that households that improved chicken husbandry practices could increase their income by an additional US $30 (from $8) while also significantly increasing their supply of chicken protein for household consumption. With improved access to higher market prices, households could bring their total income from poultry to US $50 per year, or six times current levels.
>
> These same communities lived outside the valley's game reserves in safari-hunting concessions and on average received a revenue share from hunting of about US $55 000 for an average of 1 800 households, or approximately US $30 per household. Theoretically, income derived from poultry could exceed revenues derived from safari hunting. Our research also suggested that safari-hunting revenues were more than adequate to help households finance low-cost veterinary and husbandry support costs. This raised wildlife's value by significantly improving the security of household livelihoods while also reducing the threat of illegal wildlife hunting.

In 2002 Lewis' team had introduced a low-cost vaccine against Newcastle disease and trained 'barefoot vets' to administer it. In 2003, of an estimated total of 22 000 chickens, 8 300 were vaccinated at a total vaccine cost of only $24. Families formed poultry-producer groups and shared the use of a wire fence enclosure to safeguard chicks and maintain high-quality feed for promoting growth. All so simple – and cheap. The team also assisted producer groups in marketing chickens. Lewis offered the following preliminary results based on informal household interviews:

- Incidence of Newcastle disease has become negligible in most areas.
- Value of chickens has increased relative to illegal game meat. This is because illegal game meat cannot be sold on the open market for its 'real' market value.
- The increased value and supply of chickens is reducing local demand for game meat.
- Households recognised the value of vaccinating against Newcastle disease and, to help support the purchase and delivery costs of the vaccine, households provided one free chicken to their regional trading partner for every 50 chickens vaccinated.
- Improved husbandry skills and increased market value have elevated household interest in poultry as a livelihood activity.

Lewis comments, 'Low-cost husbandry and veterinary support for poultry owners clearly can increase food security and income among relatively poor households in wildlife areas. This work also illustrates how such linkages, when understood as a basis for promoting livelihoods, can enhance rural development models for supporting wildlife conservation.'

The survey found a tougher challenge in a cattle-owning area next to Kafue National Park where poaching in the southern border region of the park had devastated its mammal populations, reaching unprecedented levels in 2000. It remains a serious problem today. 'Its consequences on tourism,' says Lewis, 'could well be in the tens of millions of dollars, a loss that will likely require years to recover.' He says a preliminary analysis of the problem suggested that increased rural poverty and chronic food shortages, precipitated by large-scale, disease-related deaths among cattle and drought-related crop loss, played significant roles in contributing to the poaching crisis.

From 1985 Zambia's Southern Province livestock numbers began declining. They dropped from about 80 per cent of all households who then owned cattle to half or less by the turn of the century. Disease was mostly to blame and most villagers have now taken to poaching as a way of life.

Lewis talks of 'faunal collapse in areas once noted for both wildlife numbers and diversity of wildlife species'. The Southern Province's Sichifulo Game Management Area (GMA) averaged US $70 244 a year from safari hunting in animal licence and hunting fee sales from 1997 to 1999 (this from tourists hunting and killing *only 70 individual animals representing 20 species*). But by 2003 this same area, because of poaching, 'was regarded as a depleted wildlife area with little capacity to sustain a hunting quota or the levels of revenues needed to encourage community compliance with laws protecting wildlife'.

Until 1990, the Zambian government provided free veterinary services for livestock owners. In the Kalomo district this included dipping to reduce tick-borne diseases. Annual cost for this service in the communities surrounding Sichifulo GMA varied between US $10 000 and $20 000 a year. But from 1990 households became responsible for their own cattle. The hardship of finding the money was compounded by a drought in 1994. Infection levels increased. Some donor assistance was available from the European Economic Commission from 1989 until 1994, but the government did not sustain tsetse control efforts after 1994 (the tsetse fly causes nagana, a fatal disease in cattle). The Swedish International Development Aid provided assistance in the form of 26 dipping tanks between 1987 and 1990, but again the government of Zambia took no interest after donations stopped and so disease-related mortality increased progressively throughout the Kalomo district. In 2002, for example, of 603 cattle sampled from outside Sichifulo GMA, two thirds were infected with trypanosomes (from the tsetse fly) whereas in the late 1980s less than one per cent was infected.

The Zambian Government was moved to create a special loan fund in 1998 to assist livestock cooperatives to buy drugs but because a number of cooperatives defaulted on repayments the local bank administering the funds closed the programme.

The Kafue story underscores the critical linkages between cattle, disease, household livelihoods, and wildlife. It also demonstrates the need for improved dialogue among potential partners that have complementary stakes in both cattle and wildlife populations. If such partners had collaborated and coordinated their needs and potential sources of help the collapse of both livestock and wildlife populations might have been prevented.[20]

It provides a vivid example of how the welfare of livestock and wildlife – and the viability of game parks and reserves – are interdependent. Perhaps the hunting industry should involve itself with animal husbandry. Lewis says 'safari operators, community leaders, local veterinary officers and officials need to coordinate information and ideas for developing a workable, low-cost programme for treating livestock against key diseases'.

Lewis' theories may be correct but the implementation was not always according to plan. His elephant-proof fences in parts of Luangwa were welcomed by the locals who were quick to cut lengths of wire to make snares, and the bushmeat trade soared.

At least in South Africa, Botswana and Namibia[21] something is being done to 'cut the people in' when it comes to wildlife-based tourism. The driving force is purely economic and has little to do with conserving biodiversity. While it is boosting the economies of remote areas, it is not really focused on resolving the human-wildlife conflict situation.

Private enterprise is more aware of the need to bring peace along the front line. In 2011 I talked to a villager, Ronald Masule, in Botswana who lives on the Chobe River a few kilometres from one of Africa's most exciting protected areas – the Okavango Delta. The 15 000-square-kilometre (5 790-square-mile) swampland is teeming with wildlife. Masule loses six head of cattle a year to lions and suffers crop damage from elephants, but he shrugs it off as a sort of tax – the price to be paid for what he considers the privilege of working in the luxury lodges in the Delta. His tolerant attitude is because he is a game guide with Wilderness Safaris, an international safari company that goes out of its way to involve and educate those surrounding their various concessions[22]. The company has 60 luxury tented camps across Southern Africa, and when it comes to winning hearts and minds it provides a useful model. They have a special programme for children; they will close a camp and bring in children to experience the luxury, learn about the more fascinating side of wildlife and understand the value of tourism. The company also sees that the outside communities receive tangible benefits from having wild animals as neighbours as well as protection from, for instance, marauding elephants. Masule's village, with help from the company, uses different methods to deter elephants, including deep trenches and, most successful of all, the planting of elephant-repelling hedges of chilli pepper plants.

One of the company's luxury lodges in South Africa, although only coincidentally, fits in with South Africa's People and Parks Programme (P&PP) – an offshoot of the Durban World Parks Congress. The idea of the P&P programme – adopted by South Africa and Botswana – was to identify 'specific activities and processes that address issues at the interface between conservation and the communities' – HWC being one of them.

A unique set of circumstances presented itself in South Africa after independence in 1994. Communities that had been forcibly removed from their tribal land under apartheid to make way for wild animals were invited to reclaim their former lands. One of the successful land claims was in the Pafuri region, in the remote but intensely beautiful far northern part of the Kruger Park. The Makuleke people had been removed from there in 1969 by the apartheid government and their territory commandeered as part of the Kruger Park. They received little or no compensation. After independence their land claim was granted and resulted in the community's becoming co-managers with the Parks Board of over 24 000 hectares (59 300 acres) of the Kruger Park. They now share in the income from tourism in that area. The community and the park's authorities, acting together, granted a concession to Wilderness Safaris to establish a luxury lodge to be jointly owned by the villagers, the Kruger Park and Wilderness Safaris. The company negotiated a 45-year lease and, using the community's skills, built a five-star lodge that employs 80 per cent local people, including on the executive staff.

The lodge also goes out of its way to integrate tourists and the communities so that the communities feel an affinity with foreign visitors and vice versa. As in most Wilderness Safari camps, the staff stages a short and colourful traditional dance before dinner; this has led to tourists' taking an interest in their culture and asking to be taken to see where and how they live outside the reserve. As a result of this unexpected development, the community planned overnight accommodation in the village. The Makuleke people's stake in the Kruger Park provides a steady income that goes towards education and other amenities. Their village is one of the few that have a library and electricity. The process and the negotiated deal was a landmark event for South Africa. In principle it has worked well, but the hunting lobby feels hunters should also be brought in, even though this would be inimical to the national park concept. The effects of hunting would not only spoil the ambience for many visitors, but it would also make the animals skittish, which would not be good for the general tourist's experience and especially for the growing photographer-tourist sector. And basic to the partnership was the principle of *protecting* the animals and ensuring that, if culling became necessary, it would be carried out in a scientific and humane manner, rather than by ad hoc hunting.

Wilderness Safaris' camps are nearly all run on a community-partnership basis – directly involving neighbouring communities in the staffing and management of the camps and in profit sharing. The rapport between the company and community goes beyond the business side. In Botswana, for instance, there are regular football fixtures when the camps play against each other (outside the protected areas) or against other communities. This involves flying teams to fixtures in the company's aircraft.

Wilderness Safaris is regarded in many ways as a private sector pioneer in the 'people and parks' initiative. The lessons learned, both in terms of its successes and failings, have been widely analysed and shared. Over time other private and public sector players have entered the field and have also implemented successful programmes.

Another initiative in South Africa came from Ezemvelo KwaZulu-Natal Wildlife, where the conflict along the front line has been pronounced. The board, noted for its bold moves in the past (in the 1960s it initiated wilderness trails in its reserves, a decade ahead of anybody else), has met with varying degrees of success in its pioneering initiatives. It worked closely with a poor rural community outside what is today the Hluhluwe-Imfolozi Park and helped it to build, operate and manage its own safari camp within the reserve itself. The deal was struck after a Neighbour Relations Programme was initiated in the 1990s. It has reached a point where the community and the rangers from various reserves play soccer against each other and where the park's staff is active outside the reserves in helping improve protective enclosures for the community's livestock and even helping in matters unrelated to wildlife conservation. As a result poaching has been reduced. A second community outside the Hluhluwe-Imfolozi Park is about to embark on something similar.

But not all is going well. More often than not it is the slowness of the pace of change and general lack of support from government departments that have resulted in the concept failing to gain momentum. In some instances, progress has been painfully slow, followed by a sudden rush of incomplete and unwise decision-taking. The bottleneck has often come from the department that deals with land affairs and land-claim processes. This lack of progress has sometimes led to frustration and communal retribution. As mentioned in Chapter Two, in 2011 a community invaded Ndumo Game Reserve on the KwaZulu-Natal–Mozambican border not far north of the Hluhluwe-Imfolozi complex. They demolished the game reserve's fence and moved in with cattle. They cut down trees and tilled the land. The uprising was quelled with diplomacy, but it underscored the need for conservation to be coupled with good governance concerning land and sound community engagement and empowerment.

The Ndumo community's land outside the reserve is at times a dustbowl from overgrazing and poor agricultural practice – in stark contrast to the lush, game-filled wetland and thornveld habitat inside the fence. This is a scenario repeated in many parts of Africa. The violent breaching of the front line was not unique and, as long as the contrast exists between exhausted farmland and well-managed or relatively resource-rich game reserves, there will be more invasions. This again suggests that conservationists need to add agriculture to their portfolio.

Jeff Gaisford, who retired as spokesman for Ezemvelo KwaZulu-Natal Wildlife in 2011, said game farms have sprouted like mushrooms in Zululand and the 'big five' (elephant, rhino, buffalo, lion and leopard) are flourishing, along with many other species of carnivores and herbivores. But the human population is also growing and all are competing for land. The Zulu is historically a pastoralist, but he can no longer move cattle around nomadically and, inevitably perhaps, outside the reserves Zululand is appallingly overgrazed and eroded. Possibly nowhere else in Africa is the competition for resources more intense than here, even to the extent that the parks administration has at times given way and allowed cattle access to game reserves. I have seen Zulu cattle inside Mkuzi Game Reserve, an internationally celebrated reserve because of its extraordinarily rich bird life.

Ezemvelo KwaZulu-Natal Wildlife, when it instituted its Neighbour Relations Programme some years ago, was motivated by the realisation that, unless the reserves had the support of neighbouring communities, conservation efforts were doomed to failure. The project, says Gaisford, has grown enormously:

'Tourism revenue provides the finance for community projects through a levy and the provincial parks board has a full-time staff working with all our neighbouring communities. It assists in the establishment of soccer teams in the camps and in the communities and has instituted the Ezemvelo Soccer Cup whose image is closely tied with wildlife conservation and tourism.'

Gaisford said, 'The thrust of our community outreach is to educate members of the communities to understand the value of a healthy environment and the need to work carefully with natural resources, given that in bad times they often rely on these resources to keep them alive. So it goes deep into the "environmental goods and services" provided by nature'[23].

Now that there is a more or less universal acceptance that our generation has the responsibility to conserve what is left of the battered natural world, how do we do it?

Nature conservation is the wise use of natural resources, and not merely preservation. And national parks and game reserves[24], no matter how large, will still amount to confined spaces and therefore will have to be managed. Each has a limited carrying capacity for different species and cannot be expected to achieve a dynamic equilibrium on its own – not without the loss of species. Biodiversity in a contained area has to be maintained – biodiversity being the whole point of a national park.

National parks and reserves are reference libraries of plant and animal species; repositories of the biodiversity that existed before the nation became paved, ploughed and plundered. My personal opinion is that the management of wild animal populations inside confined areas will require culling. But culling has a positive side – it produces protein and other by-products that can benefit the surrounding communities. To some extent, to relieve pressure, buffer areas can be opened up for community-owned safari camps and hunting. South Africa has just such a buffer-zone policy incorporated in its National Environmental Management Act as amended in 2011. The Act is based on the specific objective 'for the conservation and sustainable use of South Africa's biological diversity which addresses environmentally sound and sustainable development wherever possible around and adjacent to protected areas'. Buffer zones will promote the protection of national parks[25] and be beneficial to those within and around the zones whose active support for conservation is critical. That's the idea anyway.

Africa has to come to terms with the severity of poaching. Generally there's a tendency nowadays to give more serious prison sentences to ivory and rhino horn poachers, and scores of rhino poachers were shot dead in 2011, supposedly in gun battles. But the Far Eastern gangs who pay the poachers are running rings round the authorities in most African countries and paying off politicians and policemen. As was witnessed in the fishing industry across the world, the Far East is a conscienceless plunderer of other regions' natural resources – just as Europe was in the past. As the Orient grows wealthier, so we might soon witness a second African wildlife holocaust, similar to the days of the voracious Victorian and German colonial hunter/explorers.

Many conservationists – especially the animal-rights faction – have difficulty accepting hunting as an essential part of the long-term future of African wildlife sustainability. As I have mentioned before, I am not a hunter and would find it uncomfortable witnessing a man kill a lion, or any animal for that matter, in the name of sport. But I would be even more uncomfortable watching the workers at my local abattoir slaughtering an ox or a sheep for my consumption. Hunting is an important tool and an income earner for conservation, and the spin-offs, such as protein and animal products, are a legitimate source of wealth for communities.

In Zimbabwe and Tanzania, revenues generated by hunting clients are respectively 30 and 14 times greater than those generated by photographic clients.

While big-game hunting can be used as a tool of conservation, there is a need for hunters to show more concern for ecosystems and become a little more honest in their views. It doesn't cut any ice these days to see a hunter with a high-powered rifle posing triumphantly with one foot on a dead lion or leopard and proclaiming his love of nature or boasting of how he understands the wilds. Many have no idea of ecology and no interest in nature beyond the habits of their quarry. On the other hand, hunters are often more constructive when it comes to conservation than the average conservationist. An excellent example is to be found in the United States where Ducks Unlimited – founded and run by hunters – has become the world's largest and most effective wetland conservation organisation. Its president, John A. Tomke, says, 'It originated with a small group of individuals concerned about the future of waterfowl.'[26] This is a little disingenuous, since it was founded by hunters concerned about not having enough ducks to shoot. But, whatever the motive, Ducks Unlimited has been instrumental in re-establishing and conserving 40 000 square kilometres (15 444 square miles)[27] of wildfowl-filled wetland. It annually pumps millions of dollars into wildlife habitats.

Duck shooting takes place in only 10 per cent of the conserved wetlands and, assuming the ducks are shot for the pot, then it is a far more humane method of obtaining protein than a Kentucky Fried Chicken production line.

And it is well to remember that the Kruger National Park and, no doubt, the Selous Game Reserve and perhaps nearly all the others, were set aside because the leaders of the day could see that the 19th-century wildlife overkill would wreck their favourite pursuit – game hunting.

Africa's wildlife is a major world heritage but it must never be forgotten that the custodians are Africans. Whatever the answers are to preserving Africa's great landscapes and its wildlife, the answers must be found inside Africa. It is also imperative that the dozens of organisations that donate to African wildlife ensure that their money is being spent wisely. They must recognise that there are people sharing the same habitat with wild animals who also need help. Many of Africa's richest wildlife areas are economically handicapped and the need for overseas funding will continue if conservation is to become a sustainable way of life for such regions as Tanzania, Zambia and Uganda. With proper governance, such areas should eventually become self-supporting, even if they can never become rich.

The Zulu politician Chief Mangosuthu Buthelezi said to me many years ago in the Zulu capital, Ulundi (I paraphrase from memory):

We fully recognise that our reserves belong to the world and not just to us. We agree they are part of the world's natural heritage and that we have a responsibility to look after them. But, as our reserves are part of the world's heritage, then the world must help pay for them because we can't afford it.

NOTES

1 The conflict

1. Clarke, J. 1968. *Man is the Prey*. André Deutsch.
2. Lamarque, F., Anderson, J. et al. 2009. Human-Wildlife Conflict in Africa. An overview of causes, consequences and management strategies. International Foundation for the Conservation of Wildlife. FAO, Rome.
3. Ardrey, Robert. 1961. *African Genesis*. Collins.
4. The malarial mosquito and other arthropods kill at least a million people a year, but they are outside the scope of this book.
5. Norton-Griffiths, M. 2007. How Many Wildebeest Do You Need? *World Economics* Volume 8 No 2.

2 The front line

1. Campfire Association Zimbabwe is a conservation, educational and fundraising organisation to enable rural communities in Zimbabwe to manage their natural resources effectively.
2. Chardonnet, P., Soto, B. et al. (quoting Packer). 2010. Managing the Conflicts Between People and Lion. International Foundation for the Conservation of Wildlife (IGF Foundation), France. FAO Paper 13.
3. Packer, C., Ikanda, D. et al. 2006. The Ecology of Man-Eating Lions in Tanzania. *Nature & Faune* Volume 21 Issue 2. FAO, Accra.
4. Lamarque, F., Anderson, J. et al. 2009. Human-Wildlife Conflict in Africa. An overview of causes, consequences and management

strategies. International Foundation for the Conservation of Wildlife. FAO, Rome.

5. Packer, C., Ikanda, D. et al. Ibid.

6. Chardonnet, P., Soto, B. et al. 2010. Managing the Conflicts Between People and Lion. International Foundation for the Conservation of Wildlife (IGF Foundation), France. FAO Paper 13.

7. Anderson, J. Pers. comm.

8. Lamarque, F., Anderson, J. et al. Ibid.

9. See Chapter Twelve.

10. HuntNetwork. 4 September 2009. huntnetwork.net/modules/news/article.php?storyid=4655&keywords=gar

11. See Chapter Thirteen.

12. Rolf D. Baldus worked for 13 years in wildlife management in Tanzania, especially in and around the Selous Game Reserve. He is presently President of the Tropical Game Commission of CIC (International Council for Game and Wildlife Conservation) and contributor to and editor of *Wild Heart of Africa – The Selous Game Reserve in Tanzania* (Rowland Ward 2011).

13. Norton-Griffiths, M. 2007. How Many Wildebeest Do You Need? *World Economics* Volume 8 No 2.

14. See Chapter Fourteen.

15. *Sunday Times*. Johannesburg. 23 March 1997.

16. Packer, C., Ikanda, D. et al. Ibid.

17. Osborne, F.W. & Anstey, S. 2002. Elephant/Human Conflict and Community Development around the Niassa Reserve, Mozambique. Mid Zambezi Elephant Project, Harare, Zimbabwe.

18. The CIC with the FAO published several technical papers on wildlife management. www.cic-wildlife.org/?id=412.

19. See Chapter Five.

20. Storr, Will. *Daily Telegraph*. London. 10 August 2008.

21. See Chapter Six.

22. Guggisberg, C.A.W. 1961. *Simba*. Howard Timmins.

23. Lamarque, F., Anderson, J. et al. Ibid.

24. Ibid.

25. Among the resolutions resulting from the conference was: 'We urge commitment to ensuring that people who benefit from, or are impacted by, protected areas have the opportunity to participate in relevant decision-making on a fair and equitable basis in full respect of their human and social rights. We urge commitment to protected area management that shares benefits with indigenous peoples, mobile peoples and local communities. We urge commitment to protected area management that strives to reduce, and in no way exacerbates, poverty.'

26. Madden, Francine (executive director, HWCC). www.humanwildlifeconflict.org.

27. Nshala, Rugemeleza (co-founder and chairman of the Lawyers' Environmental Action Team). 2011. www.leat.or.tz.

28. Zululand is my preferred name for the part of KwaZulu-Natal north of the Tugela River.

29. The Peace Parks Foundation is an international partnership promoting wildlife conservation, ecotourism and job creation in Southern Africa. www.peaceparks.org.

30. It envisages the establishment of a network of protected areas linking ecosystems across international borders.

31. Pilanesberg is technically a game reserve but was created in the days of apartheid when the South African government set up 'self-governing states' for black people. Pilanesberg, being in one of these states, Bophuthatswana, was deemed to be a national park. The states were reabsorbed into South Africa when apartheid was abandoned, but the reserves are reluctant to lose their national park status.

32. Lamarque, F., Anderson, J. et al. Ibid.

33. Ibid.

34. Owen-Smith, Garth. 2010. *An Arid Eden – A Personal Account of Conservation in the Kaokoveld*. Jonathan Ball.

35. Allison, Simon. *Daily Maverick*. 31 October 2011. dailymaverick.co.za/article/2011-10-31-zambian-president-our-wildlife-is-fair-game.

36. Weaver, Tony. *Cape Times*. Cape Town. 4 November 2011.

37. Anderson, Jeremy. Pers. comm.

38. Like Pilanesberg (note 31 above), Madikwe is technically a game reserve that was created in the days of apartheid when the South African government set up 'self-governing states' for black people. Madikwe, being in one of these states, Bophuthatswana, was deemed to be a national park. The states were reabsorbed into South Africa when apartheid was abandoned.

39. Gaisford, Jeff. Pers. comm.

3 The nature of the beast

1. Patterson, J.H. 1907. *The Man-Eaters of Tsavo*. Macmillan.

2. Foran, W. Robert. 1961. *A Hunter's Saga*. Robert Hale.

3. The shark, which is outside the ambit of this book, is responsible for between 60 and 70 unprovoked fatal attacks worldwide each year, with a steady annual toll along the African coast from Cape Town and all the way north up Africa's east coast.

4. Most people do not differentiate between the white and the black rhino when speaking of the big five. A rhino is a rhino. But to hunters the black, being by far the more challenging to hunt, is the more sought-after and most hunters would have that species in mind as one of the five.

5. Rushby, G.G. 1965. *No More the Tusker*. W.H. Allen.

6. Maydon, H.C. 1925. *Big Game Shooting in Africa*. H.F. & G. Whiterby.

7. The 'big seven' usually refers to elephant, buffalo, rhino (either African species), lion, leopard (these being the 'big five') plus tiger of Asia and grizzly of North America.

8. Anderson, Jeremy. Pers. comm.

9. Brain, C. & Sillen, A. 1988. Evidence from the Swartkrans Cave for the Earliest Use of Fire. *Nature* 336: 464–466.

10. Taylor, John. 1959. *Man-Eaters and Marauders*. Muller.

11. Wood, J.G. 1854. *Illustrated Natural History*. Longmans Green. (Gordon Cumming was a colourful and wasteful Scots hunter.)

12. Perry, R. 1964. *The World of the Tiger*. Cassell.

13. Stevenson-Hamilton, J. 1957. Pers. comm.

14. Calenborne, Alan. Pers. comm.

15. Player, Ian. Pers. comm.

16. Pootman, F.J. 1959. *Secrets of the Animal World*. Souvenir Press.

17. Clarke, J. 1982. *Coming Back to Earth*. Jacana Press.

18. Wildlife Campus/Eco Training. www.wildlifecampus.com.

19. Agence France-Presse. 22 June 2002.

20. Dart, R. & Craig, D. 1959. *Adventures with the Missing Link*. Harper.

21. Ardrey, R. 1961. *African Genesis*. Collins.

4 The lion

1. Guggisberg, C.A.W. 1961. *Simba*. Howard Timmins.

2. Mesochina, Pascal, Mbangwa, Obed et al. June 2010. The Conservation Status of the Lion in Tanzania. SCI Foundation.

3. Lamarque, F., Anderson, J. et al. 2009. Human-Wildlife Conflict in Africa. An overview of causes, consequences and management strategies. International Foundation for the Conservation of Wildlife. FAO, Rome.

4. Guggisberg, C.A.W. Ibid.

5. Bulpin, T.V. (quoting Rushby). 1962. *The Hunter is Death*. Nelson.

6. Patterson, J.H. 1907. *The Man-Eaters of Tsavo and Other East African Adventures*. Macmillan.

7. Guggisberg, C.A.W. Ibid.

8. Packer, Craig, Swanson, A. et al. 2011. Fear of Darkness, the Full Moon and the Nocturnal Ecology of African Lions. Public Library of Science One.

9. Roberts, A. 1951. *The Mammals of South Africa*. Central News Agency.

10. Guggisberg, C.A.W. Ibid.

11. Packer, C., Ikanda, D. et al. 2006. The Ecology of Man-Eating Lions in Tanzania. *Nature & Faune* Volume 21 Issue 2. FAO, Accra.

12. In 2002 French zoologist Dr P. Chardonnet, under the auspices of Conservation Force and IGF, did a comprehensive study of the status of African lions and estimated Tanzania had 14 432 (10 409 minimum and 18 215 maximum) – the most in Africa.

13. Packer, C., Ikanda, D. et al. Ibid.

14. GTZ in 2011 became GIZ – the German Federal Ministry for Economic Cooperation and Development – which has conducted development cooperation activities in Tanzania since 1975. GIZ is responsible for implementation. It views Tanzania's most serious problems as 'weak public administration, corruption, and a lack of clearly defined structures within the civil society. The economy, too, is underdeveloped. Insufficient state revenues and a high level of public debt, especially abroad, have led to excessive dependence on donors.'

15. Baldus, Rolf. D. Pers. comm.

16. Baldus says it is broadly agreed that Patterson's pair of Tsavo man-eaters were not exceptional during the building of the railway to Nairobi – it is just that he wrote a book about them.

17. Packer, C., Ikanda, D. et al. Ibid.

18. Taylor, John. 1959. *Man-Eaters and Marauders*. Muller.

19. Ibid.

20. Dorsey, James Michael. 2008. 10 Extraordinary Burial Ceremonies from around the World. matadornetwork.com/bnt/10-extraordinary-burial-ceremonies-from-around-the-world. (Dorsey, explorer and author, lived among the Maasai in Kenya and Tanzania in the 1990s gathering material for, inter alia, *Christian Science Monitor* and *BBC Wildlife*.)

21. Mozambique was a Portuguese province until then.

22. Lamarque, F., Anderson, J. et al. Ibid.

23. Munnion, Christopher (reporting from Johannesburg). Big Cats Get a Taste for Illegal Immigrants. *The Electronic Telegraph* (www.telegraph.co.uk). London. 26 August 1998. (Later park officials found evidence of elephants in the area and as the girl described the animals as being 'as

big as houses' it seems the family might have stumbled into a herd of elephants. The mother's body was found with part of her buttock gone [hyaenas?] and her head compressed.)

24. Caputo, Robert. 1992. *Kenya Journal*. Elliott & Clark.

25. Lamarque, F., Anderson, J. et al. Ibid.

26. Ionides, C.J.P. 1965. *A Hunter's Story*. W.H. Allen.

27. Patterson, J.H. Ibid.

28. British South African Police.

29. *African Sporting Gazette*. 2001. Volume 10 No 4.

30. Quoted in *Giants of the Missionary Trail*. 1954. Scripture Press.

31. Rushby, G.G. 1965. *No More the Tusker*. W.H. Allen.

32. International Council for Game and Wildlife Conservation (CIC). www.cic-wildlife.org.

33. African Indaba. August 2009. www.africanindaba.co.za.

34. WFSA conference, June 2009. The WFSA claims to represent 'over one hundred million sport shooters from all around the world'.

5 The leopard

1. Stevenson-Hamilton, J. 1947. *Wild Life in South Africa*. Cassell.

2. Murray Smith, T. 1963. *The Nature of the Beast*. Jarrolds.

3. Gee, E.P. 1964. *The Wild Life of India*. Collins.

4. Clarke, J. 1968. *Man is the Prey*. André Deutsch.

5. Munnion, Christopher (reporting from Johannesburg). Big Cats Get a Taste for Illegal Immigrants. *The Electronic Telegraph* (www.telegraph.co.uk). London. 26 August 1998.

6. I have since heard on good authority that six man-eating leopards were shot in the north of Mozambique in that period.

7. Clarke, J. Ibid.

8. Hunter, J.A. 1952. *Hunter*. Hamish Hamilton.

9. Bulpin, T.V. (quoting Rushby). 1962. *The Hunter is Death*. Nelson.

10. Ionides, C.J.P. 1965. *A Hunter's Story*. W.H. Allen.

11. Rushby, G.G. 1965. *No More the Tusker*. W.H. Allen.

12. Corbett, Jim. 1947. *The Man-Eating Leopard of Rudraprayag*. Oxford India Paperbacks.

13. Gee, E.P. Ibid.

14. De Wet, Petrus (chairman of the Predation Management Forum). 2010. www.pmg.org.za.

6 The elephant

1. Lamarque, F., Anderson, J. et al. 2009. Human-Wildlife Conflict in Africa. An overview of causes, consequences and management strategies. International Foundation for the Conservation of Wildlife. FAO, Rome.

2. Siebert, C. *New York Times*. 8 October 2006, 7 May 2007.

3. *The Guinness Book of World Records*. 1997. Guinness World Records. (This is probably an exaggeration. It is not mentioned in later editions.)

4. Wood, Gerald L. 1972. *The Guinness Book of Animal Facts and Feats*. Guinness Superlatives.

5. Barnes, R.F.W. 1999. Is There a Future for Elephants in West Africa? *Mammal Review* 29(3); 175–199.

6. IUCN Elephant Specialist Group report 2008.

7. International Fund for Animal Welfare – elephant conservation conference in Bamako, Mali. February 2008.

8. Ferrar, Tony. Pers. comm.

9. Foran, W. Robert. 1958. *A Breath of the Wilds*. Robert Hale.

10. The figure of 500 deaths a year excludes deaths caused by captive elephants in Asia and Africa.

11. *Cleft Stick*. 2004. Newsletter of the Game Rangers Association of Africa No 9.

12. Thomson, Ron. 2006. *Managing Our Wildlife Heritage*. Magron Publishers.

13. Weidlich, Brigitte. *The Namibian*. 27 October 2008.

14. Ibid.

15. Safaritalk (www.safaritalk.net) is a not-for-gain organisation and volunteer-administered initiative highlighting wildlife conservation, environmental issues and community and social initiatives in Africa. Its analysis was put before the 17th Conference of the Parties Climate Change conference in October 2011 in Durban.

16. ETIS is a comprehensive information system to track illegal trade in ivory and other elephant products. The central component of ETIS is a database on seizures of elephant specimens that have occurred anywhere in the world since 1989. Since its inception, ETIS has been managed by TRAFFIC on behalf of the CITES parties and is currently housed at the TRAFFIC East/Southern Africa office in Harare, Zimbabwe.

17. Weidlich, Brigitte. Ibid.

18. Wakoli, Elizabeth Naliaka (Moi University) & Wasilwa, Noah Sitati (Eastern Africa Elephant Programme, WWF). 2009. Temporal and Spatial Distribution of Human Elephant Conflict in Transmara.

19. HuntNetwork. 12 August 2011. huntnetwork.net/modules/news/article.php?storyid=6913&keywords=Chimbuwe.

20. African Indaba. 2011. www.africanindaba.co.za.

21. Friedman, Russel (Wilderness Safaris). 2011. Pers. comm.

22. Kiiru, W. 1995. The Current Status of Human-Elephant Conflict in Kenya. *Pachyderm* 19: 15–20.

23. Lamarque, F., Anderson, J. et al. Ibid.

24. *Nairobi Star*. 6 July 2011. allafrica.com/stories/201107070074.html.

25. Draft Norms and Standards of Elephant Management in South Africa. 2007. Department of Environmental Affairs and Tourism.

26. Lamarque, F., Anderson, J. et al. Ibid.

27. *Daily Mail*. London. 30 November 2008.

28. Siebel, Tom (as told to Steven Bertoni). *Forbes* magazine. 11 October 2010.

29. Anderson, Jeremy. Pers. comm.

30. Taylor, John. 1959. *Man-Eaters and Marauders*. Muller.

31. Carrington, R. 1958. *Elephants*. Chatto & Windus.

32. Taylor, John. Ibid.

33. www.kruger-2-kalahari.com/daryl-balfour.html.

34. Chadwick, Douglas H. 1992. *The Fate of the Elephant*. Penguin.

35. Sutherland J. 1912. *The Adventures of an Elephant Hunter*. Macmillan.

36. Balneaves, Elizabeth. 1962. *Elephant Valley*. Lutterworth.

37. In musth means 'in heat' – the males, not the females, go into heat.

38. Siebert, Charles. Ibid.

39. Sanderson, Ivan T. 1964. *The Dynasty of Abu*. Cassell.

40. McFarlane, Ian. Pers. comm.

41. Douglas-Hamilton, Iain. 1975. *Among the Elephants*. Collins & Harvill.

42. Chadwick, Douglas H. Ibid.

43. *Lahore Times*. 9 July 2011.

44. Heffernan, J. 2006. *Pachyderm* No 40. (Journal of IUCN Species Survival Commission) January–June 2006.

45. Kirby, Percival R. 1958. *Jacob van Reenen and the* Grosvenor *Expedition of 1790–91*. Witwatersrand University Press.

46. Carrington, R. Ibid.

47. Sanderson, Ivan T. Ibid.

7 The hippopotamus

1. Frame, George W. & Herbison, Lory. 1991. Sizing up a Heavyweight. *International Wildlife* XXI: 4–11.

2. White, Robert Bruce. 1958. Almost Everybody Likes Hippos. *Science Digest* XLIII.

3. Klingel, Hans (Zoologisches Institut, Technischen Universität Braunschweig). Consultant to IUCN.

4. White, Robert Bruce. Ibid.

5. Willock, Colin. 1965. *The Enormous Zoo*. Longmans.

6. Ibid.

7. Caputo, P. 2002. *Ghosts of Tsavo*. National Geographic Adventure Press.
8. HuntNetwork. 24 January 2011. huntnetwork.net/modules/news/article.php?storyid=5956.
9. Kruger, Kobie. 1994. *Mahlangeni: Stories of a Game Ranger's Family*. Penguin.
10. Details of Templer's experience are based on various reports, including John Dyson's 1996 account in *Reader's Digest*.

8 The rhinoceros

1. Murray Smith, T. 1963. *The Nature of the Beast*. Jarrolds.
2. The white and the black rhino are the same colour. The term 'white' is a corruption of the Dutch word *weid* (wide) and refers to the animal's wide lips.
3. Clarke, J. 1968. *Man is the Prey*. André Deutsch.
4. Von Albensleven, Werner. Pers. comm.
5. Anderson, Jeremy. Pers. comm.
6. Guggisberg, C.A.W. 1966. *SOS Rhino (A Survival Book on Rhinoceroses)*. André Deutsch.
7. Ibid (quoting C.H. Stigand's 1906 book *The Game of British East Africa*. H. Cox.).
8. Patterson, J.H. 1907. *The Man-Eaters of Tsavo and Other East African Adventures*. Macmillan.
9. Player, Ian. Pers. comm.
10. Steele, N. 1968. *Game Ranger on Horseback*. Books of Africa.
11. According to a 2010 report by Ezemvelo KwaZulu-Natal Wildlife, parks in KwaZulu-Natal have 350 black and 1 600 white rhino.
12. The figures from the Kruger Park are hotly disputed by some who believe them to be exaggerated.

13. Anderson, Jeremy. Ibid.

14. Hunter, J.A. 1952. *Hunter*. Hamish Hamilton.

15. SANParks statement, 11 January 2012.

16. WWF press release, 12 January 2012.

17. TRAFFIC is a joint programme of WWF and IUCN that works to ensure that trade in wild animals and plants is not a threat to the conservation of nature. TRAFFIC actively monitors and investigates wildlife trade worldwide.

18. *Cleft Stick*. 2009. Newsletter of the Game Rangers Association of Africa No 4.

19. In view of the insatiable Chinese demand for rhino horn for medicinal purposes, the question has been asked whether South Africa should farm rhinos. Gerhard Damm, a German hunter now living in South Africa, founder of African Indaba (www.africanindaba.co.za), a popular web newsletter for hunters and conservationists, has introduced some interesting statistics into the debate. In African Indaba February 2011, using a 'purely hypothetical calculation', Damm worked out that the population of China is around 1.321 billion. If a tenth of a per cent of Chinese believe in rhino horn medicine it means around 1.3 million Chinese are potential consumers. If they consumed only a gram a week, 67.6 tonnes of rhino horn would be needed a year to satisfy the demand. 'That would need 15 000 rhino a year' to supply this hypothetical market sustainably. 'Neither the rhino horn stocks in private and official custody, nor the horns of all presently living rhino will be able to meet such a demand.' He says the answer lies in more energetic law enforcement and in the Chinese government cooperating.

20. Gee, E.P. 1964. *The Wild Life of India*. Collins.

9 The buffalo

1. Murray Smith, T. 1963. *The Nature of the Beast*. Jarrolds.
2. Zijlma, Anouk. 2012. goafrica.about.com/od/africanwildlife. New York Times Co.
3. wikipedia.org/wiki/African_buffalo.
4. Currin, Graham. 2005. No One Survives a Cape Buffalo Attack. The Preservation Foundation, Inc. www.storyhouse.org/select.html.
5. Taylor, John. 1959. *Man-Eaters and Marauders*. Muller.
6. Dasmann, Raymond F. 1964. *African Game Ranching*. Pergamon Press.
7. Foran, W. Robert. 1961. *A Hunter's Saga*. Robert Hale.
8. Ibid.
9. Taylor, John. Ibid.
10. Laxton, Mannie. Pers. comm.

10 The hyaena

1. Africa has three species of hyaena: the common spotted hyaena (*Crocuta crocuta*), weighing, according to Reay H.M. Smithers (*Land Mammals of Southern Africa*. Macmillan, 1986), an average 57.8 kilograms (127 pounds) for males and 64.8 kilograms (142 pounds) for females. The brown hyaena (*Hyaena brunnea*) weighs (Smithers) 40 kilograms (88 pounds) for males and 38.45 kilograms (84.5 pounds) for females. The striped hyaena (*Hyaena hyaena*) is not mentioned by Smithers but, according to Chris and Tilde Stuart (*The Larger Mammals of Africa*. Struik, 1997), weighs 40 to 50 kilograms (88 to 110 pounds). The Stuarts give the spotted hyaena as 60 to 80 kilograms (132 to 176 pounds) but according to most authorities this seems extraordinary high. The brown hyaena is scarce in the south, with the exception of Botswana and Namibia, where it can be a threat to livestock. The striped, confined to the northern third of Africa and across Asia to India, is no threat in Africa but has been known to attack in Asia.

2. Lamarque, F., Anderson, J. et al. 2009. Human-Wildlife Conflict in Africa. An overview of causes, consequences and management strategies. International Foundation for the Conservation of Wildlife. FAO, Rome.

3. Roosevelt, Theodore. 1910. *African Game Trails: An Account of the African Wanderings of an American Hunter-Naturalist.* St Martin's Press.

4. Kruuk, Hans. 1975. *Hyaena.* Clarendon Press.

5. Balestra, F.A. 1962. The Man-Eating Hyenas of Mlanje. *African Wild Life* 16: 25–27.

6. Rushby, G.G. 1965. *No More the Tusker.* W.H. Allen.

7. *African Hunter.* Volume 10 No 4. www.african-hunter.com.

11 The primates

1. Schaller, G. 1964. *The Year of the Gorilla.* Chicago University Press.

2. Merfield, Fred G. 1956. *Gorillas Were My Neighbours.* Longmans Green.

3. This is from my personal notes of the 1960s and bears no source.

4. Fallow, Allan (quoting Jane Goodall). April 2003. *National Geographic* magazine.

5. Fallow, Allan. December 2002. *National Geographic* magazine.

6. *Star.* Johannesburg. 11 March 1963.

7. *Argus.* Cape Town. 9 September 1964.

8. Marais, Eugène. 1939. *My Friends the Baboons.* Human & Rousseau.

12 The crocodile

1. Foran, W. Robert. 1958. *A Breath of the Wilds.* Robert Hale.

2. McRae, Michael. February 2008. Gustave, the Killer Crocodile. *National Geographic Adventure* magazine.

3. Lamarque, F., Anderson, J. et al. 2009. Human-Wildlife Conflict

in Africa. An overview of causes, consequences and management strategies. International Foundation for the Conservation of Wildlife. FAO, Rome.

4. Ibid.

5. Nel, Dirk. *Star*. Johannesburg. 5 March 2004.

6. *National Geographic* documentary. 15 February 2003.

7. *Sunday Mail*. Harare. 17 January 2010.

8. *Sunday Monitor*. Uganda. 14 June 2009.

9. Lamarque, F., Anderson, J. et al. Ibid.

10. Packer, C., Ikanda, D. et al. 2006. The Ecology of Man-Eating Lions in Tanzania. *Nature & Faune* Volume 21 Issue 2. FAO, Accra.

11. Ibid.

12. Murray Smith, T. 1963. *The Nature of the Beast*. Jarrolds.

13. Lamarque, F., Anderson, J. et al. Ibid.

14. Kearton, C. 1929. *In the Land of the Lion*. Arrowsmith.

15. Ruark, R. 1968. *Use Enough Gun*. Hamish Hamilton.

16. Barnes, T.A. 1922. *The Wonderland of the Eastern Congo*. G.P. Putnam's Sons.

17. Murray Smith, T. Ibid.

18. Lamarque, F., Anderson, J. et al. Ibid.

13 The snakes

1. Gear, James (South Africa Poliomyelitis Research Centre). 1968. Pers. comm.

2. Crawhall, Nigel (chairman of TILCEPA, IUCN). Pers. comm.

3. Sadly, the mouse was then fed to the snakes in the next pen. When I wrote about this incident there was a public outcry and many thought the mouse should have been given five-star accommodation for life.

4. 'Envenoming' is where venom is injected by the snake – as opposed to a bite from a non-toxic snake or a 'dry bite' where a toxic species does not inject venom.

5. WHO (www.who.int). Neglected Tropical Diseases. WHO cites several listed authorities.

6. These findings followed an International Society of Toxicology symposium in Albuquerque (1–4 June 2009) to mark Venom Week 2009.

7. Blaylock, Roger. Leslie Williams Private Hospital (Gold Fields Health Services), Carletonville, South Africa. February 2004. Epidemiology of Snakebite in Eshowe, KwaZulu-Natal. *Toxicon* 43(2): 159–66.

8. Murray Smith, T. 1963. *The Nature of the Beast*. Jarrolds.

9. Venomous snakes often deliver a 'dry bite' in self-defence when no venom is injected. They will do this when fending off a creature that is too big to eat. Delivering a deadly bite is obviously no use for defence because the venom takes too long to be effective. According to the WHO, about a third of bites from venomous snakes are dry.

10. Marais, Johan. Pers. comm.

11. Ionides, C.J.P. 1965. *A Hunter's Story*. W.H. Allen.

12. Marais, Johan. Ibid.

13. Polyvalent serum (antivenin) covers cobra and adder bites.

14. Dennis Groves was the most snakebitten man I have ever known, having survived 25 potentially lethal bites. His book *Fangs* (Bloomington) was published days after he died in 2010 (not of a snakebite).

15. Ionides, C.J.P. Ibid.

16. *Bitis arietans* is the species found in sub-Saharan Africa.

17. Warrell, D.A., Davidson, N.McD. et al. 1975. Poisoning by Bites of the Saw-Scaled or Carpet Viper (*Echis carinatus*) in Nigeria. *British Medical Journal* 4: 697–700.

18. Marais, Johan. Ibid.

19. Ibid.

20. Ditmars, Raymond L. 1960. *Snakes of the World*. Macmillan.

21. Marais, Johan. Ibid.

22. Antivenin is obtained, rather wretchedly, by injecting a horse with stronger and stronger sub-lethal doses of venom and allowing it to recover between doses. When the horse is able to reach a point where it can metabolise 70 times the lethal dose for a horse, its blood is tapped and the plasma separated. The plasma becomes the antivenin in snakebite kits.

23. *Guardian*. London. 5 January 2004.
24. BBC. 15 April 2009.
25. *Daily Telegraph*. London. 24 November 2002.
26. Marais, Johan. Ibid.
27. Ionides, C.J.P. 1966. *Mambas and Man-Eaters*. Holt, Rinehart & Wilson.
28. Pythons are listed as Cites II species and their export is restricted.
29. Lyell, Denis L. 1988. *View Larger Image African Adventure: Letters from Famous Big-Game Hunters*. St Martins Press.
30. Hillaby, John. 1963. *Journey to the Jade Sea*. Constable.
31. Ditmars, Raymond L. Ibid.
32. Marais, Johan. 2004. *A Complete Guide to the Snakes of Southern Africa*. Struik Nature.
33. Marais, Johan. Pers. comm.

14 The end of the game

1. Norton-Griffiths, M. 2007. How Many Wildebeest Do You Need? *World Economics* Volume 8 No 2.
2. Lindsey, P.A., Alexander, R. et al., Zoological Society of London. 2006. Potential of Trophy Hunting to Create Incentives for Wildlife Conservation in Africa where Alternative Wildlife-based Land Uses may not be Viable. *Animal Conservation* 9: 283–291.
3. Norton-Griffiths, M. Ibid.
4. Lindsey, Peter A. 2007. Trophy Hunting and Conservation in Africa: problems and one potential solution. *Conservation Biology* Volume 21 No 3.
5. Thomson, Ron. 2011. *A Game Warden's Report*. Magron Publishers.
6. South African National Parks' official website, www.sanparks.org.za.
7. Thomson, Ron. Ibid.
8. www.conservationforce.org/pdf/AfricanIndabaVol9-2&3.pdf
9. Baldus, Rolf D. 2006. Results & Conclusions of the Selous Conservation Programme. An examination of the crucial role of

good governance in ecosystem management. Presented at the Serengeti Conference 2006 (edited for African Indaba).

10. Convention on Biological Diversity 1998 – a UN-inspired treaty to protect the Earth's biologically rich areas.

11. Two remnant populations had survived – towards the north (near Stiegler's Gorge) about 20 animals survived and maybe as many as 25 in the south.

12. Baldus, Rolf D. Ibid.

13. Baldus, Rolf D. Pers. comm.

14. Kay, Charles E. 2009. Kenya's Wildlife Debacle: the true cost of banning hunting. *Mule Deer Foundation* magazine No 27: 22–27.

15. Baldus, Rolf D. 2006. Results & Conclusions of the Selous Conservation Programme. An examination of the crucial role of good governance in ecosystem management. Presented at the Serengeti Conference 2006 (edited for African Indaba).

16. Lewis, D. (Wildlife Conservation Society, Lusaka, Zambia). 2003. Synergies between Animal Husbandry and Wildlife Conservation: perspectives from Zambia. A paper delivered at the World Parks Congress in 2003.

17. White, Paula A. Pers. comm.

18. In 2000, IUCN adopted the following policy statement: 'IUCN concludes that: a) use of wild living resources, if sustainable, is an important conservation tool because the social and economic benefits derived from such use provide incentives for people to conserve them; b) when using wild living resources, people should seek to minimize losses of biological diversity; and c) enhancing the sustainability of uses of wild living resources involves an ongoing process of improved management of those resources.' Similarly, the preamble to the CITES recognises 'that peoples and States are and should be the best protectors of their own wild fauna and flora'.

19. Lewis, D. Ibid.

20. Ibid.

21. Botswana and Namibia often appear to be model countries when it comes to wildlife conservation. But it has to be borne in mind that, while Namibia has about five people per square kilometre and Botswana even fewer, Kenya has around 130 and South Africa around 85.

22. Friedman, Russel. Pers. comm.

23. Gaisford, Jeff. Pers. comm.

24. 'Reserves' do not usually have state protection. They are maintained by regional and local government.

25. The buffer-zone concept at present applies only to national parks and not to other conservation areas.

26. www.ducks.org/philanthropy/wetlands-america-trust.

27. Twice the size of the Kruger National Park.

INDEX

Nsungu 50
Nyasaland 33

O

Okavango 38, 43, 90, 118, 119, 213
Old Kaokoveld 24, 25
Olifants River 46
Orange County 31
Oryx 39
Osama 10, 48
Outjo 90
Owen, Sir Richard 145

P

Packer, Prof Craig 10, 11, 14, 47, 49, 65, 222, 223, 226, 227, 236
Pafuri 118, 214
Pan Africa News 149
Patterson, Di 142
Patterson, Lt-Col JH 45, 48, 50, 56, 57, 58, 59, 225, 226, 227, 228, 232
Peace Parks Foundation 23, 224
Perry, Richard 38, 226
Pilanesberg National Park 24, 85, 106, 196, 224, 225
Pitman, Col 159
Player, Dr Ian 38, 123, 124, 125, 226, 232
Pliny 45
Polokwane 155, 182
Pooley, Tony 116
Pootman, FJ 39, 226
Portuguese colonies 32, 52, 227
Pretorius, PJ 152
Primates **145–152**, 235
Puff adder 168, 170, 171, 175, 176, 177
Punda Maria 52
Python 167, 168, 182, 183, 184, 185, 186, 187, 238

Q

Queen Elizabeth National Park 80, 135

R

Reeves, Jack 164, 165
Reilly, Ted 79, 80
Rhino horn 4, 97, 98, 127, 128, 199, 218, 233
Rhino poaching 126, 127, 128, 199, 218
Rhino Specialist Group 124
Rhinoceros 1, 2, 5, 19, 28, 33, 34, 36, 37, 38, 39, 79, 91, 98, 102, 106, 113, **121–128**, 129, 159, 160, 199, 217, 218, 225, 232, 233
Rietmann, Hans 109
Rihlamfu, Thomas 77
Rinkhals 179, 181, 190
Rochat, Tobi 135, 136
Rombo district 17, 95
Ruark, Robert 160, 236
Rufiji 7, 10, 24, 48, 157
Ruponda 81
Rushby, George 35, 45, 48, 63, 64, 65, 67, 79, 80, 81, 141, 225, 226, 228, 229, 235

Ruvuma 8, 10, 49, 80, 139, 152, 198
Ruwenzori Mountains 146

S

SA Institute for Medical Research 182
SA People and Parks Programme (P&PP) 214, 215
Sabi Sabi 104
Safaritalk 92, 93, 94, 230
Saiga antelope 39
Salmon, Samaki 105
Sanderson, Ivan 107, 110, 231
Sata, President Michael 25, 26
Save the Elephants campaign 98
Saw-scaled viper 167, 177, 237
Schaller, George 147, 235
Selous Conservation Programme (SCP) 198, 200, 238, 239
Selous, FC 113, 130
Selous Game Reserve 7, 8, 9, 22, 23, 25, 43, 48, 49, 92, 93, 156, 195, 198, 199, 200, 201, 202, 220, 223
Semliki 159, 160
Senegal 68, 69
Serengeti 7, 9, 43, 100, 101, 130, 239
Sharks 16, 17, 118, 225
Sheldrick, Daphne 32
Siebert, Charles 85, 106, 229, 231
Simpson, Janice 119
Skukuza 40, 77
Smith & Wesson Forum 31
Smithsonian Natural History Museum 86
Smuts, Field Marshal JC 23, 167
Snakes 2, 11, 12, 33, 34, 70, **167–191**, 236, 237, 238
Soccer, role of 216, 217
Sofala 10, 33
Solomon, Derek 115
South Africa 15, 21, 23, 26, 27, 31, 34, 38, 39, 40, 43, 50, 52, 53, 73, 76, 77, 78, 83, 90, 91, 92, 97, 98, 102, 103, 109, 115, 118, 119, 124, 126, 127, 150, 155, 167, 170, 171, 172, 175, 179, 180, 182, 186, 189, 190, 191, 195, 196, 197, 204, 213, 214, 215, 218, 224, 225, 226, 228, 230, 233, 236, 237, 238, 240
South America 19, 21, 32, 36, 182
Southern Africa 16, 22, 23, 35, 78, 87, 92, 95, 103, 114, 179, 186, 187, 214, 224, 230, 234, 238
Speke, John 113
St Lucia 119, 160
Stanley, HM 113
Star 28, 162, 182, 235, 236
Steppes 36, 39
Stevenson-Hamilton, Col J 38, 75, 164, 226, 228
Steyn, Andries 118
Steyn, Ted 143
Stigand, CH 123, 232
Sudan 138
Sumatran rhino 128
Sunday Monitor 156, 236
Suque, Arian 80
Sutherland, Jim 105, 231
Sutherland, SK 190